SECOND REVISE

Richard's
BICYCLE
Book

Richard Ballantine
illustrated by John Batchelor

BALLANTINE BOOKS · NEW YORK

This book is
dedicated to
Samuel Joseph Melville, Hero.

ISBN 0–345–29453–X

Manufactured in the United States of America

First Edition: October 1972
Fifth Printing: December 1973

Revised Edition:
First Printing: October 1974
Second Printing: May 1976

Second Revised Edition

Layout and make-up by Mike Jarvis
and Mike Head

Cover bikes by
F. W. Evans Ltd.,
London

3 4 5 6 7 8 9

BOOK 1

1	Get a Bike!	1
2	Choosing Mounts	13
3	The Urban Commuting Bicycle	77
4	Buying and Keeping a Bike	81
5	Fitting and Gears	93
6	Riding	107
7	Traffic Jamming	115
8	Bang!	129
9	Touring	131
10	Racing	173
11	Accessories	177
12	Old Bikes	189

BOOK 2

1	Maintenance and Repair	194
	Maintenance Program	194
	Tools	197
	Lubrication	200
	General Words	205
2	Brakes	208
3	Staying Aboard	242
	Saddle	243
	Handlebars	247
	Stem	251
	Headset	254
	Forks	261
4	Wheels	263
	Removal and Replacement	263
	Tires	266
	Rims and Spokes	278
	Hubs	282
5	Power Train	286
	Pedals	288
	Cranks	289
	Bottom Bracket	293
	Front Sprocket	298
	Chain	300
	Rear Sprocket	304
	Gear Changers	307
6	Dream-Ramode-Sunfighter-Dream	348
	Index	363

"Rational Dress."

1. Get a Bike!

There is a bicycle boom throughout the world. The number of bicycles sold annually in England has climbed past the 1 million mark for the first time since the heyday 1930s, when sales in 1936 were 1.6 million. In the Netherlands 75 percent of the population own bicycles. In Japan the government has for some time energetically promoted bicycles, and there are nearly 40 million in use. In China there are no private automobiles, only public trucks and buses. *Everybody* rides a bicycle. The output of just one Chinese bicycle factory is listed as 14,000 bicycles per day!

In America the bicycle boom has crested, but for a while trading in the bicycle business was like being first in line at the 1849 California gold rush: annual sales went from 4.4 million in 1960 to 8.9 million in 1971, hit 13.9 million in 1972, jumped to 15.8 million in 1973, peaked near 17 million in 1974–75, and then subsided to the present average of between 10 and 11 million per year. The decline of interest in cycling has left countless millions of bicycles mouldering and unused in garages, attics, barns, sheds, cellars, and even broom closets. But the boom has left an enduring legacy: there are now over 100 million Americans riding on two wheels. And ten million bicycles a year, sold mostly to adults, is a hell of a lot of bicycles. Two-wheel transport in America is here to stay.

And a great bonus of the "decline" has been to clear out the deadwood. Gone are the fly-by-night bicycle dealers who did not know that a fork is a bicycle part as well as something to be used for eating spaghetti, and gone are the worst of the gilt-covered cheap trash bicycles that were fobbed off on an unsuspecting and unknowledgeable public. Most of the bicycle dealers who have survived have done so by selling good products suitable for the needs of their customers, and by knowing how to service what they sell. And the bicycle boom has done a great deal to improve bicycle quality and value. You can buy a better bicycle today, for less money, than ever before.

The typical pre-World War II American bike was sturdy but cumbersome. Equipped with a single pedal operated coaster brake and one low, slow gear, these "balloon tire bombers" hit the scales at 60 to 75 pounds. Used primarily by youngsters not old enough to drive, they were workhouse machines tough enough to withstand jolting rides over curbs and through fields, frequent nights out in the rain, and a generally high level of abuse. Fond nostalgia permeates memories of these bikes, but for the most part only people who had no other alternative used them.

After World War II returning G.I.'s brought home samples of a new kind of bike with a thinner frame and wheels, dual hand-operated caliper brakes, and 3-speed gears. Dubbed an "English racer" because of its startlingly better performance, this is actually the "tourist" bike, the common European machine for local use to and from work, shopping, mail delivery, police work, and the like. Lightweight (45 pounds) and geared for both flats and hills, the tourist bike is much easier to ride. A hit with the younger set as improved basic transportation, it provided the foundation for bicycling as an adult recreation in the U.S. of A. In the late '50s and early '60s stores devoted mainly to the sale and rental of bicycles developed steadily. Americans began spending more of their increased free time on afternoon rides in the countryside or parks. Bikes appeared in force on university campuses, and hardier souls began using them as all round transportation.

In the 1960s came the 10- and 15-speed racing-touring bikes. If the tourist bike is much better than a balloon tire bomber, the racing bike is incomparably so. Weighing about 22 pounds, they move much faster and more easily than other types of bikes. The first models came from Europe, where bike races are more important than baseball is here, and short supply made them very expensive. But adults have the economic clout to buy what they want, and while in 1965–66 only 20% of the bikes sold were adult machines, now they account for 65% of the market. High sales volume has lowered prices, so that a serviceable tourist model is about $75, with better quality machines up to $115. Ten speed models run about $90 for a poor quality cheapie, $130 to $160 for a low cost quality bike, $170 to $250 for a good quality bike, and $300 and more for a really high quality machine.

A list of all the vastly expanded applications and uses for light-weight bicycles would be dull. But the main advantages are:

Economics

With even moderate use a bike will pay for itself. Suppose you use a bike instead of public transportation or a car to get to work and back. Say it rains once a week and you live in the Northeast with an 8-month bike season. That's 4 days × 4 weeks × 8 months × $1.50 = $192 which buys a very nice bike. In sunnier climes with an 11-month season ring up $330. On a 20-mile round trip @ 25¢ a mile a car is into it for $5 a day,* or $1250 a year. For that kind of money you could ride a different color bicycle each day of the week.

Getting to and from work is just one application. Bikes are just dandy for visiting friends, light shopping, nipping down to the movies, and the like. You save money every time. And besides easing many of your chores and tasks, bikes are worthwhile in and of themselves, so that a bike easily "pays for itself" in rides taken just for fun and pleasure.

*The American Automobile Association Report for 1977 gives the following cost per mile figures:

Type of car	Low cost (rural) area	High cost (metropolitan) area
Sub-compact	14·6	22·8
Compact	15·7	24·1
Intermediate	16·8	25·5
Standard	18·5	28·2

Speed. In heavy traffic you can expect to average 10 mph, and in lighter traffic 15 mph. I regularly rode 2½ miles to midtown Manhattan from an apartment on the lower east side in fifteen minutes, usually less. The bus took at least 30 to 40 minutes, the subway about 25 to 35. When I first got into bikes it used to be my delight to race subway-travelling friends from 120th street to Greenwich Village – about 6 to 7 miles – and beat them. There have been bike versus bus, subway, and/or sports car contests in many cities, and in each case I know about the bike has always won.

One reason a bike is so fast is that it can wiggle through the traffic jams that now typify American cities and towns. Another is the fact that a bike is door-to-door. Use of public transportation involves walking to the local stop, waiting around for the bus or train, possibly a transfer with another wait, and then a walk from the final stop to your destination. Cars have to be parked. On a bike you simply step out the door and take off. No waiting, no parking problems.

The bike's capabilities make it a real freedom machine. Your lunch hour: tired of the same company cafeteria slop or local hash joint? Getting to a new and interesting restaurant a mile or so away is a matter of minutes. Lots of errands to do? A bike can nip from one place to another much faster than you can hoof it, and has a car beat all hollow in traffic and for parking. What might ordinarily take an hour is only 15 minutes on the bike. And if there is a lot to lug around, it is the bike and not you that does the work. Last minute decision to catch a film? Boom! Ten minutes and you're there before the subway even got going. If, like me, you are at all nocturnal, a bike is a tremendous advantage. Subways and buses tend to become elusive or disappear altogether as the wee hours approach. There is also a powerful contrast between a journey on a grubby, dirty, and noisy (to the point where your hearing acuity is measurably and permanently diminished) subway or bus where you run a definite risk of being mugged or raped, and a graceful, rhythmic ride in which you glide through calm and silent streets or through the stillness of a country night under the moon and stars.

All right, you say. So it takes less time than the subway. But I've got to work for a living and the subway is easier, takes less out of me. You expect me to get up in the morning and crack off 10 miles? Finish a day of hard work and do another 10? I'd never make it.

Get this. Even a moderate amount of exercise makes life *easier*. It gives your body tone and bounce which makes daily work and chores a breeze. Simply put, this is because exercise increases your range of possible effort, putting daily activities towards the center rather than the peak of your capabilities. So as you go through the day you are just cruising. It's something like the difference between a 25- and 100-horsepower automobile engine. At 60 mph the 25 horse is working hard but the 100 is just loafing. It is important to realize that you can get this increased bounce, verve, and good feeling with relatively little time and effort. Bicycling will make your work and day easier, not harder.

Are you familiar with "cleaning out" a motor vehicle? Cars today often operate in stop and go traffic for long periods of time. The engine becomes clogged with carbon and other residue. The car stumbles and staggers, it works harder than it needs to, and gas consumption goes up. The best thing for any such car is to be taken out on a highway and run fast, for at higher speeds the engine cleans itself out. Your body is a machine with exactly similar characteristics, and you will literally become more fagged out and tired just sitting still than if you run around the block a few times.

According to Eugene Sloane in his *Complete Book of Bicycling*, if you get in some sort of regular exercise you can expect:
to live for up to five years longer;
think better (more blood to the brain – and if you think this is crazy go out and run around for a while and then think it through again);
sleep better, and in general be more relaxed;
be stronger and more resistant to injury;
reduce the incidence of degenerative vascular diseases responsible for or associated with heart attacks, strokes, and high blood pressure.
As cardiovascular problems account for over 50% of all deaths

in the U.S. of A. each year this last point is worth some elaboration. The basic deal with the cardiovascular system is movement, the flow of blood through your heart, veins, arteries, and so forth. The heart normally pumps about 5 quarts per minute, and during exercise up to 30 quarts per minute. If this flow is sluggish and slow, the system clogs up. In arteriosclerosis, for example, the walls of the system become hardened and calcified. This decreases the bore of the arteries and veins, resulting in a diminished capacity to carry blood. The heart must therefore pump harder and higher blood pressure results. High blood pressure is a cause of stroke or rupture of brain blood vessels. Arteriosclerosis happens to everybody, but extent is governed by the rate of flow of the blood. Exercise stimulates the blood flow, and does not permit calcification to occur as rapidly.

Atherosclerosis is a related malady. This is when fatty substances are deposited on the lining of the blood vessels. Clots in the blood may be formed as a result, and these can jam up the system at critical points such as the brain or heart, causing stroke or heart attack. Again, exercise by stimulating the blood flow helps prevent fatty deposits.

So, the main benefits of regular exercise are first, that it will help keep your blood circulatory system cleaned out; secondly,

A COUNTRY POSTMAN.

the heart muscle, like any other, responds to exercise by becoming larger and more efficient, so that each heartbeat delivers more oxygen to the body; and thirdly, lung-filling capacity is restored or enlarged. In short, you can do more, and recover more quickly from doing it.

Bicycling in particular is a complete exercise. Not only are the legs, the body's largest accessory blood pumping mechanism, used extensively, but also arm, shoulder, back, abdominal, and diaphragmatic muscles. At the same time there is enough flexibility so that muscle groups can be worked individually, and of course pace can be set to suit the rider.

A word about weight control. Bicycling or other exercise will help your body's tone and figure. But for weight loss eat less food. A brisk ride does not entitle you to apple pie and ice cream. Regular cycling burns off about 300 calories per hour and hill climbing or racing about 600 per hour. Your body uses up about 150 calories per hour anyway, and so in the case of regular cycling this means a burn off of an extra 150 calories per hour. At 3600 calories per pound, it would take 24 hours of riding to lose this amount. It's much simpler to just eat less. Curiously enough, cycling may help you to do this. Regular exercise can change the metabolic balance of the body and restore normal automatic appetite control so that you eat no more than you actually need.

A serious health hazard for the urban cyclist is hyperventilation of highly polluted air. See Traffic Jamming for more information on this subject.

Ecology

Our country is literally drowning in pollutants and many of them come from transportation machinery. In the cities the internal combustion engine is a prime offender, contributing up to 85% of all air pollution,* and of an especially noxious quality. The effluents from gasoline engines hang in the air and chemically interact with other substances and sunlight to form even deadlier poisons. Living in a major city is the same thing as smoking two packs of cigarettes a day.**

*Reinow, L.&L. MOMENT IN THE SUN (Ballantine, New York).
**Commoner, Barry, THE CLOSING CIRCLE (Jonathan Cape, London).

All city transportation contributes to pollution. Subways run on electricity generated in plants fired by fossil fuels or deadly atomic reactors. But as anyone who has been lucky enough to live through a taxicab strike or vehicle ban knows, cars and buses are the real problem. I shall never forget a winter many years ago when a friend and I came driving into New York City late at night after a vacation in Canada. To my amazement, the air was perfectly clear. The lights of the city shone like jewels and each building was clear and distinct. From the west bank of the Hudson river I could for the first (and perhaps only) time in my life see Manhattan and the Bronx in perfect detail from beginning to end, and even beyond to Brooklyn and her bridges. As we crossed the George Washington Bridge the air was clean and fresh, and the city, usually an object of horror and revulsion, was astoundingly beautiful and iridescent. The explanation was simple: enough snow had fallen to effectively eliminate vehicle traffic for a couple of days. No vehicles, no crap in the air. A better world.

Arguments against motorized transport are usually dismissed as idealistic and impractical and on the grounds that the time-saving

characteristics of such vehicles are essential. The fact is that even pedestrians are easily able to drone past most traffic, and of course bicycles can do even better. A saving in physical effort is realized, but few of us are healthy enough to (a) need this, or (b) dismiss inhaling the poisons (equivalent to two packs of cigarettes a day) which necessarily accompany the internal combustion engine.

Walking, roller-skating, or riding a bicycle is an efficient use of energy and reduces wastage. In the U.S. of A. there are three people for each motor vehicle (as against 22,535 persons per vehicle in China),* and 80 percent of all automobile traffic is within 8 miles of home.** Transport uses 25 percent of the energy consumed in the U.S. of A., and 95 percent of this is petroleum derived.** Professor Rice in *Technology Review* has calculated that a cyclist can do 1,000 miles on the food energy equivalent of a gallon of gasoline, which will move a car only some 15 to 30 miles. Facts and figures be as they may, utilizing a 300 horsepower, 5000 pound behemoth to move one single 150 pound person a few miles is like using an atomic bomb to kill a canary. The U.S. of A. is unique in its ability to consume and waste. In fact, we utilize something like 60 percent of the world's resources for the benefit of about 7% of her population. For example, we import fish meal from South American countries where people are starving, to feed to our beef herds, and then wonder why people down there don't like us. Using a bicycle is a starting antidote to the horrors of U.S. of A. consumerism.

Which brings us to the most positive series of reasons for trying to use bicycles at every opportunity. Basically, this is that it will enhance your life, bringing to it an increase in quality of experience which will find its reflection in everything you do.

Well! you have to expect that I would believe bicycling is a good idea, but how do I get off expressing the notion that bicycling is philosophically and morally sound? Because it is something that *you do*, not something that is done to you. Need I chronicle the oft-cited concept of increasing alienation in American life? The mechanization of work and daily activities, the hardships our industrial society places in the way of loving and fulfilling relationships and family life, the tremendous difficulties individuals

*Gail Heilman, BICYCLING! June, 1977.
**CYCLATERAL THINKING, Urban Bikeway Design Collaborative, Cambridge, Mass.

experience trying to influence political and economic decisions which affect them and others?

Of course there will always be people who say that they like things the way they are. They find the subway really interesting, or insist on driving a chrome bomb and rattling everybody's windows. But the fact is that subways are crowded, dirty, impersonal, and *noisy*, and nearly all cars are ego-structured worthless tin crap junk (with bikes the more you pay the less you get).

The most important effect of mechanical contraptions is that they defeat consciousness. Consciousness, self-awareness, and development are the prerequisites for a life worth living. Now look at what happens to you on a bicycle. It's immediate and direct. *You* pedal. *You* make decisions. *You* experience the tang of the air and the surge of power as you bite into the road. You're vitalized. As you hum along you fully and gloriously experience the day, the sunshine, the clouds, the breezes. You're alive! You are going someplace, and it is *you* who is doing it. Awareness increases, and each day becomes a little more important to you. With increased awareness you see and notice more, and this further reinforces awareness.

Each time you insert *you* into a situation, each time *you* experience, you fight against alienation and impersonality, you build consciousness and identity. You try to understand things in the ways that are important to you. And these qualities carry over into everything you do.

An increased value on one's own life is the first step in social conscience and politics. Because to you life is dear and important and fun, you are much more easily able to understand why this is also true for a Vietnamese, a black, or a Tobago islander. Believe it. The salvation of the world is the development of personality and identity for everybody in it. Much work, many lifetimes. But a good start for you is *Get a bicycle!*

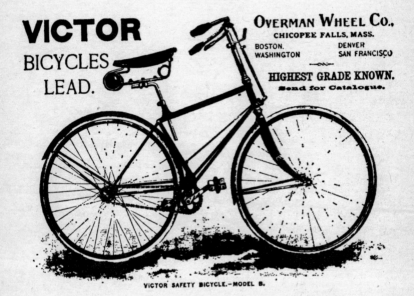
II

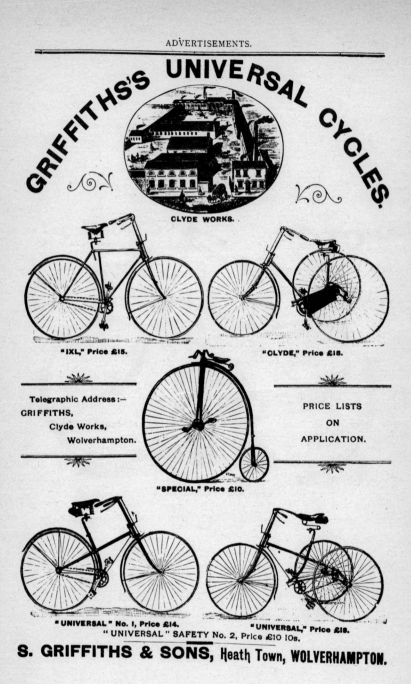

2. Choosing Mounts

What kind of bike for you? The main points are covered here, but you should also look over the sections on riding, fitting, touring, and racing to get the best idea of what's going on and what your particular needs may be before arriving at a final selection. This chapter is broken down into three sections: adult full-size bicycles; other bicycles; and children's bicycles. Technical information given for adult bicyles applies to any bicycle and will not be repeated in each section.

Adult Bicycles

Bicycle categories by function break down into six slightly overlapping groups:

(1) The balloon tire bomber, built entirely of steel, with a heavy, robust frame, wide 2" tires, and a 1- or 2-speed rear hub equipped with pedal operated coaster brake. This is the classic American bike for really tough work like riding on beaches and fields, newspaper delivery, collisions, and absolutely no care. With a weight of up to 65 pounds it can be mighty hard pedalling on anything but dead flat terrain.

(2) The heavy roadster, also built entirely of steel, with wide 1½" tires, roller lever rim brakes, and 1- or 3-speed hub gears. Weight about 50 pounds. This is the European version of the balloon tire bomber, and is sometimes called an 'Africa' model because of·its popularity in developing countries for transporting heavy loads, bouncing across deserts and through jungles and the like. They were used extensively by the North Vietnamese for transporting supplies during their last war with the Americans. A frame and forks designed for taking the sting out of bumps make them particularly steady and graceful, and for this reason they are also very popular with Netherlands housewives. The Netherlands are mostly flat however, and pedalling them where there are any kinds of hills is hard work.

(3) The sports roadster, also called tourist model or English racer, with lighter steel frame and fenders, 1⅜" tires, calliper rim brakes, and 1-, 3-, 4-, or 5-speed hub gears. This is the bike for utility use such as local errands, shopping, lots of stop-and-go riding, short trips, and gives good durability with minimal

maintenance. Weight about 35 pounds.

(4) The lightweight tourist can be as the sports roadster above, but with 5- or 10-speed derailleur gears, or it can be as the touring/commuting bike below, with a truly lightweight frame, $1\frac{1}{4}''$ tires, and steel or alloy components. In either case it usually features flat handlebars and a wide mattress saddle. Weight from 25 to 35 pounds. It is a hybrid intended to give the light weight and gear range of the touring/commuting bike with the riding position of the sports roadster, and is suitable for local errands, commuting, and short ride touring up to 25 miles.

(5) The touring/commuting bicycle features a lightweight frame, steel or alloy components depending on model, $1\frac{1}{4}''$ tires, caliper rim brakes (sometimes a disc brake is fitted to the rear wheel), 5-, 10-, 12-, 15-, or 18 speed derailleur gears, narrow "racing" saddle, and dropped handlebars. Weight from 21 to 35 pounds. These bikes are for general use, hilly terrain, and for tours of over 25 miles. Far more lively and responsive than the sports roadster, the frame is still designed for reasonable riding comfort over rough ground and easy directional stability.

(6) Racing bicycles are as the touring/commuting bicycle above, but usually feature narrow profile tires, close-ratio gears, and a "stiff" frame designed for quick handling and maximum translation of pedalling effort into forward motion. They are thus relatively more fragile and harsher riding than the touring/commuting bicycles, but on smooth roads in the hands of an experienced rider can be both comfortable and exceptionally swift. They are inappropriate for most commuting and utility use. Weight as little as 19 pounds.

Racing bicycles for use on wooden tracks are utterly stark greyhounds, with a single fixed gear, no brakes, and a weight of 16 to 17 pounds. Only the most expert of riders can use these on roads.

For the sake of simplicity I am going to speak of 3-speed bicycles, by which I mean those with 3- to 5-speed internal hub gears; and 10-speed bicycles, those with 5- to 18-speed derailleur gears. If this is Greek to you, hold on for just a bit.

I hope your decision will be to get a 10-speed bicycle. They can be set up to suit nearly any rider, job, or purpose, are dynamic, responsive, and vibrant, the most comfortable, and give the most speed for the least effort so that you will get more out of riding and will be encouraged to do even more. They are also the easiest to service. Initial cost may seem high, but experience has shown that most people who start with a heavyweight or sports roadster soon find themselves desiring (and aquiring) a 10-speed bike. It takes no longer than the first time such a machine sweeps by them going up a hill. My advice is to save money by buying a 10-speed bike in the first place. You get the most fun and turn-on for your dollar, and you get it right away.

Assigning utility functions to a 3-speed bike, and touring and

Rear derailleur and freewheel for a 10-speed bike:

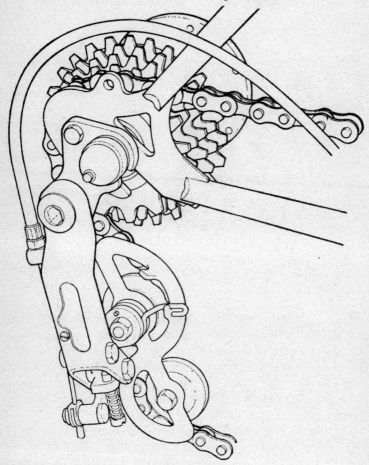

racing functions to a 10-speed bike, is only broadly accurate. Actually, a 10-speed can be set up for almost any job or purpose except beach riding. The same machine, with minor modifications, can compete in a race, go on a camping tour, be ridden cross-country through streams and muddy fields, and haul groceries or newspapers. It can even pull a trailer. The only crucial difference between the 3- and 10-speed is the method of operation for the gears: the 3-speed can be shifted to the correct gear at any time, the 10-speed must be shifted while the bicycle is in motion. It's easy once you get the knack, and the 10-speed's efficiency outweighs the disadvantage of initial unfamiliarity. If you get stopped in a "wrong" (inefficient) gear, it is easy to shift once you are under way again.

A 3-speed hub.

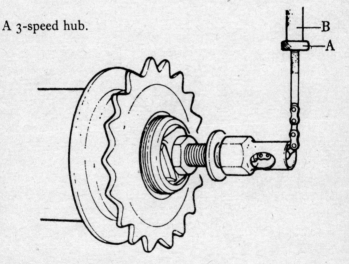

The question of durability is largely a function of bicycle model and weight and rider sense. Ten-speeds range from ultra-light (20 pounds) alloy models to heavy (35 pounds) steel models. My first 10-speed was a sturdy machine with steel wheels which I not only rode hard and fast over bumpy streets, but also used for games of bicycle tag in the woods and fields, as well as just plain cross-country and back-trail riding. It held up just fine.

The classic down-swept handlebars of the 10-speed are not a requirement; you can equip or buy such a bike with conventional tourist handlebars, although it wouldn't be to your advantage to do so (more on handlebars later). With the exception of the cheaper models, 10-speed bikes have the much better center-pull caliper brakes, rather than the coaster or side-pull caliper brakes usually supplied with 3-speed bikes. Comfort is sometimes cited in favor of the 3-speed. The fact is that the 10-speed has a wider variety of riding positions, allows you to utilize more muscles to greater advantage, and is therefore much less tiring to ride than a 3-speed.

The choice of bike is therefore largely governed by the type of person you are and how heavy you want to get into bicycling, the contents of your pocketbook, and real-life physical factors such as the quality of your neighborhood and the number of stairs you climb every day. It is the first of these which is the most relevant, and what you must assess is how much consciousness you want to bring to bicycling. Not everybody is interested in the boiling scald of blood through their veins as they spring up the highway, or the eerie desolation of a chill night. Get a 3-speed if: you are not terribly interested in bicycling and just want something you can stick in the shed or basement to use for local jaunts once or twice a month (if you're really in this category and can do so, rent machines); you or the prospective rider are not at all mechanically inclined and don't care to be; you need a knock-around bike for use by several different people or just want a worry-free machine. There is nothing degenerate about this last state of affairs. There are times when I prefer the totally casual spirit of the 3-speed, where one can just drop it on the spot, bash it around, and in general not think about what is going on. But this is the exception, not the rule. Over the long haul, the 10-speed is just so much better, so much more rewarding, that it will surely overcome any diffidence you feel about bicycling and make you an enthusiast.

Expense is a consideration only if your absolute maximum is $25.00, which restricts you to a serviceable used 3-speed. If you have $35.00 to $45.00 you can buy a used bike that at least has 10 speeds, if nothing else. More on this later.

Most of the more pragmatic considerations in type of bicycle are physical:

For hilly terrain get a 10-speed, no matter what.

If you live at the end of a long and rocky road you may want a sturdier model 10-speed. This is also a question of rider weight. For example, many years ago I gave a 100-pound cousin a Peugeot

RUSHING A RISE.

UO-8. At 27 pounds this is closer to an ultra-light 20 pound racer than a 35 pound heavyweight. My cousin lived at the top of a steep, winding, rocky dirt road about one-eighth of a mile long, and his idea of fun was to blaze down the hill as fast as he could. The Peugeot held up fine but with a heavier rider would have shown noticeably greater wear and tear. Bear in mind that "sturdier" bikes are built that way in order to overcome inherently inferior materials and manufacturing techniques. The amount of extra strength gained is debatable, and only at cost to the power to weight ratio.

Rider sense and skill also affect durability. I have ridden racing bikes equipped with lightweight tubular tires through fields and woods. It is just a question of watching where you go and not overstressing the machine. A rider who sits on his saddle like a sack of oats when his bike hits a bump needs a machine that can absorb punishment; a rider who moves with his bike, allowing it to pivot underneath him over the bumps, can use a lighter, more responsive machine.

Stair climbing apartment dwellers need to consider weight if they intend to keep their bike at home, oftentimes a necessity if the bike is not to be stolen. The two sensible answers are a 10-speed, or the Bickerton Portable (see Folding Bicycles). Other folding bikes, mini-bicycles, and 3-speeds run 35 and 40 pounds, and are a clumsy nuisance to lug up two to four flights of stairs.

Using a car or public transportation to get to a departure point for a trip is also part of carrying. Any 10-speed is easier to take apart than a 3-speed, and a good quality 10-speed will have quick release wheels which come off at the flick of a lever. The only thing easier is the Bickerton Portable, which in under 60 seconds folds into a bag 30″ × 20″ × 9″. This makes it a hands down winner when storage space is limited. Next in line is the 10-speed. With the wheels off it can be hung in a closet. It is light enough to be hung from the ceiling or a wall via brackets or pulleys. It can be kept in the bathtub or shower stall. Under any circumstances it will be easier to deal with than a 3-speed.

For frequency of repair the 3-speed has it all over the 10-speed. All the 3-speed hub will need for years is a monthly shot of oil. Once it does go however, it is much too complicated to fix, and most bicycle shops will simply replace it. It is also considerably less efficient than the 10-speed design, and transmits less pedal effort to the rear wheel. The 10-speed, while more efficient, requires more frequent adjustment and servicing. However, because the parts are all quite simple and out in the open where they are easy to get at, this is easy to do. In fact, it is part of the fun of riding. The vitality and responsiveness of the 10-speed is such that you come to enjoy fine-tuning your bike.

Perhaps now you have started to form a notion of what kind of bike you would like to have. But prices vary from $75 to $1200 for a bewildering array of bicycles. Here is some technical information to guide you through the maze and help you get your money's worth.

The significant components of a bicycle are the frame, brakes, rims, tires and hubs; gears and gear changing hardware, chainwheel, cranks, and pedals; and stem, handlebars, and saddle. According to the grade of component selected by the manufacturer, the price for a 3-speed will range from $75 to $110, from $90 to $700 for production line 10-speeds, and $500 and up for custom bikes. Manufacturers tend to assemble rather than manufacture bicycles, getting the components from a number of independent companies. Hence, two bikes in the same price category from two different brand name "manufacturers" sometimes have exactly the same parts.

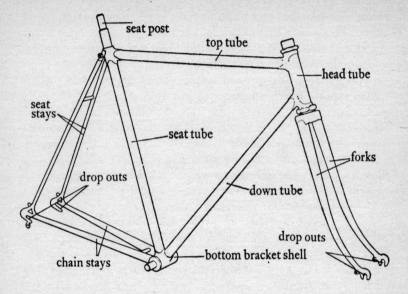

The frame

The frame is the heart and soul of a bicycle. It is the chief determinant of bicycle weight, and the more you pay the lighter the weight for the same strength. Frames are not meant to be rigid or unyielding, but rather to absorb irregularities from the road surface. Called resiliency or twang or flex, this is a function of quality of materials and manufacturing methods, and gives better bikes more springiness and vitality. There is no way to work around a cheap frame. Other components can be modified or changed but the frame endures, and it should be the first focus of your attention when considering a prospective bike.

Inexpensive coaster brake, 3-speed, and cheap 10-speed bikes use seamed tubing, made by wrapping a long, flat strip of steel into a tube and then welding it together (electrically) at high temperature. Better bikes use a seamless tubing which is even in bore throughout. The best bikes use special, cold-drawn alloy steel seamless double-butted tubing. Double-butted means that while the outside diameter of the tube remains constant, it is thicker on the inside at the ends, where greater strength is needed.

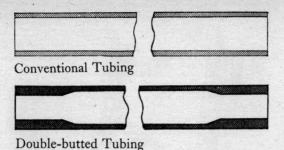

Conventional Tubing

Double-butted Tubing

The method by which the frame parts are attached to each other is important. Bikes with seamed tubing are usually just stuck together and welded, leaving a smooth joint. This is the commonest and weakest type of assembly. The welding, done at high temperatures, robs the metal of strength. High-carbon bike tube steel becomes brittle and subject to fatigue when heated. In better bikes the frame is lugged and brazed, rather than welded. Lugging is the addition of reinforcing metal at stress points, and brazing is done at lower temperatures than welding. Make sure that the job has been done cleanly and neatly on any prospective bike you examine.

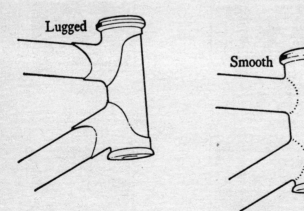

Lugged

Smooth

CENTRE & BELOW.—*Two views of high-class lug and crown work and head transfers on Evans regular models.*

LEFT.—*Fine lug and crown work on Evans Super Continental models. Anglo models are similar except crown, shewn on extreme left.*

The very, very best frames are Reynolds 531, Columbus, or Falk, double-butted, with Reynolds generally considered the finest. Reynolds 531 comes in several grades. Read the label to see what you are getting:

Only the top tube, seat tube, and down tube are Reynolds 531 plain gauge tubing.

Only the top tube, seat tube, and down tube are Reynolds 531 double butted tubing.

All the tubing is Reynolds 531 plain gauge.

All the tubing is Reynolds 531 double butted.

All the tubing is Reynolds
753 double butted.

All the tubing is Reynolds
531 Special
Lightweight double butted.

Reynolds 531 Special Lightweight tubing used in place of Reynolds 531 double butted will give a frame approximately 1 pound lighter in weight. There is no point to using this material unless you spend the money to equip the frame with ultra-light-weight components – say about $600 or more. Reynolds 531 Special Lightweight and 753 tubing are so light that tolerances in frame assembly and brazing temperatures are absolutely critical. The slightest error can result in a pile of junk. Do not buy a frame of these materials unless it is from a top quality master builder.

Chances are you will not be getting double-butted tubing unless you have elected to spend upwards of $300. However, you should at least get seamless lugged tubing, which is used even on low-cost quality bikes. Here are three tests for frame quality. Differences between price ranges should be evident.

(1) Weight. Electric welded tubing and joints are heavy in order to overcome inherent weaknesses of this type of construction and materials.

(2) Lift the bike a couple of inches and bounce it on the wheels. Better frames have more twang and bounce.

(3) Stand to one side of the bike. Hold nearest handlebar with one hand and saddle with the other and tilt bike away from you. Place one foot on end of bottom bracket axle and give a *gentle* push. A good frame will flex and then spring right back. Try several different bikes to get the feel of it and *be careful*, the idea is to find frames that will give with a gentle push, not bend anything you may encounter. If enough force is applied cheap frames will bend – permanently.

1935 BSA

Bicycle frames are also available in aluminum, aluminum and graphite, and titanium. These frames are very light and very, very expensive. I do not advise buying such a frame until you have owned at least a couple of bikes, and know exactly what you are getting into.

The design and geometry of a bicycle frame varies according to its intended purpose and weight and type of rider. The commonest design for touring and general use is 72° parallel. This means that the angle to the top tube formed by the seat and head tubes is 72°:

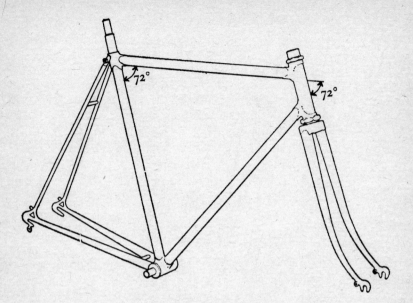

This is the standard design and gives an excellent combination of road holding, shock absorption, and power transmission. It is very good for bumpy urban streets. Many variations are possible. The frame built by Jack Taylor of England for his Superlight Tourist model uses a 73° seat and 71° head. It is designed for stability and comfort with heavy touring loads. Road and track racing frames use steeper angles, such as 73°, 73½°, 74°, or 74½° parallel, or combinations like 74° head and 73° seat. The ride is stiffer, but more power is transmitted to the wheels.

In general, bicycles for the American market have been tending towards stiffer geometry and design. For example, the Fuji Newest model is catalog listed as "the perfect all round machine, suitable both for long distance touring and racing." The frame angles are 74° × 75°. A few years ago this would have been considered suitable only for a flat-out racing bike. Some riders use these frames for touring and around town riding, but they are inadvisable on anything but very smooth roads. Out and out racing frames use shorter fork blades and seat and chain stays to bring the wheels in closer, and cannot be fitted with fenders. The rake or trail of the front fork, e.g. the distance between the front wheel axle and a line formed by extending the head tube downwards:

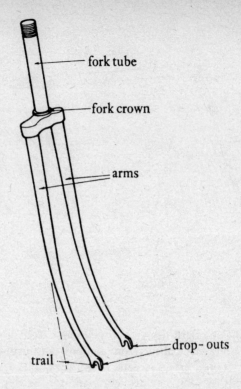

fork tube

fork crown

arms

drop-outs

trail

is usually less than on racing frames than on touring frames, and this also contributes to a stiffer ride and brighter handling. Materials play a part also. For example, the Viscount Aerospace frame has a relatively "stiff" design, but uses a "softer" fork made of aluminium.* Pedal response is quick, but the ride is not harsh. Then there is the matter of rider weight. A frame that is stiff for a person weighing 140 pounds may be soft for a person weighing 180 pounds. It is a complicated subject well covered by Albert Eisentraut in "The Frame", a chapter in Tom Cuthbertson's *Bike Tripping* (Ten Speed Press, Box 4310, Berkeley CA 94704) and by Joe Kossak in *Bicycle Frames* (World Publications, P.O. Box 366, Mountain View, CA 94040).

*At this writing Viscount no longer comes with an aluminium alloy fork. Too many of them broke. Now supplied with a conventional chrome-moly steel fork.

Summary:

One of the most satisfying and important features of a good bike is responsiveness and whip-like flex that you can feel with your whole body. The main determinants of this quality are the frame materials and construction. In 10-speed bikes, expect the following:

Under $100   – Seamed, smooth joint frame.
$100 to $300 – Seamless, lugged joint frame.
Over $300   – Seamless, double butted, lugged joint, low temperature brazed frame.

The Brakes

It is the nature of bicycling accidents that the bicyclist more often runs into something than is run into. Good, well-adjusted brakes are vital, and especially in traffic. There are three basic types of brakes: pedal or hand operated hub or coaster brakes; hand operated disc brakes; and hand operated caliper rim brakes.

Pedal operated coaster brakes are only for small children who lack the necessary strength to actuate hand levers. Although they are easy to apply, they are hard to control and can lock a wheel, causing a skid. They do not have actual stopping power. It's a skid or next to nothing. Skidding is a bad way to stop since (a) it takes too long; (b) at high speeds it is excessively exciting; and (c) wear and tear on the tires is very high. A coaster brake has poor heat dissipating qualities, and can burn out in the middle of a long down-hill descent. The sole advantage of a coaster brake is that it remains effective in wet weather, when caliper rim brakes may lose up to 80 percent of braking power.

Disc brakes are powerful, and effective in wet weather. They are often fitted to tandems and tricycles. The disc brake is a heavy unit however, and for this reason is not commonly used on lightweight bicycles. The exception is the light and very beautiful Phil Wood disc brake which costs over $200 and is not worth fitting to any but the finest machines. I would advise disc brakes only for tandems and tricycles, very heavily loaded touring bicycles, off road woods and BMX bicycles, and possibly, commuting bicycles used often in wet weather.

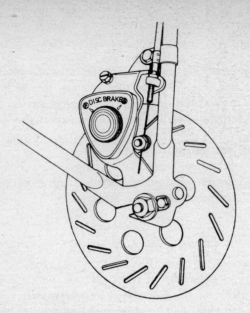

Hand operated caliper brakes come in two types, center and side-pull.

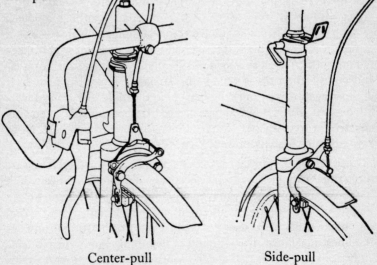

Center-pull   Side-pull

Side-pull caliper brakes are commonly used on less costly bikes. They are somewhat inconsistent in performance, although they will work if kept in constant adjustment. Center-pull brakes are better. Because they pull from the center they work in balance, and are more even, precise, and powerful. They are also more reliable and require less maintenance than side-pull brakes.

Fancy racing bikes use expensive (up to $100) special lightweight side-pull brakes with a rigid design affording precise control at high speeds. Center-pull brakes generally have a softer, less rigid design requiring less brake lever pressure for a complete stop, but which can "snatch" at high speeds, e.g. exert more deacceleration than necessary or, for a racing bike, safe. Both types stop equally well; the side-pull has the edge for speed control. However, good side-pull brakes run between $40 and $100 per set, and are only worth considering for bicycles costing over $300. For ordinary road use the much less expensive (about $15 to $30) center pull design is perfectly suitable, and since required force on the levers is less, even preferable for touring and utility bicycles. Bear in mind that distinctions between the two types are quite fine; the winning bicycle of the 1976 Tour de France was equipped with center-pull brakes.

Good brand names are Campagnolo, Shimano, Dia-Compe, Weinmann, Universal, and Mafac. Be sure that the levers on the brand you select fit your grip. Some brakes are supplied with a second "touring" or "safety" lever set underneath and in line with the top, straight section of the handlebars:

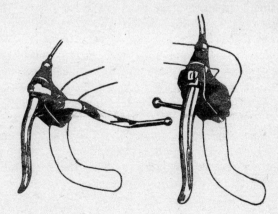

These increase the number of positions from which the brakes can be operated, and this can be very useful in traffic or for comfort when making long downhill descents. However, safety levers require a relatively greater length of travel in order to actuate the brake mechanism. If the brakes are not adjusted to close tolerances, it is possible under hard braking for the safety lever to bang uselessly on the handlebar while you carry on to destruction. Under these circumstances a safety lever is a liability rather than an asset. I therefore recommend safety levers only for those riders able to keep their brakes adjusted to close tolerances.

One development for the mechanically feeble-minded are self-adjusting brake mechanisms and levers. These units are heavy and mechanically complex, and are more trouble than they are worth. Any cyclist, at the minimum, should know how to adjust his or her brakes.

Until recently, one unnerving characteristic of rim brakes was that in wet conditions, braking power was reduced by up to 80 percent. To compensate, manufacturers redesigned brake block patterns and materials. Wet braking power is much better but now, in dry conditions, over-zealous application of the front brake can pitch the rider right over the handlebars. Anyone who has slithered helplessly down a long hill in the wet will not mind developing the ability to handle modern rim brakes in the dry. Once the skill is mastered, for ultimate braking power I recommend fitting Mathauser brake blocks ($15 from Scott/Mathauser Corp., Box 1333, Sun Valley, Idaho 83353).

A variant of the center-pull brake is the cantilever, which pivots on a boss brazed onto the fork blades and seat stays. Powerful, and less likely to "whip" (where the whole brake assembly judders back and forth), cantilever brakes are good for the heavily laden tourist, cyclo-cross, and tandems and tricycles. There is also a saving of six ounces in weight over the conventional center-pull. However, only cyclo-cross and made-to-order frames are likely to have the requisite brazed-on bosses necessary to mount cantilevers.

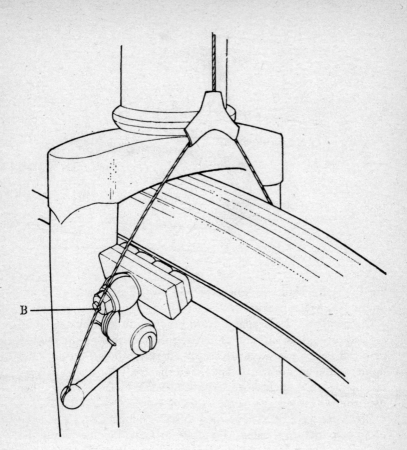

B

Rims, tires, and hubs

There are three types of rims. The Westwood, for use with $1\frac{1}{2}''$ tires and roller lever brakes, is seen only on heavy roadsters and utility bikes. Modern bikes use Endrick rims, with wire-on or "clincher" tires, or sprint rims with sew-up or tubular tires.

Clincher tires are available in a wide range of weights, and are more durable and far easier to repair than tubular tires. Tubulars offer the ultimate in light weight and minimal rolling resistance, but are expensive ($12 to $30) and puncture easily. Because the tube is sewn into the tire it is impractical to repair on the road, necessitating the carrying of whole spare tires which must be glued onto the rim. This is actually a quick process, but it is a drag to

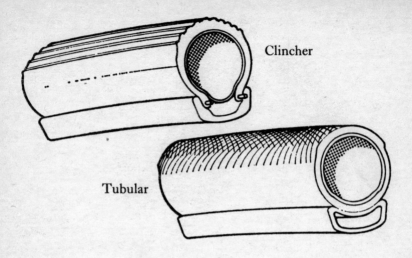

Clincher

Tubular

lug the spare with you wherever you go, since it cannot be left on the bike when parking on the street.

Clincher tires are available from heavy-duty knobby speedway models through to high pressure (90 p.s.i.) narrow profile models that will match the performance of a heavy tubular. So only the lightest tubulars are worth using, and then only for racing or very fast day rides. Clincher tires are the sensible choice for any other use.

Processes have been developed to make clincher tires puncture proof or puncture resistant. Puncture proofing involves filling the tire with a heavy foam, greatly increasing weight and harshness of ride. There is no point to the process if the ambition is to ride a lightweight, responsive bike. Making a tire puncture resistant is done by injecting a liquid sealant which adds about 2 ounces to the weight. The tire is then proofed against direct punctures, but not against slashes or cuts, as from glass. A liquid sealant is well worth considering if you regularly ride on littered urban streets. One product I know works is called STAB and is available from bike shops.

Rims are made either of aluminum alloy or steel. Less costly bikes feature steel rims, which are the most heavy and durable. Better bikes feature aluminum alloy rims which are lighter but of course more fragile. Really brutal riding over bumpy terrain may require steel rims but I have found the alloy wheels entirely satisfactory. An important consideration is that in the wet aluminum alloy rims offer much better braking power than steel rims.

Hubs also come in steel or aluminum alloy. They may use conventional bolts, requiring the use of a wrench to remove the wheel, or quick-release levers which work instantly. This is a desirable feature for bikes that will be stored in the closet, transported by automobile often, or left locked on the street (you take the wheels with you).

The hub illustrated is a high flange design used for racing and sport riding. The flange is the part with all the holes where the spokes are attached. A low flange design requires longer spokes and gives a softer ride. It is often used for touring and commuting bikes.

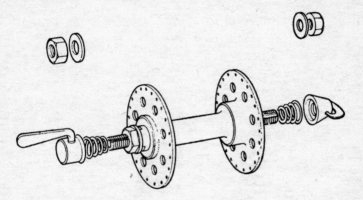

A recent development are hubs with sealed bearings which do not require lubrication or adjustment. In ordinary service these units are durable. However, very wet, muddy, or dusty conditions may make servicing a requirement, and this can be difficult to do. Good sealed bearing hub brands are Weyless, Phil Wood, and Hi-E ($40 to $70). The new Viscount hubs are OK, but avoid at all costs the old Viscount known as Lambert. Campagnolo, Shimano, Normandy, Sunshine, Zeus, and Sun Tour and all good brand names for conventional design hubs ($25 to $50).

The hubs, after the frame, are perhaps the most vital component of a bike. Cheap hubs run rough, wear out quickly, and are inclined to promote spoke breakage. Get the best hubs you can afford.

Summary: Under $150 – Steel rims and bolt on hubs, clincher tires.

$150 to $300 – Alloy rims and quick-release hubs, clincher tires.

Over $300 – Alloy rims and quick-release hubs, choice of clincher or tubular tires.

Gear changing mechanisms, cranks and chainwheel, and pedals

Nearly all 3-speed bikes use Sturmy-Archer, Sun Tour, or Shimano multi-speed hubs, no matter what price range. At the core of the design of the 10-speed bike are the derailleurs, which shift the chain from sprocket to sprocket. Differences between brands are to be found in weight, smoothness and precision of shifting, and durability. However, each manufacturer offers several different grades of derailleurs in two different categories, competition and touring. For example, the Campagnolo Nuevo

Record (competition) and Rally (touring) are top of the line products of irreproachable beauty and performance, as well they might be with price tags of about $50 each. Campagnolo's Vallentino economy model on the other hand, has not been well received, and there are plenty of other inexpensive units which are better.

Simplex is a popular brand noted for smooth shifting and lightness. Newer models feature main bodies of alloy rather than of delrin, a plastic that was prone to disintegrating. Huret is another popular brand, although some models are constructed so that just a little dirt and oil will gum up the works. They have to be kept clean. A most attractive new Huret model is the Duopar, which uses a double parallelogram design instead of the conventional single parallelogram. The result is exceptionally easy shifting, particularly under heavy loads such as generated by tandems and touring bikes. The Duopar is made of aluminum alloy and titanium and weighs only 11 ounces complete with mounting bracket. At this writing the Duopar leaves a massive $75 hole in the pocket, but a new model sans titanium parts is anticipated and should go for a more reasonable price.

The Japanese have justifiably cornered the derailleur gear market for some years. Shimano produces a comprehensive line of derailleurs. Their low cost Lark and Eagle models are reliable but heavy. The medium cost Titlist and 600 series derailleurs are much lighter and give excellent performance. The Dura-Ace and Crane units are fully competitive with the best European units, and have the edge on price. Shimano also produces a semi-automatic derailleur called the Positron, which positions the chain correctly for any gear selected, thus avoiding missed shifts and chain grind. It has the disadvantage of dual cable control, which is just that much more to go wrong, but I have found the Positron a good unit for novice riders who are all thumbs.

Best value for money today are the Maeda Sun Tour series derailleurs, popular with tourists and a good choice for beginning riders. They have wide range, and positive shifting under load, e.g., when pedalling pressure is maintained while shifting. This is a common novice error, and a recurrent problem for heavily laden tourists climbing hills. Campagnolo and Shimano units perform perfectly when shifted correctly, but can jam up and grind when shifted under load.

Gearing is a major factor to consider in the choice of derailleurs, and this subject is covered under Fitting. Read this chapter before purchasing a bike.

There are four different places on a bicycle commonly used to mount the levers for shifting derailleur gears:

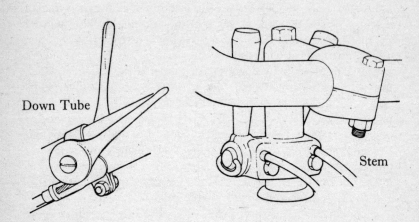

Down Tube

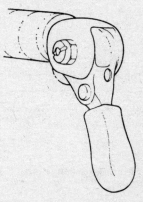

Stem

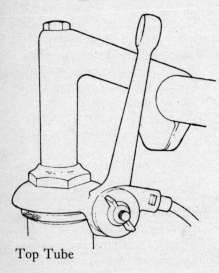

Top Tube

Handlebar

Each method has advantages and disadvantages. In my own opinion, simplest is best. Down tube mounting allows the use of short cables giving maximum feel and quick response when shifting. Stem and top tube mounts are more convenient when flat or all-rounder handlebars are used, but in a crash can dig you nastily in the gut or crotch. Handlebar end mounting requires long cables which give a sloppier response. It also requires the drilling of holes in the handlebar, and I know of instances where this led to corrosion and a complete snapping apart of the handlebar while the rider was under way. Down tube mounting is simplest and safest.

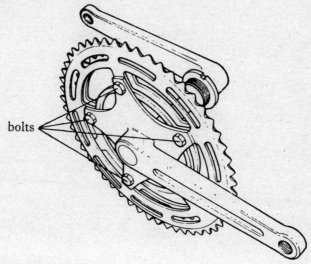

bolts

Cranks and chainwheels are made of aluminum alloy or steel. Design varies in the method of fastening to the bottom bracket axle:

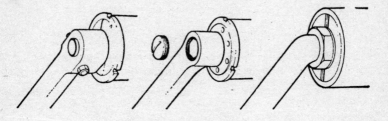

The Ashtabula is a one-piece cranks, chainwheel, and bottom bracket axle design. Quality bikes use aluminum alloy cotterless, medium quality bikes use aluminum alloy or steel cotterless, and low cost quality bikes use cottered steel. Good brands are Campagnolo, Shimano, Stronglight, T.A., Zeus, and Williams. Best value for money is Sugino.

An elliptical chainwheel known as the Durham is available as an accessory (Durham Bicycles, 3944 Marathon Street, Los Angeles CA 90029, about $26).

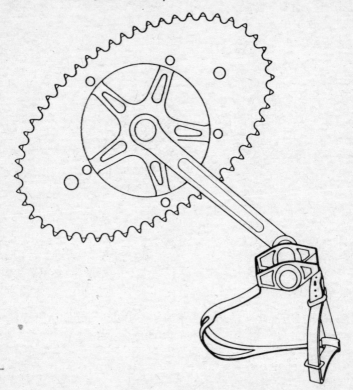

Elliptical chainwheels are not as effective as circular chainwheels when used for racing. However, at low speeds and under load, as when hill climbing or in frequent stop-and-go traffic riding, they can have a power advantage. Elliptical chainwheel enthusiasts claim that over long distances the lowered cadence rate (pedal revolutions per minute) is less fatiguing. Other cyclists disagree.

There seems to be no hard and fast rule. It is something you have to try for yourself. One limitation of current elliptical chainwheel designs is that no front gear changer can be used, so that the maximum possible number of gears is six with a derailleur system. Combining a multi-gear hub with a derailleur system could give between 9 and 25 speeds (up to 50 if a conventional double front chainwheel is used), but this is a complex and elaborate arrangement suitable only for meeting very specific needs.

Pedals come in three basic types: (1) the classic rubber tread platform; (2) cage design; and (3) metal platform.

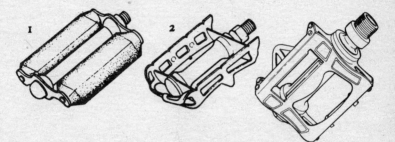

Cage and metal platform pedals can be used with toe clips and cleats, rubber platform pedals cannot. Metal platform pedals offer good foot weight distribution. The thin cage design can induce foot cramps on long tours. Pedals may have no ball bearings, adjustable bearings, or sealed bearings. Pedals with no ball bearings are found on only the cheapest and most chinzy of bikes, and should be avoided like the plague. Adjustable ball bearing pedals are found on low cost quality bikes through to superbikes, and range in price from $12 for the good value KKT Top Run to $100 for the Campagnolo Super Record road pedals with titanium spindles. Sealed bearing pedals are lubrication and maintenance free, but only to a point. In very wet or dirty conditions even a sealed bearing pedal (or hub or bottom bracket) will require maintenance. In this event, adjustable bearing pedals are easier to service. But in ordinary conditions sealed bearing pedals will not require lubrication or adjustment.

At this writing the most water resistant sealed bearing pedal is the Phil Wood platform (about $50). The Weyless sealed bearing pedal (about $65) gets wet easily, but features interchangeable cages for road, track, and or touring. At 105 mm wide the Weyless touring cage is one of the widest available. It has a center plate for good weight distribution. A top quality sealed bearing pedal is the Barelli Supreme (about $50), which features replaceable platform cages and a lifetime exchange warranty.

Saddle

Three-speed bikes generally have a mattress design wide saddle with coil springs. Racing and touring saddles for 10-speed bikes are long and narrow to minimize friction between the legs.

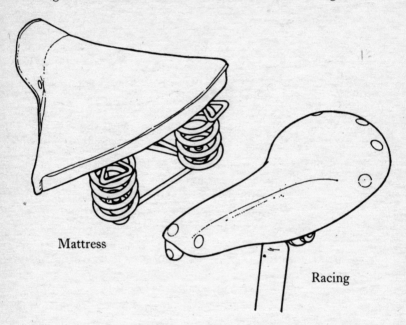

Mattress

Racing

Less expensive saddles are of plastic, the best of leather, with Brooks the acknowledged leader. A choice between the two depends somewhat on the type of riding and conditions. Leather wants a minimum of 500 miles of riding to become supple and properly broken in, but once done the fit is so good you will keep the saddle from one bike to another. Plastic needs no breaking in, and is impervious to weather, making it a good choice for cycle-cross machines and bikes that will be left out in the rain. A plastic saddle such as the Unica (12 ounces) is half the weight of the leather Brooks Pro (25 ounces) and this is a decisive factor in short distance and track competition events. The problem with plastic is that in warm weather it has you slipping about in your own sweat. A compromise has been sought in models such as the Milremo Super de Luxe, which are plastic covered with foam and leather, softer to ride, and a good choice for riders who will cover a lot of rough roads or paths.

I own and ride a number of different cycles, and have not got the time to switch my Brooks Pro from bike to bike, or spend a year breaking in half a dozen saddles. I find the suede covered plastic Milremo Professional excellent. Other good brands are Cinelli and Unica. Advocet saddles come in racing and touring models, with different designs for men and women. The women's models are slightly wider to accommodate the larger female pelvic structure. Both touring models feature additional padding where the pelvic bones touch the saddle.

In leather saddles only the good ones are worth buying. But whatever kind of saddle you buy, don't skimp. If you buy a bicycle and the saddle is of poor or unsuitable quality, exchange it immediately for a better one and pay the price difference. You will spend many, many miles and hours on your saddle, and if you pinch pennies you will be so oftimes reminded, for truth, by a sore ass and inflamed crotch.

Handlebars come in four standard designs:

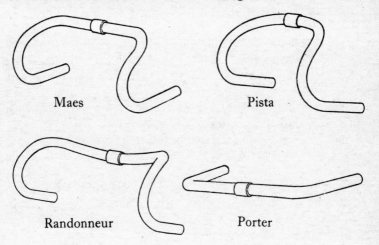

Maes

Pista

Randonneur

Porter

The Maes pattern is the most common downswept version, and is suitable for either touring or racing. The Randonneur and Pista patterns are more specialized, and respectively are for touring and racing. On inexpensive bikes the bars are of steel, and on better bikes of aluminium alloy. The virtues of downswept bars as opposed to flat bars are discussed in Fitting.

General summary:

There are many different bicycle brands, and each manufacturer usually produces upwards of a dozen or more models in different price grades. As you move from the under $100, all steel bike with seamed, smooth-joint frame, to the $700 and over superbikes, you find an increasing use of aluminum alloy for all parts of the bicycle, except the frame, which in quality machines is of cold-drawn alloy steel, and increasing sophistication of manufacture, such as lugged and brazed frame joints, double-butted frames, and cotterless cranks.

Broadly speaking, bicycles divide by function into: hub gear utility bikes designed for a soft ride and very stable handling; derailleur gear touring and commuting bikes also designed for a soft ride and stable handling, but with definitely brighter performance and lighter weight than the utility bike; combination touring and racing bikes designed for a medium ride and fairly brisk handling, and suitable for fast day rides or touring on smooth roads; and racing bikes designed for maximum speed, giving a stiff ride and very quick handling.

Now, clearly if most of your riding will be commuting on rough paved city streets, your interests will be best served by a bike with a long wheelbase 72° parallel (73° at maximum) frame with $1\frac{1}{4}''$ tires mounted on sturdy rims with 14 gauge spokes. Such a machine will also suit touring of a type where you frequently wander off into the boondocks down unpaved roads or paths. Suppose you are more interested in fast tours and sport riding. A stiffer frame with narrow profile high pressure tires will best suit your needs.

I find that beginning riders make two common errors: they under- or over-buy with respect to their needs. They are interested in cycling, but "don't need all that fancy stuff." So they buy an all steel machine which turns out to be good enough for local

"CORONA" CONVERTIBLE TANDEM.
For two ladies, or lady and gentleman. As a
single, suitable for lady or gentleman.
32 guineas; non-compressible, **31 guineas.**

use, but just gives a taste of what is possible when touring or racing.
Two or three years later they are back at the shop laying down the
bread for a better quality machine.

Alternatively, a prospective cyclist wants "the best money can
buy." He purchases a lightweight racing bike for regular commuting and quickly tires of a sore behind, endless punctures, and
buckled rims. The bike goes off to moulder in a closet.

Evaluate and understand your own needs carefully, and then
try to buy a bike that has some potential in reserve. For example,
a 3-speed is perfectly adequate for local utility use, short commuting trips, and off-road use. A sturdy 10-speed will serve all
these functions *and* be suitable for moderate touring. A lighter
combination touring/racing bike can still, with careful riding, be
used for commuting and even off-road riding.

Conversely, do not buy more machine than is comfortable.
Own the bicycle rather than having the bicycle own you. An
expensive touring/racing bike requires a certain amount of maintenance. It wants to be ridden with some degree of sensitivity. It

needs protection against theft. If you know for a fact that you just want a thrasho utility bike to get you from here to there, then buy that sort of machine. A bike should be used, not be an object of deification and worry about investment.

The first B.S.A. Safety Bicycle, 1884.

Recommended Bicycles

I can't possibly cover and evaluate every available bike and therefore am going to make recommendations by category only, and largely to set standards. The bikes that I list are fair values for the money. Diligent shopping may net you a better buy. Many bike shops have one or two specials where you may compromise on color or some other consideration for a good break in price. In any case apply and use the technical information I have given you. There are many fine bicycles which are not listed here and you will be doing yourself a disservice if you pass them by.

In standard 1- and 3-speed bicycles the large manufacturers offer good quality and value. In 10-speed bicycles the products of smaller firms that specialize in this kind of bicycle are usually better. Decent 10-speed bicycles are fairly refined and exact pieces of machinery, and while the use of mass production tech-

44

niques for their manufacture is far from impossible, it is difficult. Bicycle dealers, mechanics, and riders report that 10-speed models from large manufacturers are sometimes poorly prepared, and are subject to breakdowns. Products of the smaller, more specialized firms are more likely to come from the factory properly assembled and ready to go, and give less trouble in service. They are also more likely to have quality features such as leather saddles and ball-bearing pedals.

On the other hand, there are many bicycle dealers and riders who swear by the large firms, and say their products are the best value in any model or price range. In the next chapter I tell you where and how to buy a bicycle, and extol the virtues of your friendly local bicycle shop. I suggest you be guided by the shop. If they say that a big brand bike is good, and are willing to back that statement up with a service guarantee, that is a very important consideration. Many, many, many are the miles I have gone on popular brand name bicycles. For the more esoteric racing and touring machines – say over $175 – I personally would favor a smaller company whose main business is this sort of bike. In any case, I repeat, use the technical information I have given you. In any given model there is often little to choose between three or four different manufacturers, as the components supplied (brakes, derailleurs, chainsets, and so forth) may be exactly the same. Variations in manufacturing quality control can mean that in one batch of bikes manufacturer A's is the best, while in another batch of exactly the same models, manufacturer B's is "better". Look for yourself.

Do not be put off if the bike you find on a showroom floor has a slightly different specification than listed here. The desirability and/or availability of components can change rapidly. Manufacturers will generally provide the best components affordable within a given price range.

Heavy-duty Roadster

Raleigh Tourist DL1. Sturmey-Archer 3-speed gears, roller lever (uses metal rods in place of cables) brakes, lockable front fork, leather saddle, saddlebag, and 28″ wheels. Sizes: men's 24″, ladies' 22″. Black color only. Virtually an "Africa" model, with robust construction and frame geometry and fork trail designed for comfortable riding over rough ground. A modern museum piece.

Heavy Roadster

Raleigh Superbe DL24. Sturmey-Archer 3-speed gears, self-adjusting side-pull caliper brakes, lockable front fork, Dynohub generator and lights, leather saddle, rear carrier, and 26″ wheels. Sizes: men's 21″, 23″, ladies' 21″. Coffee color only. Not as massive as the Raleigh Tourist, but a heavyweight nonetheless.

Sports Roadster

(1) Raleigh Sports DL22. Sturmey-Archer 3-speed gears and self-adjusting side-pull caliper brakes, or 3-speed coaster brake hub, lockable front fork, leather saddle, saddlebag, and 26″ wheels. Sizes: men's and ladies' $19\frac{1}{2}$″, 21″, 23″. Colors: silver, green, coffee, blue, and yellow (not all sizes). Classic quality reliable and comfortable sports roadster.

(2) Raleigh LTD DL32. As Raleigh Sports DL22 above, but vinyl saddle, coaster brake hub option single-speed only, and no saddlebag. Sizes: men's 21″, 23″; ladies' $19\frac{1}{2}$″, 21″, 23″. Colors: black, red, and blue (not all sizes).

Lightweight Tourist

(1) Raleigh Sprite DL90 and DL95. Huret 5- or 10-speed derailleur gears, self-adjusting side-pull caliper brakes, flat handlebars with stem mounted geat shift levers, vinyl mattress saddle, alloy rear carrier, 27″ steel wheels with low flange bolt-on steel hubs. Sizes: men's $21\frac{1}{2}$″, $23\frac{1}{2}$″, 25″; ladies' $19\frac{1}{2}$″, $21\frac{1}{2}$″, $23\frac{1}{2}$″. Colors: red, coffee, and yellow (not all sizes). Basically a sports roadster with derailleur gears and not a true lightweight. Will stand rough use.

(2) Fuji Sports 5. Steel throughout. Dia Compe side-pull brakes, Sun Tour gears, 27″ wheels with medium flange hubs, vinyl saddle, flat handlebars with stem mount shift lever. Sizes: men's 21″, 23″; ladies' 20″. Colors: red or blue (men's) and cream or blue (ladies'). Also basically a sports roadster with derailleur gears. Durable.

(3) Raleigh Super Tourer DL140. Frame, forks, and stays of Reynolds 531 double butted tubing. Huret Jubilee 10-speed derailleur gears, Weinmann alloy side-pull caliper brakes, cotterless chainset, alloy flat handlebars with stem mounted shift levers, 27″ alloy wheels with high flange quick release alloy hubs, leather mattress saddle. Sizes: men's 21½″, 23½″, 25½″. Color: green. A proper lightweight suitable for commuting and limited touring.

(4) Falcon Model 88 and 89. Frame of Reynolds 531 plain gauge tubing. Shimano 5-speed derailleur gears with down tube mounted shift lever. All alloy components throughout, including Sugino cotterless chainset, Weinmann center-pull caliper brakes, flat handlebars, and 27″ wheels with low flange bolt-on hubs. Mattress saddle. Sizes: men's 21″, 22″, 23″, 24″, 25″; ladies' 21″. Color: black or red. The Falcon 88 has a very good finish and excellent handling qualities. It wants only dropped handlebars, a narrower saddle, and a double chainwheel, for conversion to a long-distance touring bike.

Nine-speed bicycles

These are commuting/touring bicycles created by combining a 3-speed derailleur gear freewheel with a 3-speed hub. The complete kit for this conversion, consisting of a 3-speed freewheel, derailleur, and shift lever and cable is manufactured and sold by the Cyclo Gear Company.

The disadvantage of this system is the inherent inefficiency of the internally geared hub, and the more bits and pieces that can go out of order. The advantage is that gears can be shifted quickly and positively through a wide range whether the bike is moving or not. This can be handy for people who are fumble-fingered, and for cyclo-cross types riding through fields and woods where most of the attention goes into staying upright. Here are the gear ratios commonly obtained through this conversion (read the section on Gearing for an explanation of the meaning of the numbers):

A 36-tooth front chainwheel and 26″ wheel gives:

3-speed hub		freewheel	
1st	30.5	40.7	54.3
2nd	36.9	49.3	65.7
3rd	43.9	58.5	78

and a 40-tooth front chainwheel and 26″ wheel gives:

1st	33.9	45.2	60.3
2nd	41.1	54.7	73
3rd	48.7	65	86.7

Bicycle - Galley 12

Five-, 10-, 12-, 15-, and 18-speed derailleur gear commuting, touring, and racing bicycles

A word for females: a ladies' pattern frame is structurally weaker and less responsive than a men's frame. They are not available in all models, frame sizes are limited, and often a mattress saddle and flat handlebars are supplied in place of the racing saddle and downswept bars supplied with the comparable men's model. You will get better value and performance from a regular "men's" bike. Incidentally, if you are on the short side (male or female), and are having a frame built to order, discuss the possibility of a raked top tube with the builder. This allows adequate bottom bracket height, a comfortable straddle when stationary, and, because a longer head tube can be used, increased frame flexibility (conventional design small frames tend to be stiff).

And a word for everybody: if you have less than $130 to spend I recommend the purchase of a used machine (see next chapter). This way you can get the fundamental quality in a machine which makes for really enjoyable cycling.

I have looked at a lot of low-price 10-speeds in the $85–$120 range, and they are mostly junk. Things are better now than in the bad old days of the bicycle boom, when two-bit factories throughout the world cranked out shiploads of rubbish to dump on the market, and unscrupulous importers retired almost overnight, but there are still a few manufacturers and bicycle dealers pandering to unprincipled consumerism. Many people don't know much about bikes. They want, say, a 10-speed with chromed fork tips and quick-release wheels, and look for the bike with these features at the lowest price. They don't know if the frame is a bathtub of old lead pipe. Bright paint and fancy transfers hide the truth. Wheels are out of true. Saddles are liquid, floppy plastic. Bearings bind. Derailleurs are low grade units that either slip or jam or break easily. Brakes are often crummy. Riding one of these machines is such a grinding painful torment that in short while you decide the whole idea is worthless. And there is very little that a bicycle repair shop can do, even if they are willing, about bad frame welds or low grade components. You wind up wanting back Old Invincible Ironsides, the faithful heavyweight that at least always worked.

The problem is not to save money, but to be sure you get what you pay for. Most reputable shops will tell you to avoid the $85–$120 bikes as pain and grief for everybody – you and the shop, where you will spend a lot of time if you buy one of these machines. Do not be hyped by colorful brochures filled with pictures of happy people sporting about on garbage machinery. Ignore the junk. Know the fundamentals in this chapter and buy a bicycle that really will bring you joy and pleasure.

The bicycles recommended below are grouped in arbitrary price ranges of $140 to $160, $160 to $225, $225 to $340, and $340 and up, and listed in order of increasing cost. Prices will change; the idea is more to indicate what specification to expect in basic, medium, high, and best quality grades of bicycle.

Basic quality bicycles, $140 to $160

(1) Fuji Sports 10. High tension steel tubing frame, angles 73° × 73°, men's sizes 19", 21", 23", 25"; ladies' 20". Sun Tour Spirt (front) and 7 GT (rear) derailleurs, Sugino steel cotterless chainset 42 × 52T to Sun Tour 14-28T freewheel, Dia Compe center pull brakes with dual levers, Sunshine semi large flange steel bolt on hubs with steel rims, and vinyl padded saddle. Steel handlebars, stem, seat post, pedals, and chain and spoke guards. Ladies' model with flat handlebars and stainless steel fenders. Weight 31 pounds. Colors: men's blue, red, or green; ladies' blue

or cream. Sturdy, comfortable, and good value for money.

(2) Azuki Gran Sport. High carbon steel tubing frame, angles $72° \times 72°$, men's sizes 19″, 21″, 23″, 25″; ladies' 19″, 21″. Shimano 600 derailleurs, Sugino Maxy 1 alloy cotterless chainset $40 \times 52T$ to 14-28T freewheel, Dia Compe center pull brakes with dual levers, alloy quick release high flange hubs, and vinyl padded saddle. Alloy handlebars, stem, seat post, pedals, and chain and spoke guards. Ladies' model identical, except in blue color, which has flat handlebars and wide mattress saddle. Colors: blue, silver, yellow, or red. Very predictable, forgiving handling, and very good value for money.

(3) Motobecane Nomade. Light steel tubing frame, men's sizes 19½″, 21″, 23″, 25″; ladies' 19½″. Huret or Sun Tour 7GT derailleurs, Tourney luxe alloy cotterless chainset $40 \times 50T$ to 14×28 or 14×32 Atom or Maeda freewheel, Weinmann center pull brakes with dual levers, alloy high flange bolt on hubs with steel rims, alloy stem, and vinyl padded saddle. Steel handlebars, pedals, and chainguard. Weight 29 pounds. Colors: silver or silver green. Good specification, and a particularly handsome finish.

Medium quality bicycles, $160 to $225

(1) Fuji Gran Tourer. High tension steel tubing frame, angles $73° \times 73°$, men's sizes 19″, 21″, 23″, 25″; ladies' 19″, 21″. Sun Tour Spirt (front) and 7GT (rear) derailleurs, Sugino New Maxy 1 alloy cotterless chainset $42 \times 52T$ to Sun Tour 14-30T freewheel with six cogs giving 12 speeds, Dia Compe center pull brakes with dual levers, Sunshine semi large flange alloy hubs (bolt on rear, quick release front), steel rims, and vinyl padded saddle. Steel handlebars, pedals, spoke guard and seat post. Alloy stem. Weight 31 pounds. Colors: men's silver, champagne, burgundy; ladies' silver or burgundy.

(1-A) Fuji Dynamic 12. As above, but men's sizes only, 21″, 23″, 25″. Alloy handlebars and wheel rims, and leather saddle. Dia Compe center pull brakes with hooded levers. Sun Tour Compe V (front) and VGT (rear) derailleurs. Colors: blue, red, or brown. Weight 29 pounds.

In the normal way, 6 cog freewheels require additional dishing of the rear wheel, which weakens it. Fuji have instead redesigned the rear axle and freewheel so that there is no increase in dishing.

The Fuji GT and 12 are very stable bikes, good for commuting and for touring trips with heavy loads. The 12 gears are usefully well spaced. The GT is included in this listing on account of the steel wheels, which might be a better choice for regular commuting on bumpy city streets, the extra men's 19″ frame size, and the ladies' mixte 19″ and 21″ models. If you can ride a 21″, 23″, or 25″ men's frame then I definitely advise springing the extra $20 or so for the Dynamic 12 model, which with a better specification is a superior value.

(2) Peugeot Super UO10. Carbon steel tubing frame, angles 72° × 72°, men's sizes 21″, 23″, 24″, 25″. Simplex AV-3-SC (front) and SX-800T (rear) derailleurs, Stronglight T. S. chainset 40 × 52T to Maillard 14-28T freewheel. Mafac center pull brakes with hooded levers, Normandy large flange alloy hubs with alloy rims, alloy handlebars and stem, and vinyl saddle. Steel seat post and pedals. Weight 28 pounds. Colors: red, white, blue, green, or black.

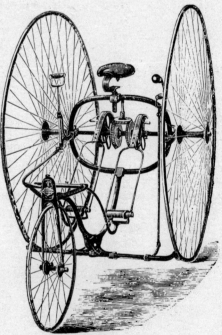

The Omnicycle.

A rose by any other name . . . this is the workhorse UO-8, a very stable bike especially suitable for commuting and heavy touring loads, but with a new and much better derailleur, the Stronglight T.S. chainset, and the Rigida rims. Lots of room for fenders and pannier racks.

(3) Panasonic DX-2000. Double-butted 1020 tubing frame, angles 73° × 73°, men's sizes 21", 22", 24", 26". Sun Tour V Luxe derailleurs, Shimano Tourney alloy cotterless chainset 42 × 52T to Sun Tour Pro Compe 14-24T freewheel, Dia Compe side pull brakes with hooded levers, Shimano 600 alloy large flange quick release hubs with alloy narrow $1\frac{1}{8}$" clincher rims, and vinyl padded saddle. Alloy handlebars, stem, and seat post. Steel pedals. Weight 29 pounds. Colors: black or red. Definitely more a racing than a touring bike. Suitable for fast one-day rides with light loads.

(4) Windsor Super Carrera. Columbus plain gauge tubing frame, angles head 73° × seat 74°, men's sizes $19\frac{1}{2}$", $21\frac{1}{2}$", 23", 25". Sun Tour Cyclone derailleurs, S. R. Apex alloy cotterless chainset 40 × 52T to Sun Tour Pro Compe 14-32 freewheel, Dia Compe side pull brakes with dual levers, Sunshine small flange quick release alloy hubs with alloy narrow $1\frac{1}{8}$" clincher rims, and suede saddle. Alloy handlebars, stem, and seat post. Steel pedals. Colors: silver, red, blue, or orange. A very lively and quick bike suitable for fast one-day rides but factory quality control is sometimes poor. If you are capable of dealing with minor mechancal imperfections, and poor paint finish, the Windsor gives outstanding performance for the price.

High quality bicycles, $225 to $340

(1) Fuji S10-S. Fuji double-butted high tension steel tubing frame, angles 73° × 73°, sizes men's 21", 23", 25"; ladies' 19", $21\frac{1}{2}$". Sun Tour SL (front) and VX-L (rear) derailleurs, Sugino New Maxy 2AL alloy cotterless chainset 42 × 52T to Sun Tour 14-30T six cog freewheel, Dia Compe center pull brakes with hooded levers, Sunshine alloy quick release low flange hubs with alloy rims, and leather saddle. Alloy handlebars, stem, and pedals. Steel seat post and spoke guard. Pump. Weight 26 pounds. Colors: men's black, platinum, blue, or jade; ladies' black or blue. A stable and good handling bike suitable for roughish roads and

heavily laden long distance touring. High class performance at a budget price.

(2) Motobecane Grand Touring. Vitus 172 double-butted main tube frame, angles head 74° × seat 73°, sizes men's 21″, 23″, 25″; ladies' 19½″, 21″. Sun Tour VGT Luxe derailleurs, Tourney SP alloy cotterless chainset 40 × 52T to Sun Tour 14-32T freewheel, Weinmann center pull brakes with dual levers, Normandy high flange alloy quick release hubs with alloy narrow section 1⅛″ clincher rims, and suede saddle. Alloy handlebars, stem, seat post, and pedals. Weight 25 pounds. Colors: gun metal grey or champagne.

Wheee! This is really rather more of a fast club riding than touring bike, although it can be used very nicely for this purpose on smooth roads. The performance is very exciting and especially in light of a price (like the Fuji S10-S above) under $250. The finish of the Motobecane GT is just about the nicest I have seen anywhere. There are some bikes that draw you on the moment you see them, and if you are a fast rider on a budget be sure to look this one over.

(3) Raleigh Gran Sport. Reynolds 531 double-butted tubing frame, men's sizes 20½″, 21½″, 22½″, 23½″, 24½″. Simplex Maxi derailleurs, alloy cotterless chainset to 14-28 freewheel, Weinmann center pull brakes with hooded levers, Normandy high flange alloy quick release hubs with alloy narrow section 1⅛″ rims, and Brooks B17 leather saddle. Alloy handlebars, stem, pedals, and seat post. Toe clips and straps. Pump. Weight 25 pounds. Color: blue and white. A comfortable bike suitable for touring on fairly good roads.

Best quality bicycles, $340 and up

(1) Fuji America. Fuji double-butted chrome molybdenum steel tubing frame, angles 73° × 73°, men's sizes 21″, 23″, 25″. Sun Tour SL (front) and VX-L (rear) derailleurs, Sugino New Maxy 2AL8 alloy cotterless chainset 42 × 52T to Sun Tour 14-30T six cog freewheel, Gran Compe center pull brakes with hooded and drilled levers, Sunshine alloy small flange quick release hubs with alloy 700 × 28C rims, and alloy handlebars, stem, seat post, pedals, and spoke guard. Toe clips and straps. Pump. Weight 24.5 pounds. Color: burgundy.

You've surely noticed by now that Fuji bikes are represented in every category here. Simple reason: Fuji bikes almost always have very good lug work and finish, an excellent well balanced selection of components, and a value for money price tag. The Fuji America is no exception. It is a good long distance tourer that will also serve as an ace commuting bike.

(2) Raleigh Competition Mk. II. Reynolds 531 double butted tubing frame, men's sizes 21½″, 22½″, 23½″, 24½″. Huret Jubilee derailleurs, T. A. Criterium alloy cotterless chainset, Weinmann center pull brakes with hooded and drilled levers, Normandy high flange alloy quick release hubs with alloy sprint rims for tubular tires, and Brooks B17 narrow leather saddle. Alloy handlebars, stem, seat post, and pedals. Toe clips and straps. Zefal pump. Weight 23 pounds. Color: black. A distance racing bike that can be used for fast club riding and light touring.

(3) Centurion Pro-Tour. Tange champion no. 2 double-butted chrome moly tubing frame, angles 73° × 73°, men's sizes 21½″, 22½″, 23½″, 24½″, 25½″. Sun Tour Cyclone derailleurs, Sugino Mighty Tour alloy cotterless chainset 36 × 52 to Sun Tour Pro Compe 14-30 freewheel, Dia-Compe G-type brazed on center pulls with hooded levers, Sunshine small flange alloy quick release hubs with alloy rims, and YFC Professional saddle. Alloy handlebars, stem, seat post, pedals, and spoke guard. Weight 26 pounds. Color: orange.

The Centurion Pro-Tour is purely, firmly, and beautifully, a touring bike. It is made for comfort, and stable handling of heavy touring loads. The brazed on Dia Compe brakes have strong stopping power. The Pro-Tour is also an excellent and durable commuting bike.

(4) Bob Jackson Gran Prix 16. Reynolds 531 double-butted frame, angles 73° × 73°. men's sizes 19″ through 26″ in 1″ increments. Sun Tour VT Lux (rear) and SL (front) derailleurs, Sugino Mighty Compe alloy cotterless chainset 42 × 52T to Sun Tour Pro Compe 14-24T freewheel, Gran Compe side pull brakes with hooded levers, Sunshine Pro Am small flange alloy quick release hubs with alloy Fiamme Red Label rims for tubular tires, all alloy components, and suede or leather covered plastic saddle. Weight 22 pounds. Colors: any.

The Gran Prix 16 is an English frameset with components selected and supplied by the mail order firm of Bikecology (P.O.

Box 1880, Santa Monica, CA 90406) and sold in kit form. You assemble the bike yourself. Optional extra cost components may be substituted for those listed above for a still better grade bike. However, as it stands the Gran Prix 16 is a very smooth running, lively, quick handling bike with an over-all springiness and dynamic feeling that is particular to European framesets. Strictly a racing bike, although an experienced rider would find it a joy for ultra-light fast touring on smooth roads.

(5) Bob Jackson Super Tourist. This is identical to the Gran Prix 16 above, except: frame angles 72° × 72°, Sugino Mighty Tour chainset, Gran Compe center pull brakes, and clincher rims.

(6) Austro-Daimler Vent Noir. Reynolds 531 or manganese molybdenum tubing frame, angles 73° × 73°, men's sizes 21″, 23″, 25″, ladies' 19½″, 21″. Shimano Dura-Ace equipment throughout, gearing 42 × 52T to 13-21T freewheel. Tubular tires, Gilux 3000 leather saddle. Weight 23 pounds. Color: black.

Sexy. Flat black frame, brakes, derailleurs, chainrings, saddle, and stem, with contrasting gold pinstriping, chain, freewheel, and rims. It is rather similar to my own black bike on the cover of this book. And it is a goer, a quick handling road racing machine that is still stable on fast downhills and through bumpy corners.

(7) Schwinn Professional Road Racing Paramount P-13. Reynolds 531 double-butted tubing frame, angles head 73° seat 73½°, men's sizes 20″ to 26″ in 1″ increments. Optional short-coupled frame sizes 21″ to 25″ in 1″ increments. Other frame modifications to order. Campagnolo Record (front) and Nuovo Record (rear) derailleurs, Campagnolo Nuovo Record alloy cotterless chainset 49 × 52T to Regina Oro 14-26T freewheel, Schwinn-Approved (Weinmann, most likely) alloy center pull brakes with hooded levers, Campagnolo Record large flange alloy quick release hubs with alloy tubular tire rims, Campagnolo Superleggeri alloy pedals with Christophe toe clips and straps, Campagnolo alloy seat post, Cinelli alloy handlebars and stem, and Unicanitor suede saddle. Weight 23 pounds. Colors: many.

Very fine top class machinery. Custom frame building to order and optional components available for an extra charge. Pricy, but with the advantage of the very large Schwinn dealer network. Paramounts also come in a touring model and a track model, men's sizes 20″ to 26″ in 1″ increments, and a ladies' touring mixte, sizes 20″ and 22″.

(8) Fuji Professional. Fuji double-butted chrome molybdenum tubing frame, angles head 74° seat 75°, men's sizes 20½″ to 25″ in ½″ increments. All Sun Tour Superbe components, gearing 47 × 52T to 13-22T six cog freewheel. Nitto alloy handlebars and stem. Fujita Pro King saddle. Tubular tires. Pump, water bottle, toe clips and straps, and spoke guard. Weight 20½ pounds. Color: silver mink.

A very fast handling bike excellently suited to short course criterium races, and therefore a tad too stiff and sensitive for general riding or even long stage races.

(9) Panasonic Professional. Double-butted tubing frame, angles 73° × 73°, men's sizes 21″ to 25″ in 1″ increments. Shimano Dura-Ace equipment throughout, gearing 42 × 52T to 13-23T six cog freewheel, Gran Compe handlebars and stem, and suede padded nylon saddle. Weight 23 pounds. Color: gold. Chainrings, hubs, and headset in black.

Expressly designed for long distance stage races, with relatively stable handling and a comfortable ride. Suitable club riding and ultra-light fast touring.

THE NEW CLUB CRIPPER TANDEM QUADRICYCLE ROADSTER.

Twelve-speed derailleur gear bikes

Twelve speeds are obtained by using a 6-cog freewheel gear cluster on the back wheel. The extra cog requires additional "dishing" – offsetting the hub into the rim so that the middle of the cluster is in line with the middle space between the front chainrings. The wheel is thereby slightly weaker, and for this reason 6-cog clusters are ordinarily used only on racing bikes, and not on touring or commuting bikes. The exception is the Fuji line of 12-speeds, which utilize a redesigned rear axle to minimize dishing.

Fifteen-speed derailleur gear bikes

Fifteen speeds are obtained by using triple front chainrings. Experienced tourists are the main users of this arrangement, because it gives a very wide range of closely spaced gears. Wide range 10-speed gearing usually leaves large gaps between each gear. But 15-speed gearing also has drawbacks: shifting requires more skill, and the chain will sometimes fall between chainrings; the chain is required to deflect greater distances from side to side, increasing chain wear and often rubbing the chain against various parts of the gear system; and the selection of components must be exactly right if the whole system is to work at all. Only an experienced cyclist who has to handle severe mountain grades and/or very heavy touring loads should even consider a 15-speed system.

A very comprehensive series of articles about 15-speed gear systems was done by Frank Berto in the March, April, and May, 1977 issues of *Bicycling!* I strongly suggest reading them before undertaking a 15-speed project.

In a price range of $300 and up are the offerings of small manufacturers and custom shops. Several are listed in the next chapter. They have models for touring, road racing, hill climbs, time trials, track, cyclo-cross, etc. Frames are hand built, and price depends on specification (grade of components supplied). The usual range is $500 to $800, with super de luxe models costing over $1000. The design and specification of these bikes reflects considerable experience, and they can be a most worthwhile investment for a keen cyclist. Often gear ratios, fittings, and color will be done to suit your own particular needs.

For about $300 and up you can construct your own bike. A factory produced double-butted frame runs about $125, with hand made jobs starting at about $200. For about $300 you can have a frame custom built to order. If the frame builder knows his business, and many do, you can have a bike that fits you and your kind of riding to absolute perfection. It is grand fun to have a superbike, but I would advise leaving this until you are an experienced cyclist and know exactly what you want – any mistake will be expensive.

Herewith a list of frame builders. There is no way the list can be comprehensive.

Ben Serotta
35 Maple Avenue
Saratoga Springs, NY 12866

Ray Gasiorowski
4434 Steffani Lane
Houston, Texas 77041

Thomas A. Boyden
Fastab Cycles
2706 S. Glenbrook
Garland, Texas 75041

Ron Boi
RRB Cycles
38 Greenbay Road
Winnetka, ILL 60093

Al Eisentraut
910 81st Avenue
Oakland, CA 94621

F. Matthew Assenmacher
104 E. May
Mt. Pleasant, MICH 48858

Jim Redcay
82 George Street
Lambertville, NJ 08530

W. L. Boston
38 Franklin Street
Swedesboro, NJ 08085

Colin Laing Racing Cycles
3454 N. First Avenue
Tucson, Arizona 85719

Rick Green
Talbot Frames
3237 Kingsway
Vancouver, V5R 5K3
British Columbia, Canada

Jeff Lindsay
WJL Custom Bike Frames
P.O. Box 3923
Chico, CA 95926

Angel Rodriguez
5627 University Way N.E.
Seattle, WASH 98105

R. T. Jansen Bicycles
Worcester, Vermont 05682

Barry Koenig
Proteus Design
9225 Baltimore Blvd.
College Park, Maryland 20740

Rob Horwitz
Tanguy Cycles Co.
331 Sommerville Avenue
Somerville, MASS 02134)

See also the section on Great Britain in the Touring chapter for a list of British framebuilders.

Other Bicycles

Small-wheel bicycles

These are mini-bikes with 16″ or 20″ wheels, available with a variety of options, including hinged, folding frames. Their virtues are: (1) easy storage; (2) good luggage capacity; (3) manuverability; and (4) easy adaptation to any size rider. Their drawbacks are: (1) high price; (2) a weight of 40 to 50 pounds which makes them heavy to carry and hard to pedal; (3) an unstable ride due to the small wheels; and (4), poor brakes. This last is critical, since the net effect of the mini bike's design is to restrict it to short local trips in urban areas, where good brakes are vital.

Many people who take up cycling for the first time since childhood get a mini. They like the crisp looks and easy way it goes. If you are in this category I want to caution you specifically that these bikes are good for some things and not for others.

For getting the groceries it is hard to beat one of the shopper versions with baskets front and rear that come off quickly to carry around with you in the store. The manuverability and small size

of the bike make handling and parking easy. However, a conventional 10-speed with quick-release touring panniers will carry as much and more – and go touring.

The mini-bike is ideal for exploring urban locales.It will U-turn right and left as fast as thought. You can get on and off effortlessly. The price is unsteadier handling at speed, and sudden dumps on slippery surfaces like oil or leaves. Mini-bike brakes are just adequate so long as the sun shines and the rims and brake blocks are dry. While in the wet any rim brake tends to piffle out, the mini-bike's brakes go down to near zero. As a choice for steady all weather commuting, or habitual use by a rider weighing more than 170 pounds, they are just not on.

Most mini-bikes come with quick-adjust seat and handlebars. This can be a very useful feature if several members of the family will be using the same bike.

In sum, the mini-bike is a local use machine with characteristics that give it the edge for multi-rider use, light shopping, urban exploring, and zesty handling. It is not so good for commuting or longer tours.

Folding bicycles

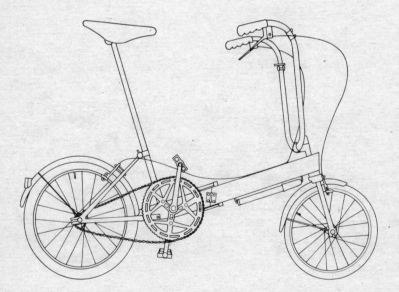

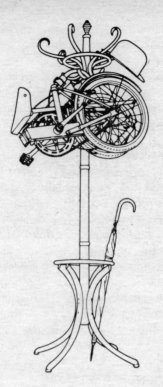

In all the world there is only one folding bicycle to consider seriously – the Bickerton. Conventional folding bicycles weigh 40 to 50 pounds and are bulky and difficult to manage. The Bickerton, constructed of aluminum alloy throughout, weighs only 18 pounds (20 pounds for the 3-speed model) and folds down in 45 seconds to an astonishing 30″ × 20″ × 9″ – about the size of a small suitcase. A stout canvas bag fitted on the front handlebars will hold up to 40 pounds of groceries or whatever, and also doubles as a carrier for the folded bike.

The portability of the Bickerton has to be experienced to be believed. It is no trouble at all to take along in a taxi, train, or bus. I would guess that 8 Bickertons could be carried in the trunk of a conventional American car. More importantly, the Bickerton obviates security problems. There is no need to bother with locking it up, because you can take it wherever you go. A folded

Bickerton will slide under a desk or workbench. It can hang from a cloakroom coathook. Storage in an apartment or home with limited space is a snap.

The portability of the Bickerton is a great asset for touring. Hopping by train, bus, airplane, or car from one interesting touring area to another is easy. On back trails the Bickerton can be carried in a backpack when the going becomes too rough for riding.

In performance a Bickerton will keep up with anything short of a flat-out racing or touring bicycle. The very light weight gives quick acceleration and easy uphill pedalling. Design and materials give the frame a surprising flexibility, so that despite the use of small wheels, the ride is very comfortable.

Of course the Bickerton is a mini-bike, and the handling is quick. Rapid downhill descents are unnerving. Very powerful pedalling from a standing start can "bounce" the front wheel. The initial riding sensation on a Bickerton is distinctly odd. But once the distinctive characteristics are mastered the Bickerton becomes a very tractable and enjoyable bicycle to ride.

Is there a catch? Of course – at this writing the Bickerton, which is manufactured in England, is not available in the U.S. of A. An export model conforming with American regulations is planned for 1978, but this cannot be taken as gospel. You can order one by post or airfreight from:

F. W. Evans Ltd.
77-79 The Cut
London SE1   ENGLAND

Price is about $250 for the 3-speed, and if this seems steep, remember that most 20 pound derailleur gear bikes cost $350 and up. And the Bickerton cannot even be compared to conventional folding bikes. It is in a class of its own for combining portability, easy riding, and load carrying ability.

Tandem bicycles

A tandem bicycle offers a number of advantages and disadvantages over a conventional solo bicycle. Two strong riders can move a tandem along very briskly, as over-all bicycle weight

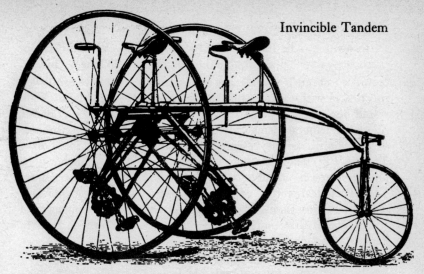

is less, and wind resistance is cut in half. A tandem will outrun a solo on a downhill run. Uphill, a tandem is slow. But over gently undulating terrain the greater mass of the tandem increases momentum, "ironing out" small hills.

Two riders of unequal strength can have rest periods for the weaker rider on the easy parts of a ride, and put in the muscle together when climbing hills. Togetherness is a very definate plus feature of tandemning. It is easy to talk, and there is something very pleasant about the shared physical effort. The rear rider, or "stoker", is free to enjoy the scenery to the maximum. Disadvantages include awkward handling in traffic, which riding should be done only by experienced cyclists, and the sheer size of a tandem, which necessitates a roof rack for transport by automobile, and generous storage space.

Only a lightweight (35 to 45 pounds) derailleur gear tandem is worth owning. The heavyweight (90 pounds) models are just too much work to pedal. At double the weight of a solo bike, a tandem requires first rate brakes. At the minimum it should have cantilever rim brakes with oversize blocks, or with Mathauser blocks. This would be for a lightweight racing tandem for use by experienced riders. Touring tandems should have drum brakes or disc brakes, or better still, cantilever rim brakes and a drum or disc brake. Tandem tires take a beating. Tubular tires and $27\frac{1}{4}''$ clincher high pressure tires are suitable only for racing or ultra-fast day riding. The Technical editor of *Bicycling!*, Fred DeLong, who has racked up many thousands of miles on tandems, recommends the sturdy 650-B tires and rims for durability, comfort, and stable handling even on unpaved roads.

A good tandem is expensive – $500 to $1500 – but think of it as one bicycle for the price of two. The Gitane Tandem Super-Sport at about $700 is a very good value. The Schwinn Paramount Tandem at about $1000 is a quality bike backed up by a nation-wide dealer system. Other good names are Follis, Urago, Jack Davis, and Southern Cross. My personal favorite is Jack Taylor of England, whose sports, touring, and track tandem models have a justified reputation for quality (about $1000 and up). Address: Jack Taylor Cycles, Church Road, Stockton-on-Tees, Teesside TS18 2LY, England. Another British tandem builder is Bob Jackson, 148 Harehills Lane, Leeds LS8 5BD. A number of American bike shops sell both domestic and imported tandems and the simplest way to find one near you is to check the adverts is a current issue of *Bicycling!*

Tricycles

These are popular items in retirement areas and cities in Florida and California. They usually have 20" wheels to keep the weight down low and are quite stable as long as they are not driven briskly. A large rear basket carrier handy for carrying groceries, gold bricks, golf clubs, or whatever, is a popular accessory. People with poor balance or coordination, brittle bones, or other problems, should seriously consider a tricycle. But bear in mind also that many old folks do just fine with conventional two-wheelers, and in fact there are a number of bicycle clubs whose members are all over seventy.

One type of tricycle has a fixed gear on which there is no free-wheeling and the pedals turn when the wheels turn. People who have limited motion in their legs have sometimes found that the exercise provided by this type of machine helps recovery of leg mobility. Cost is about $125 to $175. For hilly terrain get a 3- to 10-speed freewheel and expect to spend $150 to $225.

Humber Cripper Tricycle

People with a taste for the unusual might want to consider a lightweight racing or touring tricycle with 26″ or 27″ wheels. In no way is this an old age toy. Many an experienced bicyclist has come a cropper first time out on a trike. It must be steered around a corner, a sensation completely at odds with the handling of a bicycle, and rider weight must be counter-balanced to the inside on even a moderate bend. It is quite easy to lift a wheel, and downhill bends in particular must be approached with caution. Changes in the camber of the road also easily upset balance.

At first I was into trikes simply because I found them challenging. Now that I am more familiar and comfortable with their handling characteristics a number of advantages have emerged, and in fact the "family" cycle is a tandem trike. It has very good load-carrying capacity, does not require a dismount when stopped, will park without having to be propped up, and will stay upright under slippery conditions. The baby's seat is located between the two rear wheels, giving some measure of protection should there be an accident. When the next little 'un comes along it will be easy to add another seat. All in all, the tandem trike works out as a very comfortable family bike for relaxed and social cycling. The handling does not inspire rapid downhill descents, but this is immaterial on a family bike.

Higgins Ultralight.
    ca. 1950

A lightweight solo trike costs about $350 and up, and a tandem about $450 and up. Solo and tandem models are available from Ken G. Rogers, 71 Berkeley Avenue, Cranford, Hounslow, Middlesex TW4 6LF, England, and solo models from Jack Taylor Cycles, Stockton-on-Tees, Teesside TS18 2LY, England.

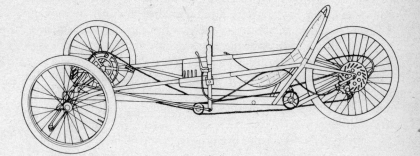

Another racing tricycle design is the recumbant, where the rider lies parallel with the ground, head at the rear. Two front wheels are steered through a system of rods and levers. The low center of gravity increases cornering ability, and the streamlining contributes to a high cruising speed, but the riding position gives poor visibility in traffic. They are suitable only for racing, and are obtainable in this country from Recreation Imports, 1329 Fee Drive, Sacramento CA 95815.

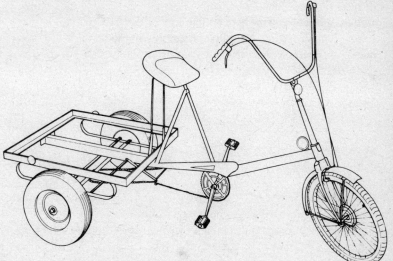

At the opposite end of the scale is the utility tricycle, weighing in at about 100 pounds. These feature a rear platform with a load capacity of 500 pounds, and have a great variety of industrial and commercial uses. A few examples would be: moving gardening equipment and lawnmowers around estates and parks; moving TV sets (or lawn furniture, or lace undies, or bags of cement – anything that a human being can pick up) around a warehouse; mounting a hot dog, ice cream, or vegetable stand; collecting rubbish from small litter bins. The great point in favor of the utility trike is that it is highly economical, and uses only the amount of power appropriate for the job at hand. It is also noise and pollution free. If you can think of and suggest an application for a utility trike where you live or work, you will be doing yourself and everybody else a big favor. One utility trike is called the Pedi-Porter, made by Alco Cycle Products, 451 3rd Street S.E., Largo, FLA 33540.

Quadricycles

These are 4-wheel cycles with seating for one or two persons. They generally aim to provide protection from the weather, and good load carrying capacity. To date they have been too heavy for practical urban use, but research and development continue, and the near future may well see such vehicles available to the general public. A fun quadricycle popular in holiday resort areas is the Surrey Selene, which roughly resembles a model T Ford and comes complete with a fringed awning top. Available from Recreation Imports, 1329 Fee Drive, Sacramento, CA 95815, and from Cliff Marshall Imports, 184 Old Wharf Road, Dennisport, Mass 02639.

Sailing Tricycle

The Rans Company, East Highway 40, Hays, Kansas 67601 manufactures and has sold about 350 sailing tricycles. Their product looks well made, and like a lot of fun. It is literally a tricycle with a (30 sq. ft.) sail just like on a boat, and will do up to 50 m.p.h. The Windhawk model sells for about $500, and the Eagle V model for about $700. Just be sure you have a lot of room.

Unicycles

These are becoming increasingly popular with kids, and one of these days I'm going to get one myself. Columbia's is well thought of, as is Matthew's.

From time to time small firms take up producing reproduction antique bicycles. If you are interested in something really different, this may be for you.

The "Boneshaker" bicycle is completely misnamed, as it is actually a penny-farthing or "ordinary" design, with a 48″ front wheel and 16″ rear wheel, but it is still a lot of fun to ride. Realize, of course, that the term "come a cropper" was first used in connection with bicycles in the days of the ordinary, which had and has a marked tendency to pitch the rider head-first over the handlebars if the front wheel encounters an obstacle such as a small stone. Write to The Boneshaker, 2111 South Green Road, Cleveland, Ohio 44121 for the name of a dealer near you.

Another manufacturer of a reproduction penny-farthing is the High Step Bicycle Co., P.O. Box 847, Milwaukee, Wisc. 53201.

Children's Bicycles

One attitude towards buying clothes, toys, and other materials for children is something like, "Well, the kid'll grow out of it soon, so let's not waste money. Just get him/her something good enough." Another ploy is, "Well, let's first see if she/he is really interested–then we'll get him/her something better." The victim of this faulty reasoning is the helpless child, who is saddled with some worthless or even painful piece of junk and who is expected to be grateful for it. Cheap bikes for children run from $35 to $40, and good ones from $40 to $60, so the price difference is at most $25. The cheap bike is difficult and unpleasant to ride, and shoddy workmanship and materials guarantee that it will grace the junkpile within a year. Result: total financial loss and total lack of stimulation for the child. The better bike is not only a pleasure to ride, thus insuring your child's fun and interest, but will also survive for a number of years through the hands of several children. It can be passed down in the family or sold for at least half the purchase price. Result: happier *children*, and less net expenditure. If you would like to save money or are on a tight budget, put up 3 × 5 cards advertising for what you want at laundromats, PTA meetings, etc., and get a used bike for $15 to $25.

Incidentally, the use of training wheels will only make learning to ride more prolonged and difficult for your child. He has to learn how to balance, and training wheels only postpone and make harder the inevitable. The best way to teach anybody, young or old, to ride is to let them do it themselves. Lower the seat so that they can comfortably touch the ground with their feet when mounted. All they need to do is push themselves along with their feet, like scootering. Balance and steering ability will come quickly.

Children are ready for their first two-wheel bicycle at about the age of 5, depending on the development and co-ordination of the individual child. The first bike for a child aged 5 to 7 should be a small-frame 20″ wheel featuring:

* Pneumatic tires for a comfortable ride, easier pedaling, and effective braking. Solid rubber tires are three times harder to pedal, provide a jolting ride, and give bad braking.
* A coaster brake. Caliper brakes cannot be managed by small hands.

* Steel steering head bearings. The plastic sleeve bearings used on cheap bikes result in bad handling and steering characteristics, and wear out quickly, compounding the problem.
* A sturdy frame with at least two permanent members welded to the steering head. Anything less won't take the punishment kids dish out.
* A large seat range adjustment so the bike can grow with the child.

Good, sturdy bikes with all of these features in a price range from $40 to $60 are:

(1) Schwinn J357 Bantam
(2) Vista M901 Speedy
(3) Ross 13613 Deluxe
(4) Columbia 9051 Deluxe Convertible
(5) Raleigh Mountie DL-80

The Raleigh Mountie comes in boy's and girl's models. Any of the other bikes may be converted to a girl's model by removing a bolt-on frame member.

For children between the ages of 7 and 9, a 24″ wheel coaster brake bicycle such as the Schwinn Fleet or Raleigh Space Rider DL54 is good. Children between 9 and 12 should have a small frame 26″ wheel bicycle with caliper brakes front and rear, and a 3-speed trigger control hub, such as the Schwinn L12-6 Typhoon or the Raleigh Colt DL58. Be sure your child has a strong enough hand grip before switching to caliper brakes. Children over the age of 12 can use adult bikes.

Declining in popularity with children is the hi-riser bicycle, with 20″ or smaller wheels, small frame and wheelbase, extra high handlebars, banana seat, and an excess of flashy hardware. Highly manuverable at low speeds, the hi-riser is otherwise unsafe and difficult to control. This is reflected in bicycle accident studies published in the *British Medical Journal*, which found that serious accidents with head injuries, broken bones, etc., involved these bikes all out of proportion to the number in use. Often it was a new, first bike (Christmas! Birthday!) or a first ride on a barrowed machine. Hi-risers are not much good for anything except hanging out at the local pizza parlor, and under no circumstances should they be a first bicycle.

Hi-risers are on the way out, but they have helped birth a new type of bicycle and sport – BMX. This is off road bicycle racing for kids, usually around a dirt course with features such as waterholes and jumps. BMX bicycles are light, extremely tough, and many even feature suspension systems. BMX racers need helmets, gloves, heavy boots and clothing, and plenty of ooooomph! But the BMX bikes are also just great for general off road use. Kids can mess about to their heart's content, and very importantly, do not have to be anywhere near cars and other motor vehicles. If you live near a park or out in the country I would rate a BMX bike very high for fun value, and just adequate for local utility use. It is not suitable for a first bike.

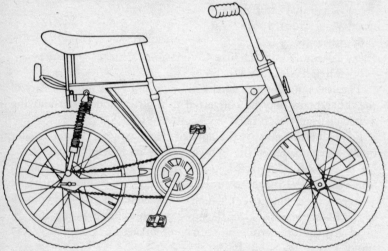

BMX bikes litter the ground, from manufacturers large and small. A good BMX bike should be light, obviously robust and sturdily built, and functional. Bikes with non-operative shocks or fake gas tanks are just for show. Good brand names are Kawasaki, Yamaha, Dan Gurney Eagle, and Matthews, with price from $100 to $200. Many kids save money by building up their own customized BMX bikes, but make sure the job is properly done: reinforced frame, MX handlebars and seat, and heavy-duty wheels and tires.

If your youngster is the sort who would like to really cover some ground, perhaps touring with the family, then consider a junior racer (suitable ages 8 to 12). These are 18″ frame 24″ derailleur gear bikes such as the Peugeot G45 CXE Junior Sports, or the Raleigh Record 24 Model DL128, price about $125.

3. The Urban Commuting Bicycle

Road racing, cyclo-cross, and track bicycles each have distinctive characteristics appropriate to their intended use. So does the urban commuting bicycle. Many city streets are obstacle courses filled with bumps, potholes, uneven surfaces, "temporary" steel plates which are slippery when wet, broken glass, and bits of sharp metal and other rubbish. In heavy traffic there is often not enough room for a cyclist to avoid an obstacle. A machine for these con-

LUDGATE HILL.

ditions must be tough. Theft is a constant problem in cities. An obviously expensive bicycle is more likely to be stolen, or stripped for parts. Finally, most regular commuters prefer a bike that requires a minimum of maintenance.

Several different types of bicycle are best capable of coping with urban conditions. Each has advantages and disadvantages according to your particular situation and needs.

The classic heavy-duty roadster offers a soft frame design which helps to iron out the worst of the bumps, enclosed hub gears which are well protected from wet and grit, robust $1\frac{1}{2}''$ tires which have a fighting chance of surviving glass and other road litter, and an upright riding position which allows a good view of traffic conditions. However, at 50 pounds weight, the heavy-duty roadster is hard work to pedal, and is not suitable for long journeys or steep terrain. It is available only in a 24″ men's frame, or 22″ ladies' frame, with 28″ wheels, and only tall people will find it comfortable to ride. As far as security is concerned it is an odd-ball bike with a low black market value and in theory would be less likely to be stolen.

The 3-speed sports roadster is much the same as the heavy-duty roadster except that it is lighter in weight, uses 26″ wheels with $1\frac{3}{8}''$ tires, and is available in a wide range of frame sizes. It is still not much of a speed machine or hill climber. One performance improvement is to fit alloy 26″ × $1\frac{3}{8}''$ rims and high pressure tires. An inexpensive way of improving hill climbing ability is to fit a

larger rear sprocket of 20 or 22 teeth. This limits top speed to around 20 m.p.h., but this is adequate for most traffic conditions. The bike is then also very suitable for off-road riding. Sports roadsters are not the most valuable of bicycles, but are easy to re-sell. Security is a problem.

Derailleur gear 5- and 10-speed bicycles are the obvious choice for long journeys and/or steep terrain. A longish wheelbase and fork trail, strong rims with thick spokes, and stout tires, will maximize comfort and stability over rough surfaces. Three stock bikes noticably good for commuting on bad roads are the Raleigh GP, Peugeot UO-10, and Fuji Dynamic-12 (see chapter 2 for specification details).

There are a number of modifications to make a 10-speed more suitable for regular commuting. Fitting sealed bearing hubs, bottom bracket, and pedals will increase maintenance intervals. Ultra-Glide cables with teflon lined housings do not need lubrication. Spokes should be at the minimum 14 gauge plain, cross four laced on small flange hubs, with steel rims or strong alloy rims such as Super Champion. Stout tires such as the Michelin Sports should be kept inflated *hard*, to help absorb bumps. The addition of a puncture resisting sealant such as STAB will increase tire weight by 2 ounces, but may spare you frequent tire repairs.

Ten-speed bike security is a hassel. For locking up on the street the only answer is a lock such as the Citadel or Kryptonite KBL4 (see Chapter 4 for details). Many people disguise high quality frames with a coat of dull looking, sloppy paint, and substitute low grade components (saddle, derailleurs, chainset). The resulting bike looks like an old banger but still goes fairly well. Some people booby-trap their bikes by slacking off the brakes or wheels, or removing the saddle. These are last ditch measures, however.

One way of obviating the security problem is with a folding bicycle such as the Bickerton (see chapter 2 for details). The bike goes where you go. A Bickerton is light and fast, comfortable over rough surfaces, and easy to take on a bus, train, or taxi if it rains and you don't feel like getting wet. It is in many ways the ideal urban bicycle, but for some people its quick handling characteristics are a drawback in crowded traffic, where predictability is important. Other people feel just the opposite, and like being able to manuver quickly in traffic. The Bickerton is a specialized bicycle, and only personal investigation can tell if you will enjoy riding it.

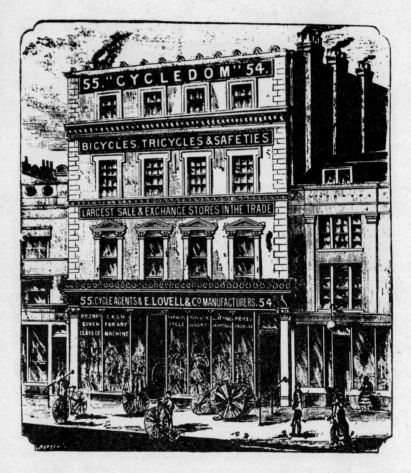

55. "CYCLEDOM" 54.

BICYCLES, TRICYCLES & SAFETIES

LARGEST SALE & EXCHANGE STORES IN THE TRADE

55. CYCLE AGENTS & E. LOVELL & Co MANUFACTURERS. 54

4. Buying and Keeping a Bike

New Bikes

The best place to buy a new bicycle is a bike store. You can sometimes save money at a department or discount store, but you are virtually guaranteed disproportionate headaches and problems. In the first place, the quality of merchandise is almost always inferior. Secondly, the sad fact is that not even the finest machines are defect-free when they come from the manufacturer. Department and discount stores do not employ trained bicycle mechanics, and so the bikes they sell are often unassembled, or have been put together by some cretin who has literally done more harm than good. It takes a good bicycle mechanic to assemble a new bike without damaging anything, check all the parts, and iron out the inevitable defects. Even then, problems are not likely to be over. If a department or discount store gives a guarantee – few do – they have no mechanics to take care of in-service problems. And if there is some totally basic defect in a machine you buy, it takes weeks for a refund or replacement.

A bike store will assemble the machine. Although you must check their work carefully, chances are they'll do the job right. If some problem comes up later they are available right away to fix it, and so are replacement parts. You get a guarantee, and sometimes a really good one. And you will want to deal with a bike store anyhow, for servicing, parts, accessories, and advice.

The kind of bike store makes a difference. Try to find one that deals only in bicycles. Many major cities now have at least one such shop. Usually they sell machines with a guarantee on parts and labor good for a year and more. Three-year guarantees are not uncommon. Due to a high volume of sales, prices are usually very competitive with discount stores.

The more local a shop you can deal with, the better. Any bike store must meet certain basic requirements in quality of bikes and in service, but convenience means a lot. A guarantee on a store 50 miles away is useless for anything except a major disaster. If there is a local shop and they don't have what you want, talk it over with them. Perhaps they can order a bike for you. If their "brand" of bike is not the one you had in mind take a good look at what they offer. All other things being equal, as they may well be since many manufacturers use the same components, the convenience of a local shop is an excellent reason to switch "brand". Just make sure you get a fair value. Ask about servicing and parts. If their guarantee isn't good enough, explain the problem. Don't expect however, that they will be able to offer as good a deal as a high-volume super-powered bike store. What you pay a little extra for is the fact that they are around the corner. Also, perhaps the general feeling and vibes are better.

At any rate, stay away from discount and department stores. I have not regaled you with horror stories about machines purchased from such sources, but they are legion, and cover everything from kids' tricycles to ultra-fancy racers. The tiny bit extra you spend in a bike shop buys an awful lot.

Taking Delivery

Anticipate that any new bike will have something wrong with it. Dealing with a good bike store minimizes this possibility but by no means eliminates it. When I picked up a new dream machine from one of NYC's finest stores I was too bedazzled to give it anything but the most cursory inspection. As I accelerated away from the store the rear hub and freewheel exploded in a blizzard of metal flakes and chips. Most problems you are likely to encounter are not apt to be so spectacular, but the point cannot be emphasized too strongly that a thorough inspection of any new bike is necessary. The best way to learn what to look for is to read the Maintenance and Repair sections of this book. Here are the main points to watch:

* Check the frame for straightness. Stand behind or in front of the bicycle and see that the wheels are in line. Next, hold the bicycle by the saddle only and wheel it around the shop. If the frame or forks are bent, it will tend to veer to one side. Finally, if you do a test ride, at some point when you are clear of traffic hold the handlebars as lightly as possible, even riding hands off if you have this skill. The bicycle should go straight, in control, without pulling to one side. Reject any bicycle which fails these tests. A bicycle which will not track accurately is tiring and unsafe to ride.

* Check quality of lug welds on frame. Sight down frame to check for bends.

* Wheels should spin easily. When held off ground weight of valve stem should pull wheel around so valve is in six o'clock position. Wheel should be centered in fork arms or chain stays. If wheel can be moved from side to side and there is a clicking sound hub cones are out of adjustment. Check that rim is true by holding a pencil next to it and spinning the wheel. Brace the pencil on a fork arm or chain stay to keep it steady.

* Pluck spokes. All should be evenly tight and give the same "twang".

* Brake blocks should hit rims squarely and not drag when released.

* Gears should work smoothly and with no slippage. Test first with wheels off ground and then on a ride.

* Pedals and chainwheel should spin easily but without side-to-side play.

* Ride the bike around the vicinity of the store for a few miles.

You may think that all this is a lot of trouble to go through. I have bought a fair number of new bikes for myself, family, or friends. There was something wrong with every one of them, and a few I rejected outright. You will save yourself a lot of grief if you invest some time at the outset on a careful inspection.

After you purchase a bike, check that all nuts, bolts, and screws are secure. Every last one. After riding 50 miles or so, repeat this operation. New bicycles "bed in", and it is very common, for example, for the brake bolts to work loose. Cranks, particularly the cotterless type, are bound to need tightening. See the appropriate section under Maintenance for details.

You may be far from a suitable bike store. Here are some that sell bikes and parts by mail:

Bikecology
2910 Nebraska Dept B
P.O. Box 1880
Santa Monica, CA 90406

Cyclo-Pedia
311 N. Mitchell
Cadillac, Michigan 49601

Big Wheel, Ltd.
Dept K
310 Holly Street
Denver, Colorado 80220

Bike Warehouse
8063 Southern Blvd. B8
Youngstown, Ohio 44512

Cycle Goods Corporation
17701 Leeman Drive
Minnetonka, MN 55343

Lickton's Cycle City
Telephone orders only.
0-312-383-4433

Just to help out (these lists are very incomplete) here are some of the better-known bike stores, and probably some do business by mail:

Pleasant Valley Shop
P.O. Box 293
Livingston, New Jersey 07039

Turin Bicycle Co-op
2112 North Clark St.,
Chicago, Illinois 60614

Hans Ohrt Lightweight Bikes
9544 Santa Monica Blvd.,
Beverly Hills, California 90210

Thomas Avenia
131 East 119th St.,
New York, New York 10035

Vel-Sport Cyclery
1650 Grove Street
Berkeley, California 94709

Thomas Avenia
10205 Rio Hondo Parkway
El Monte, California

John's Custom Bike Center
741 East Dixie Drive
West Carrolton, Ohio

Lifecycle
1005 Massachusetts Ave.
Cambridge, Mass 02139

The Bicycle Exchange
3 Bow Street
Cambridge, Mass 02138

Stuyvesant Bicycle
10 East 13th Street
New York, NY 10003

Fulton Street Cyclery
3038 Fulton Street
San Francisco, CA 94118

Cupertino Bike Shop
2098 Sunset Drive
Pacific Grove, CA 93950

Bud's Bike Shop
217 West First Street
Claremont, CA 91711

The Spoke
1301 Pennsylvania
Boulder, CO 80302

General note: if you live in a remote area the way to a quality machine may well be through mail order. Firms such as Bikecology have survived through dedication to fair business practice and satisfied customers. But nothing can duplicate the thrill of going to a bike shop, looking at the merchandise, and plunking down your money for your very own bike. Check the adverts in current issues of *Bicycling!* and *Bike World* for a shop near you.

Used Bikes

Used bikes are a good way to save money. Expect to pay about 75% of list price for a machine in excellent as-new condition, and about 50% of list for one in average condition.

Sources of used bikes depend on where you live and your own initiative. A lot of the bikes sold during the Bicycle Boom now moulder away in garages, attics, and sheds. They often have some minor fault like a broken brake or gear shift cable, and are no problem to make roadworthy. The problem is that they have been forgotten. If you just start asking around your neighborhood, put up WANTED notices in laundromats and on bulletin boards, you may well turn up a prize bike for a song.

Some bike shops sell used machines. Most cities and counties have local classified publications listing all kinds of stuff – including bikes – for sale. Check also the classified ads in the regular papers. Often a sale of household effects includes a bicycle. Auctions are sometimes good. A good bet in the spring are local bulletin boards at universities and colleges. Put up some cards yourself or take an ad in the student newspaper. Naturally, the more prosaic a bike you seek, the faster you will be likely to find it. But if you just put the word out wherever you go something will eventually turn up.

Understand exactly what sort of bike you are looking for. Converting a 10-speed racing bike to a touring bike can be expensive – new freewheel, chain, chainwheel sprockets, and possibly new derailleurs and new wheels. Be particularly careful of winding up with a lemon. Try to find out the history of the machine. It's best if you can talk to the owner. Was he or she interested in the bike and in taking care of it? Or did they just leave it out in the rain? Where did they ride? I would rather pay a little extra for a well-loved bike than save a few dollars on a machine with a dubious or unknown past.

In inspecting the bike, cover all the points listed for a new bike. Pay particular attention to the frame. Wrinkled paint on the forks or where the top and down tubes meet the head tube can indicate that the bike was crashed. So can a coat of nice new paint. I know of instances where badly repaired crash damaged bikes have fallen apart, killing their unfortunate new owners. What you want to see are a certain number of the inevitable nicks and scrapes, but no major dents, rust spots, or welds.

Count into the cost of a used bike a complete overhaul and lubrication, including possible replacement of the cables, chain, and sprockets. Read the sections on Maintenance and Repair in this book to learn how to assess components for wear and useful life.

A final word about used bikes related to the next problem, keeping your bike. There are plenty of stolen bikes for sale. Newspapers publish articles about marketplaces for stolen machines, and in some areas you can even order the type of bike you want. Price is usually about 25% of list, often less. With such a flourishing industry it hardly seems a crime to get a bike this way. It is. Legally and morally. Simply put, you are helping to steal. Additionally, it is not some giant dollar-hungry corporation's candy bar or rip-off piece of junk which you are stealing, but a possession somebody quite probably loves and cherishes.

Carriage propelled by dogs, from France

The figures on stolen bikes are impressive. As near as I can figure out, about 20% of the bikes in use at any given moment will be ripped off within a year. Conditions are barbaric. One day I came out of school to find a gang of urchins swarming over my bike. They had a five foot long steel far filched from a construction project with which they were busily trying to break the chain. I noticed with some amusement that not only were passers-by oblivious to the drama, but so were two of New York's finest in a patrol car directly across the street. In fact, should your bicycle be stolen and recovered by the police, there is still a good chance that you will not get it back. Many police forces have not got the time or inclination to check serial numbers against lists of stolen bikes.

The point is, you can expect little help. You have to rely almost entirely on out-thinking the opposition, and on the strength of your locking system. Unfortunately there is no such thing as a fool-proof system. One luckless individual used a "burglar-proof" lock to affix his bike to a parking sign post outside the Bicycle Exchange in Cambridge, Massachusetts. He returned the next morning to find only a stub of the parking sign post.

When locking up on the street you must:

* Use either a Citadel or Kryptonite KBL4 lock. These cost about $25 at bike shops and you have no alternative. Any other kind of lock or chain is easy to defeat. At this writing Citadel and Kryptonite back up their locks with a guarantee of replacement, maximum value $150 and $200 respectively, should your bike be stolen.

* Lock your bike to seriously immovable objects like lamp-posts, parking signs, heavy fences, etc.

* Lock the frame, and both front and back wheels.

* Be very selective about where and when you lock the bike. Slum neighborhoods are a bad bet at any time. Even if the bike itself is not ripped off, kids will often strip away the seat, handle-bars, brakes, and other components. Business and industrial districts are OK during the day. Always try to pick a busy spot with plenty of people around. NEVER leave your bike locked on the street overnight.

* Try to enlist help. The cashier for a movie theatre will

usually keep an eye on your bike. Newsdealers and other merchants will often help, and particularly if you do business with them. The local greasy spoon may give you indigestion, but if the cook waves a meat cleaver at anybody who bothers your bike the place is worth cultivating.

Successfully locking your bike is only one part of the problem. Depending on your age, sex, and the value of your bike, you are also subject to direct assult while riding. Usually this crime occurs in parks and other semi-isolated places, and to a lesser extent on slum streets. In form it can vary from seemingly friendly and casual interest on the part of strangers who would like to "try your bike out", to people leaping out of the bushes, knocking you flat with a club, and riding away on your bike. This once happened to an entire pack of racers in New York's Central Park. The attacking gang got away with 10 bikes.

Once assaulted, there is little you can – or should – do unless you are an action freak or have experience in physical combat. No bike is worth a cracked skull or a knife in the gut. You would not have been jumped in the first place if your opponents did not have an advantage.

On the other hand, being a coward is sickening. If you are confronted by three guys with knives or clubs, OK you quit. That's sensible. But if you and half a dozen people see a thug knock someone off their bike, and do nothing about it, then you are a low-grade yellow-bellied coward not fit for the name human. You've been hurt worse than if you had collected a black eye or lump on the jaw. There are lots of circumstances where you can and should fight. Where you draw the line is up to you. Fighting takes experience. You have to feel that you have a chance of winning. One person may be able to take on an assailant armed with a knife; another person may be better off to run away. In any case, do not let a violent encounter take you by surprise. Think about and prepare for it now.

For example, one kind of attack consists of a group of people fanning out across a street with the obvious intention of stopping you. What do you do? Stop and negotiate? You might as well just hand your bike over. Is that what you want to do? There may be room enough for a quick U-turn and fast sprint away. Suppose there isn't? William Sanders in a October, 1974 *Bike World* article has a sustinct answer: CHARGE! Pour on the power, yell like a maniac, and head directly for one of the people blocking you. Don't aim at a gap between people, aim at somebody and genuinely try to hit them. In the end, most anybody will make a scrambling effort to get out of the way. This is the kind of thing you can do only if you are prepared. Otherwise you will just roll to a dumb stop, wondering what if anything you can do, and one of the crowd will "try your bike out".

Of course if you can avoid confrontations in the first place, so much the better. Stay out of isolated areas in parks at any time, and stay out of parks altogether at night. If you travel through slum areas move along at a smart pace, and try to stick to well-lit streets. Stay out of lonely business and shipping districts at night. Above all else, be alert. Look for likely ambushes and for people who seem to be unduly interested in you. Keep moving in areas you think are dangerous. You can do 30 mph and easily outrace people on foot.

I won't say that you shouldn't let these problems discourage you from owning a bike. You have to make a realistic evaluation of your own situation. If you work in a crummy neighborhood and your employer won't let you bring your bike inside you're screwed (and should get another job). If you are a woman in a major metropolitan area you are a more likely victim of direct assault. I think that the advantages of owning a bike outweigh the disadvantages. But it

would be unfair not to tell you about the problems you may encounter.

If you do get a bike you must accept the possibility that it will be stolen. I succeeded in keeping one bike for years and years. It went when my apartment was ripped off. It can hurt a lot when a cherished and loved bike that you have shared all kinds of experiences with suddenly vanishes to feed some junkie's habit. Try not to forget that it can happen to you, accept it, and the elaborate security precautions you must take will have a slightly less paranoid tone.

A final word about attitude: I used to forgive thieves on the grounds that they were poor. Now that I have seen plenty of places where poor people do not steal this idea is invalid. Still, if you catch somebody trying to steal a bike I think the best thing to do is just tell them to split. Punitive measures, if you are capable of them, will accomplish little, as will moralizing or sermonizing. Calling the police or authorities will only result in teaching the thief how better to steal. The most practical thing would be simply to shoot such people, but this is noisy, messy, and of course illegal. Anyway, the drift of what I am saying is to not blow your cool. You'll only become frustrated. If you don't like this state of affairs, and it is abhorrent to any civilized, sensitive human being, then LOVE AMERICA OR LEAVE IT. Or change it.

5 . Fitting and Gears

Getting the most out of your bike requires careful fitting, e.g. placement of handlebars, seat, and controls. The standard formulas for this process are the result of considerable work and study by genuine experts and will probably work the best. After you have finished setting your bike up "according to the book" the resulting position may feel a bit odd. Give yourself at least 50 miles to get used to the new arrangement before making alterations. You may find the "odd" position considerably more efficient and less fatiguing than a "comfortable" position. At the same time, no two people are exactly alike, and some variation from the norm may be in order. Just give the orthodox position a fair trial, and make alterations gradually.

For how to make alterations in the position of seat, handlebars, stem, and brake levers, look up Adjustment under the relevant heading in the Maintenance and Repair sections.

Frame

Frame size is measured from the seat lug to the center of the bottom bracket. There are two methods of calculating the proper size:

Inside length of leg from crotch bone to floor, measured in stocking feet, less 9″, and

Height divided by 3.

Thus, a person with a 32″ inside leg measurement should have a 23″ frame, and somebody 6′ tall would get a 24″ frame. Be sure in any event that you can straddle the frame comfortably with your feet flat on the ground. An under-sized frame can be compensated for to some degree through the use of an extra-long seat post and stem, but an over-sized frame will inevitably slam you in the crotch.

Saddle

The position of the saddle determines the fitting of the rest of the bike. For most riders the correct fore-to-aft position is with the nose of the saddle $1\frac{3}{4}″$ to $2\frac{1}{2}″$ behind a vertical line through the crank hangar:

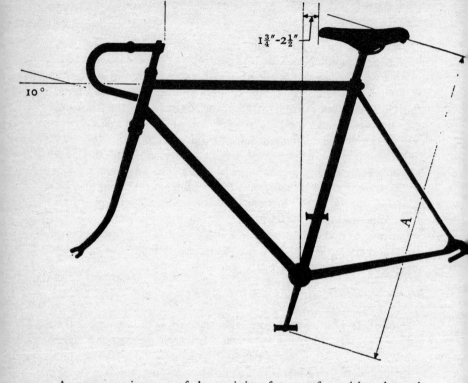

$1\frac{3}{4}''-2\frac{1}{2}''$

$10°$

A

A more precise way of determining fore-to-aft position depends on rider height. A person 5′6″ tall would normally have the nose of the saddle 1″ back of the bottom bracket, while for a person 6′3″ tall the distance would increase to 3″. Thus for someone 5′10″ tall the usual position would be 2″ back. However, there are many variations. Touring riders often use a slightly rearward saddle position together with handlebars set on the high side. They are interested in comfort and steady power output over long distances. Sprint riders and traffic jammers who use brief bursts of sharp energy often use a more forward saddle position. This is the reason sprint frames come with a steeper seat tube angle. For around town use, if you are a vigorous rider, you may like a more forward saddle position. For extended going and best over all efficiency however, stick to the normal position.

The horizontal tilt of the saddle, i.e., height of the front relative to the rear, is crucial. There is, in your crotch, a nerve. Pinching it even just slightly over a long ride can disable you with numb crotch for weeks. Start with the nose and rear of the saddle dead level, and if you experience any discomfort, immediately lower the nose a degree or two. It can make all the difference. This is where a good quality seat post with micro-adjusting bolts is important.

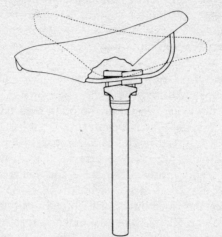

I have never seen a serious racing or touring bike with a back tilted saddle.

Most saddles are set too low. A rough rule of thumb is that while sitting on the bike with your heel on the pedal at its lowest point, your leg should be straight. This means that when riding with the ball of your foot on the pedal, your leg is almost but not quite fully extended at the bottom of the stroke.

A precise formula for the best saddle height has been worked out in a series of scientific tests. Measure inside length of leg from crotch bone to floor without shoes. Multiply this length (in inches) by 1.09. Example: $32'' \times 1.09$ equals 34.88, or $34\frac{7}{8}''$. Set saddle so distance A from top of saddle to center of pedal spindle in down position with crank parallel to seat tube is $34\frac{7}{8}''$.

This formula has been put together by experts. They found that an alteration in saddle height of 4% of inside leg measurement from the 1.09 setting affected power output by approximately 5%. So once the saddle is set, give it a good long trial before making changes.

Let's settle one thing now: there are many reasons why dropped bars are more efficient and comfortable than flat bars. Here are a few:

(1) A much greater variety of positions is possible. Not only can you select the best position for conditions – like low down when headed into the wind – but being able to shift about and bring different groups of muscles into play greatly increases comfort, to say nothing of power.

(2) Because weight is supported by both the hands and seat, road shocks and bumps rock the body rather than jar it. With conventional flat bars the whole weight of the body rests on the saddle. With dropped bars, not only is weight supported by the arms, but because the body is forward, it tends to pivot at the hips going over bumps. As it happens this is also very desirable from an anatomical point of view: leaning forward stretches the spine, allowing the absorption of shocks, and increases breathing capacity. Conventional bars force the rider into a stiff-spined position where the individual vertebrae of the spine are pinched together. Further, because there is no pivoting give at the hips, each and every jolt and bump is transmitted directly up the spine, greatly increasing fatigue.

(3) The better distribution of weight allowed by dropped bars provides improved stability and steering characteristics.

Positioning of the handlebars is crucial. For conventional use they should be set so that the top bar is just level with the nose of the saddle. Sprint bikes have the bars a whole lot lower, and if you do a lot of traffic riding you may want to set yours down a bit. Mine are about $1\frac{1}{2}''$ lower than the saddle. Just remember that if you opt for short-term speed it will be at some cost to over-all efficiency.

The stem should position the bars so that the distance between the nose of the saddle and the rear edge of the center of the handlebars equals the distance from your elbow to your outstretched finger tips. Another way to determine this distance is to sit on the bike in your normal riding position while a friend holds it steady. Without changing position, remove one hand from handlebars and let arm dangle fully relaxed. Now rotate your arm in a large arc without stretching. If, as your hand comes back to the bar, it is ahead or behind the other hand, the bars need to be moved.

Stems come in increments of length, or you can buy an adjustable stem. This costs and weighs more.

The standard rake for the ends of drop bars is 10° from the horizontal:

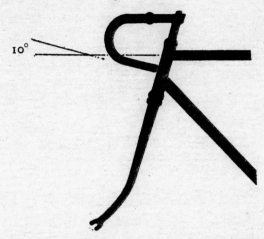

Start with this setting, which makes the tops of the bars level and thus affords the greatest variety of riding positions, and make changes as you desire.

Brakes

Do not tape new bars until you have ridden the bike enough to fully fiddle with and set the position of the brake levers. Most levers are too low. Almost all braking is done from above:

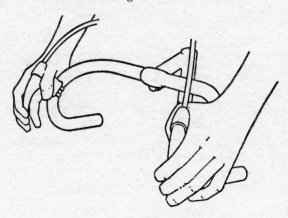

and the levers need to be high enough so that you can stop quickly and without undue effort.

Toe clips

Use them! They virtually double your pedalling efficiency. They may be a little awkward at first, but soon you will be able to slip in and out of them without a thought (see Riding). Be sure to get the size which corresponds to your shoe size. To avoid scratching up fancy shoes, tape the fronts of the clips with a little cloth tape.

Cleats

Cleats are metal strips fastened to the soles of bicycling shoes. Used in conjunction with toe clips they hold your foot to the pedal with a vengeance, and are quite unsafe for traffic riding unless you use very loosely set straps. But they are essential for racing and great for touring. To fit cleats properly ride your bike for a few miles without toe clips so that the soles of your shoes take an impression from the pedals. Then simply position cleats so cleat tunnel is aligned exactly with the pedal marks. Then fit toe clips.

Gearing

Fitting also includes the selection of gearing. Understanding this subject requires some knowledge of basic riding technique. Some of the information I am going to give you now is rather technical. Just use it as you need it.

When I bought my first 10-speed I was surprised to find that the gears, instead of each having a separate range like on a car, overlapped considerably. One gear really wasn't much different than the other. The reason for this is that there is a rate of cadence – the speed with which the cranks are spun around – which is the most efficient. For most people this rate is from 65 to 85 strokes per minute. Racers run 120–130 and up. The idea behind a multitude of gears is to allow the rider to maintain the same cadence regardless of terrain.

In consequence, a racing bike will have close ratio gears, each one much the same as the next, while a touring bike will have wide-ratio gears, with much greater differences between each gear. The reason for this is that touring bikes frequently pack heavy loads up steep grades. They are also – rightly – usually the choice of the novice rider. Only expert riders in good condition can comfortably use close-ratio gears.

What determines ratio? The number of teeth on the front sprocket divided by the number of teeth on the back sprocket. Thus a 60 front and a 15 rear give a 4 to 1 ratio. For competition a typical set-up might be a rear cluster of 23, 21, 19, 17, 15 matched to front sprockets of 49 and 52. For touring it might be 28, 24, 20, 17, 14 rear and 40 and 50 front.

To make everything a little simpler, gear ratios are expressed as a single number. The formula is:

$$\frac{\text{Number of teeth on front sprocket}}{\text{Number of teeth on back sprocket}} \times \text{wheel diameter} = \text{gear ratio}$$

Here is a chart of the commonly available gears:

Number of teeth on chainwheel

Number of teeth on rear sprocket	24	26	28	30	32	34	36	38	40	42	44	45	46	47	48	49	50	51	52	53	54	55	56
12	52	56·2	60·6	65	69·2	73·6	78	82·2	86·6	91	95·2	97·5	99·6	101·7	104	106	108·2	110·5	112·6	114·7	117	119·1	121·2
13	47·8	52	55·9	59·8	64	67·9	71·8	75·9	79·8	84	87·9	90	91·8	93·9	95·9	97·8	99·8	101·9	104	105·8	107·9	110	111·8
14	44·5	48·1	52	55·6	59·3	62·9	66·8	70·5	74·1	78	81·6	83·5	85·3	87·1	88·9	91	92·8	94·6	96·5	98·3	100·1	101·9	104
15	41·6	45	48·4	52	55·4	58·8	62·4	65·8	69·2	72·8	76·2	78	79·6	81·4	83·2	84·8	86·6	88·4	90	91·8	93·6	95·2	97
16	39	42·1	45·5	48·6	52	55·1	58·5	61·6	65	68·1	71·5	73·1	74·6	76·2	78	79·6	81·1	82·7	84·5	86·1	87·6	89·2	91
17	36·7	39·5	42·6	45·8	48·9	52	54·9	58	61·1	64·2	67·1	68·6	70·2	71·8	73·3	74·9	76·4	78	79·3	80·9	82·4	84	85·5
18	34·6	37·4	40·3	43·2	46	48·9	52	54·9	57·7	60·6	63·4	65	66·3	67·9	69·2	70·7	72	73·6	74·9	76·4	78	79·3	80·9
19	32·8	35·4	38·2	40·8	43·7	46·3	49·1	52	54·6	57·5	60·1	61·4	62·9	64·2	65·5	66·8	68·4	69·7	71	72·3	73·8	75·1	76·4
20	31·2	33·8	36·4	39	41·6	44·2	46·8	49·4	52	54·6	57·2	58·5	59·8	61·1	62·4	63·7	65	66·3	67·6	68·9	70·2	71·5	72·8
21	29·6	32	34·6	36·9	39·5	41·9	44·5	46·8	49·4	52	54·3	55·6	56·9	58	59·3	60·6	61·9	62·9	64·2	65·5	66·8	67·9	69·2
22	28·3	30·7	33	35·4	37·7	40	42·4	44·7	47·1	49·4	52	53·1	54·3	55·4	56·7	57·7	59	60·1	61·4	62·4	63·7	65	66
23	27	29·4	31·5	33·8	36·1	38·2	40·6	42·9	45	47·3	49·7	50·7	52	53	54·1	55·4	56·4	57·5	58·8	59·8	60·8	62·1	63·2
24	26	28·1	30·2	32·5	34·6	36·7	39	41·1	43·2	45·5	47·6	48·6	49·7	50·7	52	53	54	55·1	56·2	57·2	58·5	59·5	60·6
25	25	27	29·1	31·2	33·3	35·4	37·4	39·5	41·6	43·7	45·8	46·8	47·8	48·9	49·9	51	52	53	54·1	55·1	56·2	57·2	58·2
26	23·9	26	27·8	29·9	32	33·8	35·9	38	39·8	41·9	43·9	45	45·8	46·8	47·8	48·9	49·9	51	52	52·8	53·8	54·9	55·9
27	22·9	25	26·8	28·9	30·7	32·5	34·6	36·4	38·5	40·3	42·1	43·2	44·2	45·2	46	47·1	48·1	48·9	49·9	51	52	52·8	53·8
28	22·1	23·9	26	27·8	29·7	31·5	33·3	35·1	36·9	39	40·8	41·6	42·6	43·4	44·5	45·5	46·3	47·3	48·1	49·1	49·9	51	52
29	21·3	23·1	25	26·8	28·6	30·4	32·2	34·1	35·6	37·4	39·3	40·3	41·2	42·1	42·9	43·7	44·7	45·5	46·5	47·3	48·4	49·1	50·2
30	20·8	22·4	24·2	26	27·6	29·4	31·2	32·8	34·5	36·4	38	39	39·9	40·6	41·6	42·4	43·2	44·2	45	45·8	46·8	47·6	48·4
31	20	21·6	23·4	25	26·8	28·3	30·2	31·7	33·5	35·1	36·7	37·7	38·5	39·3	40	41·1	41·9	42·6	43·4	44·2	45·2	46	46·8
32	19·5	21·1	22·6	24·2	26	27·6	29·1	30·7	32·5	34·1	35·6	36·4	37·2	38	39	39·8	40·6	41·3	42·1	42·9	43·7	44·5	45·5

For 26″ wheels

	24	26	28	30	32	34	36	38	40	42	44	45	46	47	48	49	50	51	52	53	54	55	56
12	54	58·3	62·9	67·5	71·8	76·4	81	85·3	89·9	94·5	98·8	101·2	103·4	105·6	108	110·2	112·3	114·7	117	119	121·5	123·7	126
13	49·7	54	58	62·1	66·4	70·5	74·5	78·8	82·9	87·2	91·3	93·4	95·3	97·5	99·6	101·5	103·7	105·8	108	110	112·1	114·2	116·1
14	46·2	49·9	54	57·8	61·6	65·3	69·4	73·2	76·9	81	84·8	86·7	88·6	90·4	92·3	94·5	96·4	98·3	100·2	102	104	106	108
15	43·2	46·7	50·2	54	57·5	61	64·8	68·3	71·8	75·6	79·1	81	82·6	84·5	86·4	88	89·9	91·8	93·6	95·3	97·2	99	100·8
16	40·5	43·7	47·2	50·5	54	57·2	60·7	64	67·5	70·7	74·2	75·9	77·5	79·1	81	82·6	84·2	85·9	87·8	89·4	91	92·1	94·5
17	38	41	44·3	47·5	50·8	54	57	60·2	63·4	66·7	69·6	71·3	72·9	74·5	76·1	77·7	79·4	81	82·6	84	85·6	87·2	88·9
18	35·9	38·9	41·8	44·8	47·8	50·8	54	57	59·9	62·9	65·8	67·5	68·8	70·5	71·8	73·4	74·8	76·4	78	79·4	81	82·3	84
19	34	36·7	39·7	42·4	45·4	48·1	51	54	56·7	59·7	62·4	63·7	65·3	66·7	68	69·4	71	72·4	73·7	75·4	76·7	78·1	79·3
20	32·4	35·1	37·8	40·5	43·2	45·9	48·6	51·3	54	56·7	59·4	60·7	62·1	63·4	64·8	66·1	67·5	68·8	70·2	71·5	72·9	74·2	75·6
21	30·8	33·2	35·9	38·3	41	43·5	46·2	48·6	51·3	54	56·4	57·8	59·1	60·2	61·6	62·9	64·3	65·3	66·9	68	69·4	70·5	72
22	29·4	31·9	34·3	36·7	39·1	41·6	44	46·4	48·9	51·3	54	55·1	56·4	57·5	58·9	59·9	61·3	62·4	63·8	65	66·2	67·5	68·6
23	28	30·5	32·7	35·1	37·5	39·7	42·1	44·5	46·7	49·1	51·6	52·6	54	55·1	56·2	57·5	58·6	59·7	61	62·1	63·2	64·5	65·6
24	27	29·2	31·3	33·7	35·9	38	40·5	42·7	44·8	47·2	49·4	50·5	51·6	52·6	54	55·1	56·2	57·2	58·5	59·4	60·7	61·8	63
25	25·9	28·1	30·2	32·4	34·6	36·7	38·9	41	43·2	45·4	47·5	48·6	49·7	50·8	51·8	52·9	54	55·1	56·2	57·2	58·3	59·4	60·4
26	24·8	27	28·9	31	33·2	35·1	37·3	39·4	41·3	43·5	45·6	46·7	47·5	48·6	49·7	50·7	51·8	52·9	54	54·8	56	57	58·1
27	23·8	25·9	27·8	30	31·9	33·7	35·9	37·8	40	41·8	43·7	44·8	45·9	47	47·8	48·8	49·9	50·7	51·8	52·9	54	54·8	55·9
28	22·9	24·8	27	28·9	30·8	32·7	34·6	36·4	38·3	40·5	42·4	43·2	44·3	45·1	46·2	47·2	48·1	49·1	50	51·1	52	53	54
29	22·1	24	25·9	27·8	29·7	31·6	33·5	35·4	37	38·9	40·8	41·8	42·6	43·7	44·5	45·4	46·4	47·2	48·3	49·1	50·2	51	52·1
30	21·6	23·2	25·1	27	28·6	30·5	32·4	34	35·9	37·8	39·4	40·5	41·3	42·1	43·2	44	44·8	45·9	46·8	47·5	48·6	49·4	50·2
31	20·8	22·4	24·3	25·9	27·8	29·4	31·3	32·9	34·8	36·4	38·1	39·1	40	40·8	41·6	42·6	43·5	44·3	45	45·9	47	47·8	48·6
32	20·2	21·9	23·5	25·1	27	28·6	30·2	31·9	33·7	35·4	37	37·8	38·6	39·4	40·5	41·3	42·1	42·9	43·7	44·5	45·4	46·2	47·2

For 27″ Wheels

Number of teeth on rear sprocket

In general, 100 is the top range and is hard to push, 90 is more common, and 80 the usual speed gear. 60 and 70 are the most often used, 40 and 50 are for hills. Below 40 is for extremely steep terrain and heavy loads. Most people gear too high and pedal too slowly. This increases fatigue. It is much better to pedal briskly against relatively little resistance.

There are other factors besides range to consider in setting up gears. Ease of transition from one gear to another is important. If you have to shift both front and back sprockets every time it is laborious. For example:

		Rear			
	14	17	21	26	31
Front	52	100.2	82.3	66.9	54	45
	47	90.4	74.5	60.2	48.6	40.8

means that to run up through the gears consecutively requires continuous double shifts. On the other hand, a set up like:

		Rear			
	14	15	17	19	21
Front	54	104	97.2	85.6	76.7	69.4
	38	73.2	68	60	54	49

means that you can run up through the gears using only one shift of the front derailleur. (Never use the small front to small rear or big front to big rear. I will explain why later.)

If you use wide gaps front and rear there is almost bound to be some duplication of gears:

		Rear			
	14	17	21	26	31
Front	52	100.2	82.3	66.9	54	45
	42	81	66.7	54	43.5	36.4

and yet curiously enough, many good bikes are set up this way. It really depends on what you want the bike for, because in balancing the various factors of range, ease of shifting, and number of different gears, you are just going to have to make some compromises. For novice riders I would suggest the following:

Hilly terrain
Competition – 45 × 52 front, 14, 16, 19, 20, 23 rear.
Touring – 36 × 52 front, 14, 16, 19, 23, 28 rear.

Flat terrain
Competition – 49 × 52 front, 15, 17, 19, 21, 23 rear.
Touring – 40 × 54 front, 14, 16, 19, 23, 26 rear.

Compromise
Touring – 40 × 50 front, 14, 17, 20, 24, 28 rear.

I make these recommendations with some misgivings for there is one problem or another with all of them. There always is, but these are stock gearings with which you can do quite a bit. Each person of course has his own personal preferences, and you should work out gearing to suit your own needs. On my all-time favorite bike (lost to a junkie) I had 46 × 60 front and 13 through 30 rear, which got me incredulous and pitying regard from bike-wise friends. It suited me perfectly. The 46 front running through the 30 rear gave me a 41 gear which got me up nearly everything. When in town I used only the 60 front and the three middle gears of the back sprocket, thus minimizing shifting. Down hills and long shallow gradients the super-heavy 60 front and 13 rear drove the bike along like a bomb. In short, it was ultra-wide range gearing also suitable for short sprints.

If you do elect to muck around with gear ratios you will have to take derailleur capacity into account. Besides shifting the chain from sprocket to sprocket, the rear derailleur also keeps the chain taut. A 14 through 30 rear and a 36 × 54 front gives a variation in chain slack (between the 36 to 14 and 54 to 30) which exceeds the capacity of some derailleurs. Derailleur capacity is a function of design: competition units do not have to cover a wide range and can therefore be much lighter; touring units are heavier and sturdier. Generally, capacity is marked on the box as for example 13-24-36-53. The outer figures give the high gear, inner, the lower. Some advertised figures are as follows:

Brand	Rear Range	Front and Rear
Simplex Prestige	13–28	37
Huret Allvit	13–28	28
Campagnolo Nuevo Record	13–30	32
Campagnolo Gran Turismo	13–36	43
Sun Tour GT	13–34	40

You will have to decide for yourself which elements in the weight *vs.* range balance are the most important. Here is the final tidbit to take into account and round out an already confusing picture: you don't need the full range of the derailleur. You should not ever run the big front sprocket to the big rear, or the small front to the small rear, because it causes the chain to cut across at too severe an angle, causing excessive wear, usually rubbing of the derailleur gates, and reduced efficiency.

So . . . the important range is between the large front sprocket to the next to largest back sprocket and the small front sprocket to the next to smallest rear sprocket. Since this is a more limited range with a little diddling you can use a competition derailleur with relatively wide range gears. The advantage is lighter weight and improved performance.

This business of cross-angle strains on the chain bears on the subject of triple front chainwheels. These units are the choice of many experienced tourists for mountain country and packing heavy loads, as they give the most range. Because of cross-over problems however, you do not get that many extra gears. In addition, triple chainwheels are difficult to adjust and align, and the derailleur cages tend to get screwed up. Unless you really need the extra range I'd advise staying away from this combination.

A DANGER BOARD

6. Riding

Anybody can ride a bicycle. You just get aboard and pedal. Heh. Try following an experienced tourist on an 100-mile run or a competition rider around the track. Physical condition of course plays a part, but here technique counts more than anything else. Fifty-year-old grandmothers can and do run rings around fit young adults. Attention to the basics of technique will make riding easier and more enjoyable, and give you greater freedom than if you had not bothered with the subject at all.

Of course even basic technique varies somewhat with conditions. And there is a lot more to riding than technique. The following chapters on traffic jamming, and touring and racing, amplify considerably on the information you need in order to cycle safely and comfortably.

Shifting

Take it easy when first learning to shift. Once you get the knack you can make smooth split-second gear changes, but let your skill develop gradually and avoid damaging "clunk" sounding shifts.

3-Speeds: To shift up to a higher gear, ease pressure on pedals, move selector to next gear, resume pressure. Extra-fast shifts may be made by maintaining pedal pressure, moving the selector, and then pausing momentarily when the shift is desired. If done too hard this may damage gears. Going down to 1st from 2nd or 3rd and coming to a stop, back-pedal slightly. If not stopping, use same procedure as for upshifts.

10-Speeds: Never, ever shift a 10-speed unless pedalling. To see why, hang your bike up so that the rear wheel is off the ground, rotate the cranks, and manipulate the gear shift levers so you can see how they work. Shifting a 10-speed without pedalling may result in a bent or broken chain or gear teeth. If you park your bike on the street always give the gears a visual check to make sure passers-by have not fiddled with them. It happens often.

When going up or down through the gears ease pedalling pressure during shift. The shift levers do not have stops for the different gears. and you have to learn where they are by feel. Do not let the derailleur cages rub the chain. Sometimes it is necessary

to make a small adjustment in the front derailleur when using a wide range of rear sprockets in order to prevent this. Do not run the big front sprocket to the big rear sprocket, or the small front to the small rear. It causes the chain to cut across at too severe an angle, greatly increasing. wear and reducing efficiency. Proper shifting should also take into account the demands of cadence (see below).

Pedalling

Ride with the ball of your foot on the pedal, not the heel or arch. The fundamental technique for easy cycling is called ankling. This is where the foot pivots at the ankle with each revolution of the crank. Start at the top of the stroke (12 o'clock) with the heel slightly lower than the toes. Push with the ball of the foot and simultaneously pivot at the ankle on the downstroke so that the foot levels out between 2 and 3 o'clock, and continue this motion so that at the bottom of the stroke the toes are lower than the heel:

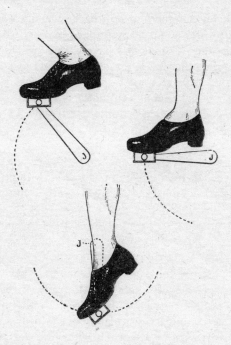

With toe clips pull up on the upstroke as well. The main thing to strive for is smoothness and steady, even pressure. Practice this slowly, in a high gear, and away from traffic so you can concentrate on watching your feet.

Toe clips are a great boon. By allowing you to pull up on the pedals as well as push down they virtually double pedalling efficiency. They are completely safe. Smooth-soled conventional shoes can always be slipped out even when tightly strapped down. If using bicycling shoes and cleats, keep the straps loose in traffic. The technique for setting underway is simple: start with loose straps. Straddle the bike, slip a foot into a pedal at the 1 o'clock position, and tighten the strap. Push off, using the downstroke of this crank to get you underway, and simultaneously reach down with the free foot, give the pedal a light tap to spin the toe clip around to the proper position, slip foot in, bring crank around to 12 o'clock position, and tighten strap. It sounds more complicated than it is. The key is the deft, light tap to the pedal to bring the toe clip around so you can slip your foot in. Practice will soon make it second nature. When coming to a stop reach down and loosen one strap so you can get your foot back in easily when underway again. Do not worry about being trapped by toe clips. I have made zillions of emergency stops and have always been able to get my feet free. On the other hand, do not tempt fate by riding in heavy traffic with ultra-tight straps. And if you use sneakers or other soft-soled shoes (bad – not enough support), or cleated bicycling shoes, keep the straps loose when conditions warrant.

Cadence

This subject was mentioned in connection with gearing. Briefly, human beings pedal most efficiently at a certain number of strokes per minute. The optimum cadence varies with the physical condition and technique of the individual rider. Generally, novices run from 60 to 85 strokes per minute, experienced tourists approach 100, and racers run 120–30 and up.

Most people gear too high and pedal too slowly. They don't think they are getting anywhere or getting any exercise unless they are pushing against resistance. It is precisely this pushing which creates needless fatigue. It is much better to pedal rapidly against relatively little resistance. Especially when first starting with a bike, always try to pedal as rapidly as you can without going into orbit. Soon you will find your natural cadence, and should always try to maintain this as a uniform rate of pedalling. Allow this to be one of the primary functions of the gears, and always shift up or down as necessary to maintain an even cadence. Learn to shift just before you need the new gear. Do not let a hill slow down your cadence, for example, but shift just before you hit it, and as needed going up. The way you will be able to churn along will be absolutely amazing.

Bumps

When you come to bumps, pot-holes, cables, etc., put most of your weight on the pedals and handlebars. This allows the bike to pivot underneath you, reducing shock for both you and the bike. You know how motorcycle scramble riders stand up on the pegs? Like that.

The American Star machine

Braking

Try to use your brakes as little as possible. This will help you to "look ahead" and anticipate traffic conditions in advance. Be careful of braking too hard and skidding or pitching yourself over the handlebars. It is the front brake which does most of the work, and the more rapidly you deaccelerate, the more work it can do.

This is because weight is transferred forward, increasing the co-efficient of friction between the front tire and the road surface. Simultaneously, weight on the back tire is lessened slightly, decreasing the coefficient of friction and making it more liable to skid. The technique for a rapid or panic stop is thus one of keeping the body weight as far back as possible, progressively increasing pressure on the front brake, and holding pressure on the back brake to just below the point where the wheel will lock and skid. It is a question of feel and can only be learned by practice. Start with quick stops from low speeds and gradually increase velocity. After you feel reasonably adept, have a friend give you emergency stop signals at unexpected moments.

In slippery conditions or when banked hard over in turn favor the rear brake. The rear wheel does have a greater tendency to skid, but if it goes you may still be able to keep yourself upright, and at worst will land on your hip. A front wheel skid will pile you on your face.

In wet conditions frequently apply the brakes lightly to wipe water off the rims. Otherwise you may need four or five times the distance for stopping with dry brakes.

Going down long hills avoid overheating the brake shoes or wheel rims by pumping (on-off-on-off-on, etc) the brakes. Always be able to stop.

Turning

If you can ride a bicycle then by definition you can turn it. But there are different methods and styles of turning.

Underway, a bicycle is in a constant state of imbalance. A tendency to lean one way will be corrected by the rider, the bike will move through center of balance to a lean the opposite way, and the rider will correct again. Most turning consists simply of taking advantage of a lean in the desired direction. Instead of correcting, the rider allows the lean to continue and thus effects a turn. The *feeling* is that the rider has changed balance and the bike has followed to suit, and in that bicycle geometry is designed for a certain amount of self-steering, the feeling is accurate enough. The rider does in fact change balance. This type of turn has two faults: it is slow, and it puts rider and bicycle weight in one single line down to the point of tire contact with the road.

The police have strict orders to arrest any Bicyclist riding without a bell or whistle

In racing, and in traffic riding, it is often necessary to turn QUICK! This can be done by hauling back on the handlebar end opposite to the direction in which you wish to go. The bike will move out from under you, you will start to fall, and then you will TURN. Can you see it? In the "normal" turn you topple to one side gradually; in the "haul handlebar" turn you snatch the bike out from underneath you, and immediately fall into a turn. It is very handy for avoiding unexpected obstacles such as broken glass. In effect, you go one way, the bike goes the other, and afterwards you catch up with each other. Like panic braking, this type of turn must be learned slowly, and with lots of room for manuvering.

Another type of turn consists of laying down the bike, while you remain relatively upright, i.e., the bike "leans" more than you do. This is useful when the road surface is rough, because then a percentage of the rider weight pivots as the bike moves up and down, lessening the load on the wheels. Better for the bike, better for you. It is also a quick turn, tho not as fast as hauling handlebar.

Another type of turn consists of leaning the body more than the bike. I think – but cannot assure you – that this helps lessen the chances of a skid. At any rate, when I unexpectedly encounter a wet manhole cover or oil slick while turning I throw the bike *up* while keeping my own weight down. This, and the lay down turn, can be done by moving the whole bike underneath you while you pivot sideways at the hips, and can be accelerated by hauling on the handlebars as well.

Haul, lay down, and set up turns are esoteric in description but relatively simple in practice. For your own safety you should be able to execute a haul turn instantly and automatically, whenever circumstances require.

7. Traffic Jamming

Every rider must know how to ride on streets and highways shared with motor vehicles, the same way if you walk you have to know how to cross the street. Beyond this, for many people 99% of their riding is in traffic, and they might as well make it as safe and enjoyable as possible. I have the worst misgivings about this chapter, for on the one hand I want you to use a bicycle as much as possible, but there is no way I can tell you that riding in traffic is safe. In plain fact it is dangerous. The other side of the coin is that taking a bath is dangerous too. There are some things one has or wants to do, accepting and attempting to prepare for attendant dangers. Each person needs to make her/his own evaluation of the amount and kind of traffic riding that suits him/her. Although the basic principles are the same, there is a considerable difference between mixing it up with heavy weekday commuter traffic and cycling a few blocks to the park on Sunday.

This chapter contains a multitude of facts and suggestions, but the most important thing I have to tell you about riding under any conditions, *and especially in traffic*, concerns psychological attitude and attentiveness. You must at all times be alert, and know everything that is going on, from the size of the pebbles on the road to the debris which might fall on you from a construction project to the number and type of vehicles before and behind you – absolutely everything. Traffic riding requires total concentration. There is no place for woolgathering here, or idyllic pastural pleasures. If you don't pay attention, you may die.

Attentiveness has benefits. First of all, total engagement is refreshing. For example, I like physical challenges but spend most of my time pushing a pencil. For me the change of pace represented by traffic jamming is at times exhilarating. It does, as they say, take your mind off your troubles. Secondly, once you gain a little experience you will hopefully still be alert, but relaxed. Is crossing the street a C. B. DeMille production for you? In a more relaxed state you will appreciate the benefits of attentiveness, and see more, notice more, feel more. Getting from one place to another will be a distinctly real experience, and something *you* do.

I would like to deal with two other drawbacks to traffic jamming which unfortunately have no redeeming features:

Hyperventilation*

The inhalation of exhaust fumes and other pollutions is a serious health hazard. The automobile contributes up to 85% of all air pollution in urban areas. As a cyclist not only are you at nose level with the maximum concentration of the pollution, but you are breathing harder and faster (hyperventilation). Estimating the precise degree of possible or actual damage is difficult. One statistic is that the average urbanite inhales the equivalent in particles and poisons of two packs of cigarettes a day. Does this translate for the bike rider as 4 packs of cigarettes a day? Five? Six?

Cars emit lead, unburnt gas, nitrogen oxides, sulphur oxides, carbon monoxide, and small quantities of grit. The worst for the cyclist are lead and carbon monoxide.

According to Dr. Derek Bryce-Smith, Professor of Chemistry at Reading University, there is a good chance that airborne lead is causing real physical damage to large numbers of children today. He has also suggested that a portion of mental illness may be due to otherwise undetectable brain damage from lead pollution. Lead poisoning has been listed as a cause in the death of zoo animals.

Carbon monoxide is the greatest immediate risk for the cyclist. It is a classic poison which interferes with the oxygen-carrying capacity of the blood. Long before it kills, this action results in decreased alertness, headaches, vague dizziness, and nausea. This dehabilitation adds to the hazard of traffic jamming.

The concentration in the air in many urban areas of both lead and carbon monoxide is already far above recommended levels. These levels are themselves suspect, for in the Soviet Union the permitted concentration of lead is 100 times lower than in the U.S. of A. Considering that the auto industry has now for decades resisted building pollution-free engines for reasons of profit, it is most likely that we have false standards and a tremendous minimizing of the real hazard.

Mental illness, headaches, animal deaths, Soviet standards, two packs a day, and other tidbits of information are not readily translatable into an accurate assessment of damage, and particularly not for the cyclist, who rides through the very worst of the pollution. But the simple fact is that I get sick with headache, eye pains, nausea, and general malaise when I ride on smoggy days, and

*Thanks to Francis Arnold for much of the information here.

particularly the days which have a yellowish tint.

I would advise against riding at all on high air pollution count days. Try to stay clear of smoke-factory trucks and buses, and pick roundabout routes that favor parks and less travelled streets. Most gas masks will only filter out grit, but of course the sight of you using one would be wonderful guerilla theatre.

The hazard of air pollution should not be minimized at all: the benefits you gain from the exercise of riding may well be offset by the damage caused by inhaling the chemicals, poisons, and other wondrous substances freely released into the air we breathe.

Females

I am ashamed to write about this, yet it is a reality. Females are subject to harassment from motorists and passersby. This ranges from relatively harmless if insulting lewd comments to outright assault, where a motorist will reach out of his car to knock a moving female cyclist to the pavement. I don't have statistics on this latter sort of thing, but have heard of enough incidents so that there is no question but that it happens, and is something any female cyclist must take into account. Incidentally, if you witness such an assault and can possibly do so, beat the assailant up black and blue. Such people are cowards who can be kept in check only through fear and intimidation. Get license numbers and all that, but the wheels of justice tend to miss these characters. An attack from a car on a defenseless bicyclist merits putting the assailant in a hospital.

There are innumerable physical hazards to keep a lookout for while riding in traffic, but it is motor vehicles which are your main concern. In riding your bike you are something of a pioneer. The U.S. of A. is not really ready for the bicycle. Theory and law say that the bicycle is a vehicle which must be operated according to the rules of the road and which has the same privileges as other vehicles. Fact says otherwise. The American motorist is absolutely convinced that his vehicle gives him the complete right of way. Anything which obstructs his forward progress – like a slow moving bicycle – just shouldn't be there. He may be wrong, but it is essential for your survival to understand how he thinks. As a cyclist you don't really exist for him. As often as not he will cut you off, make turns in front of you, or sit on your tail honking furiously when there is no room to pass. It never even occurs to him to put on his brakes and give you room to maneuver, as he would for another car.

Riding successfully in traffic requires a blend of determination and knowing when to give in. For example, try never to block overtaking cars. At the same time if it is unsafe for you to let them pass, don't hesitate to take full possession of your lane so that they *can't* pass. Both you and the other human have exactly the same right to use the street or highway. Just because he/she has a motor vehicle confers no additional rights or privileges, and in fact the wasteful consumption of energy and vicious pollution of the environment for which her/his vehicle is responsible is a serious infringement of your rights. It is important that you understand and believe this. You have nothing to apologize for. You are not "blocking" or "in the way". At the same time you have to be practical. You are in a land of primitive savages. A lot of people behind the wheel are authentic maniacs. No matter how right you are, any confrontation with a motor vehicle will wind up with you the loser.

There are enough aspects and tricks to traffic jamming so that I am simply going to run them as a list. Before doing so, a brief discussion about traffic regulations.

The rules of the road, which you are legally required to obey, need to cut both ways. In England for example, cyclists meticulously observe traffic lights, signs, and regulations. Riders signal all turns, stops, and the like. In turn, motorists treat the cyclists as equals. Nobody ever leans on a horn and crawls up somebody's behind if a bicycle leads a pack of cars away from a light. The English are fond of traffic circles which resemble a Dodge-em at Coney Island. It takes a little cool, but you can confidently sail out into the middle of one of these on a bike. Because a cyclist is in fact accorded proper privileges and vehicle status, it is really unthinkable not to obey traffic regulations. In England, even when the coast is clear I always stop for a red light. I desperately want the protection equal status gives me.

In the U.S. of A. no such rules apply. Most books tell you to abide by the traffic regulations. This often is not practical. Moreover, because you can never rely on your "rights" to protect you, you have to engage in a form of defensive riding which assumes that if there is some way for somebody to get you, they will. According-

ly, when the coast is clear rules have little binding effect. You just aren't thinking that way. Remember however, you can get a summons for traffic violations on a bicycle, and if you supply a driver's license as identification (which you are not required to do), any convictions become part of your driving record.

Rolling

* Hands near or on brake levers at all times. If you need to stop as quickly as possible and are not going too fast, twist the front wheel as you apply the brakes. The bike will melt into the ground in a controlled crash as the wheel and forks buckle.

* Be alert. There is plenty to watch for. Keep your eyes constantly moving. When looking behind don't twist your head, duck it down. Easier to do, quicker, and smoother. Do this constantly. You might have to swerve to avoid an obstacle or serious accident, and must know if you have the room or not.

* Be definite. Save meandering for country lanes where you

can see for a long way in both directions. Ride in a straight line. Signal all turns clearly. Make right turns from right lane and left turns from left lane, if on a wide street. If you are going to do something, do it. Being definite takes the form of a certain amount of aggressiveness. Don't get bulldozed into immobility – nobody is going to give you a break. Make and take your own breaks. As far as most other drivers are concerned you either don't exist or are some alien foreign object which they want behind them. Draw attention to yourself and be super-clear about your intentions. Colorful clothing and/or a bright hat are a good idea.

* Be defensive. Always assume the worst. You can't see around the stopped bus? *Assume* a pregnant lady who is the sole support of 21 children is going to come prancing out. There is a car waiting to cross your lane? *Assume* it will, because *it will*. In 4 out of 5 accidents involving bicycles and motor vehicles, the motor vehicle committed a traffic violation. Always ride within a margin of control which allows you to stop or escape should absolutely everything go wrong.

* Look for openings in traffic, driveways, streets, garages, etc. that you can duck into should the need arise. Try to plan where you would go should you and the bike part company. The natural tendency in a collision situation is to try desperately to stop. Many times your interests will be better served by launching yourself over an obstacle. Far better to hit the pavement at an angle than a car head-on.

* While not exceeding a speed which gives you control, try to keep moving. Within reason, avoid using brakes. This will have the effect of making you figure out well in advance what traffic situations are going to occur. There is a car double-parked in the next block. Are you going to be able to swing out? Also, a lot of the danger from other vehicles in traffic comes from differences in velocity. If you are going slow, cars bunch up behind, crowd, become impatient, etc. A racing bike can easily keep up with and pass a lot of traffic. You may find it a bit unnerving to run neck and neck with cabs and trucks at first, but it is safer than offering a stationary target. Try to *integrate* yourself with the traffic.

* To this end, always be in a gear low enough to give you power and acceleration. In heavy traffic an even cadence is difficult to maintain, but try to keep your feet churning away and avoid getting stuck in a "dead" high gear. As a cyclist you

have only a fraction of the power available to the motorist. To stay integrated with traffic requires that you be prepared to accelerate hard and quickly.

* On the other hand, do not tailgate. Car brakes are better than bike brakes. Most bike accidents consist of the bicycle running into something. Leave plenty of room up front. This is where motorists accustomed to running bumper-to-bumper will try to pressure you from behind, even though you are moving at the same speed as the car you are following. Maintain position and if they give you the horn give them the finger.

* Be extra-cautious in intersections where you already have right of way. Cars coming from the opposite direction and turning left will frequently cut right across your path. Even if the vehicle is seemingly waiting for you to pass, don't trust it, for at the last moment it will leap forward. Cabs are particularly bad for this. Letting a motor vehicle precede you to clear the way is often a good tactic.

Another danger at intersections is cars coming up alongside from behind and then making a sudden right turn. Cabs love to do this. One way to stop it is for you to be in the center of the lane. However, if the intersection you are entering has a light which is going to change soon, then traffic from behind may be storming up at a breakneck pace. You'd better be out of the way.

* In any city anywhere in the world taxicab drivers are your worst hazard. All things are relative, and in London for example, most cabbies are decent. In the U.S. of A. cabbies have the highest ulcer rate of any occupational group, as well they might considering their working conditions and how they drive. Abilities vary, but most are just no good. New York City cabbies are the bottom of the barrel.

The cab driver is your enemy. He is *accustomed* to bulldozing and bluffing his way around by main force. It is second nature, and does not even require hostile intent on his part. It is just something he does. Every day. You, on a 30-pound bicycle just haven't got a chance against his 5000-pound cab. And many cabbies do take a perverse pleasure out of screwing you up. Perhaps they are resentful of anyone having fun on a bike. Who knows. At any rate, if there is anybody who is going to cut in front of you, brake suddenly, etc., it is the cabbie. Cabs are the enemy.

* Very often you will be riding next to parked cars. Be

THE CITY CYCLIST.

especially careful of motorists opening doors in your path. Exhaust smoke and faces in rear-view mirrors are tips. Even if a motorist looks right at you and is seemingly waiting for you to pass, give her/him a wide berth. Believe it or not, you may not register on his/her consciousness, and she/he may open the door in your face.

* In most states the law requires you to ride to the right of the right lane as far as is practicable. This is a very elastic and sometimes abused definition. Cyclists have been ticketed for causing an obstruction by riding too far to the left, and there have also been instances of opening car door/cyclist accidents where the cyclist was held at fault. Take "as practicable" to mean "as is safe", and always allow enough manuvering room to avoid road litter and potholes. Pass parked cars with room to spare should a door open. If somebody objects to your "obstructing" let them stuff it. If you get a ticket, it is a far better deal than a trip to the hospital.

When the road or street is too narrow for overtaking vehicles to pass you with enough room, then ride bang out in the center of the lane. Do not let them pass, or if it is a two-way road or street, make them pass in the opposite lane. Vehicle drivers may object and cavail, but this is far safer for you than letting them pass with only inches to spare..As said before, if they don't like it, let them stuff it. You are equally entitled to road space and safe passage.

* On multi-lane roads or streets where there is a right turn only lane at an intersection, and you intend to go straight through, get into the left through lane well before the intersection. Ditto if there is a bike lane. In fact, even if there is no right turn only lane, it is better to move out of the bike lane into the next lane left for going straight through an intersection. This helps minimize the chance of a right turning vehicle cutting you off.

Lane changing into fast, thick traffic can take muscle. John Forester does it by eyeball to eyeball contact with a particular motorist while positioning himself with the clear intention of moving left.* If the motorist makes room Forester then changes lane. The method has a distinct advantage in that both hands stay on the brakes, where they belong in heavy traffic. However, if you

*Forester, John. EFFECTIVE CYCLING. Custom Cycle Fitments, 782 Allen Court, Palo Alto, CA 94303. The best and most comprehensive book on cycling that I know of.

have enough room in front to take one hand off the bars and stick it out in a jabbing, emphatic signal, the situation is then much clearer to other road users.

* Keep an eye on the road surface. Watch out for broken glass – endemic to the U.S. of A. – stones, potholes, etc. Plenty of bumps and potholes are big enough to destroy a bike – and you. Going over bumps, cables, etc. get off the saddle and keep your weight on the pedals and handlebars.

* Quite a few things can dump a bike:

Oil slicks in the center of traffic lanes at busy intersections and on sharp curves. When cars stop or turn hard a little oil drops off. The resulting slick can send you off the road or sliding out into the middle of a busy intersection.

Newly wet streets. There is a light film of oil which until it is washed away mixes with the water to make a very slippery surface.

Wet manhole covers and steel plates can dump you in a hurry. I have seen this happen often.

Wet cobblestones.

Wet autumn leaves.

Gravel and sand.

* Storm sewers. American storm sewers are just the right size to swallow up a bicycle wheel.

* Ride with the traffic. Sometimes when there is no traffic coming the other way, it is better to ride in the opposite lane.

* The velocity of traffic on free-way streets which have no parking is usually too high to permit safe cycling. If you run in the center of the lane, you block traffic. If you go to the side, cars whiz by you at high speeds with only inches to spare. Stick to streets with parked cars and look out for opening doors.

* Cars and trucks pulling out. They do it unexpectedly and without signaling. Look out for driveways, building entrances, construction projects, cab ranks, and any other possible source of a vehicle. Remember, you don't exist for many drivers. They look right at you, the image is flashed on their brain, but they don't comprehend. They don't *see* you.

And perhaps some do. One time I had the light going into an intersection with a police car waiting on the cross street. The eyes of the driver fixed steadily on me and he waited until I was just going through the intersection before pulling through a red light and right in front of me.

* Pedestrians are another unreliable bunch. They don't think 200 pounds of bike and rider coming toward them at 30 mph means anything, and will frequently jaywalk right in your path. Your odds are much better here than when mixing it up with a car, but even so any collision is going to hurt you, the pedestrian, and your bike. Use a horn, yell – and give them the right of way if you have to.

* Kids. As much of a hazard to the cyclist as to the motorist. Any child has the potential to suddenly race out into the street.

* Other cyclists. I don't know why, but many cyclists and especially children cyclists are erratic. Give them a wide berth.

* Yellow glasses are good for city riding to keep the dirt out of your eyes.

* Lights are a legal requirement at night. I have learned from bitter experience that they don't make much difference to motorists. There is a French-made white front/red rear flashlight which straps to the arm or leg and therefore gets waved around a lot. It weighs only 5 ounces. See Accessories for a fuller discussion of lights. I like a large, permanently mounted rear reflector. Lights have a habit of failing.

* Alcohol and cannabis. In a recent experiment a group of drivers were tested for driving ability. Then half the group was stoked up on booze, the other half stoned out on hash or grass, and driving ability measured again. The booze group became more belligerent and aggressive, for example passing more often, and demonstrated slowed reaction times, while the dope contingent slowed down, became easy going and accommodating, but showed no diminishment of reaction time to emergency situations.

All these endless cautions are depressing. It seems that riding in traffic involves girding yourself for battle and inducing a constant state of morbid apprehension for your life. This is true. The idea of mixing cars and bicycles together is crazy. Cars themselves are an atavistic idiocy responsible for millions of deaths and injuries. It is entirely logical to want to have nothing to do with them.

On the other hand you can get used to it. If you are an alert, defensive rider you are reasonably safe. In return for the risks there are many benefits and it is up to you to decide how they balance. It isn't all bad by any means, but never deny the stark reality: in traffic there is a chance that you will be killed.

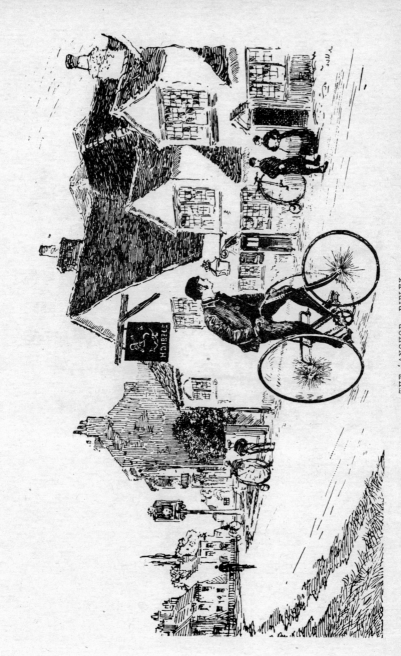

THE 'ANCHOR, RIPLEY

"An aged woman on her back,
Two babes in gutter prone."

8. Bang!

As William Sanders pointed out in a *Bike World* article (October 1973) it is all very well to preach Defensive Riding, but the cyclist should also know what to do should an accident actually occur. The problem is not so much knowing what to do, as being able to do it.

Most people react to an imminent crash situation with panic. They may freeze into immobility and do nothing, or blindly clamp down on the brakes and lose directional stability. This can make a bad situation fatal. For example, if a car is about to hit you from the side and you death grip the brakes, locking up the rear wheel and sending the bike down in a slide, then when the car hits you are likely to be rolled up underneath it. If, on the other hand, at the moment of impact you try to get clear of the bike and make a dive for the hood of the car, you may slide along to the windscreen and perhaps even over the roof. Not fun, but the survival chances are much better than if you are underneath the car.

Panic induced muscular tension increases physical damage in a crash. The person who falls or is thrown and is able to stay loose and relaxed will suffer less injury than the person who tenses and tries to save him or herself.

The ability to exercise the best of a series of bad options, and stay physically relaxed in a situation offering damage, can only be learned through experience and practice. I have been an avid skiier since I was four, a high diver since I was seven, and when I suddenly find myself flying through the air upside down I am automatically loose, looking to tuck and roll when I hit.

If you do not know how to fall, try to have someone with training – fighting experts, skydivers, skiiers – give you pointers. I find that fast woods riding with an old trasho bike is useful. A few spills are inevitable, and as long as they are in loose dirt, usually little damage results.

Practice the braking and turning techniques discussed in the Riding chapter. Think of how to use them in various circumstances. If a car pulls up alongside you and then unexpectedly turns right, cutting you off, a sudden application of the brakes will simply pile you into the car. A rapid haul turn however, just might avoid an accident, and if you do hit, you will both be going more or less in the same direction. Suppose a car pulls out in front of you from a side road or driveway. There may be enough room for a haul turn so that you hit the car a glancing blow. If there is not enough room to turn, then brake as hard as possible without skidding, and just before hitting the car launch yourself clear of the bike. You may be able to sail right over the car. Stay loose and roll when you hit the pavement.

If you are hit from behind DO NOT BRAKE. Try to get away by steering to the side.

9. Touring

Touring is the real joy in biking. The only better way to see the country is to walk or roller skate. A bike has advantages in mobility and luggage-carrying however, and the aesthetic sacrifice is not too great. Touring can be done in a tremendous variety of ways. You can go for an afternoon's jaunt or spend a summer or more travelling thousands of miles. You can go as a self-contained unit with your own camping gear, or ultra-light and stay in inns and motels. You can count the miles travelled, or concentrate on the scenery (yeah!). Your journey can include transit by auto, bus, train, boat, and plane, so that you can hop from one interesting place to another. You can have a plan, or absolutely none at all. Touring is a call to adventure, beauty, new sights and experiences.

There's a lot to touring, and plenty for you to think about. At the same time it can be kept simple. Any bike headed for the boondocks should have a tool kit, unless you don't mind pushing your bike a few miles to a garage and/or the possibility of an overnight stay until it opens. Equipment makes a difference, but the main thing is to get out there. My greatest, happiest tour was on a battered 1935 BSA whose vital parts shed like water.

'A merry heart goes all the way,
Your sad tires in a mile, a.' – *Shakespeare.*

Part of the fun of touring is figuring it out and planning or not planning for yourself. Some people insist that the only way to tour is with a meticulous and detailed plan; others heave map and

compass into the bushes and go wherever fancy takes them. For some the fun and relaxation comes as a result of planned and concentrated effort; for others it is through not thinking about anything. There is no "right" way to tour. Each to its own. Accordingly, this chapter tries to simply give basic information about touring. It is not a step-by-step guide. It's up to you to decide where and when you want to go, and what sort of equipment you expect to need.

One source of detailed information is books. *Bicycle Camping and Touring* (Dell, $4.95) has a lot of solid information on techniques and equipment. *The Best of Bicycling* (Pocket Books, $1.95) has all sorts of wonderful stories about short and long distance touring and a pot-pourri of technical information. *North American Bicycle Atlas* (American Youth Hostels, $2.25) gives detailed, mapped tours throughout the U.S. of A. So does *The American Biking Atlas and Touring Guide* (Workman, $5.95). Good reading is *Bike Tripping* by Tom Cuthbertson (Ten Speed Press, $3.95). Full of really useful specific information is *Traveling by Bike* (World Publications, P.O. Box 366, Mountain View, CA 94040, $1.95).

Another good way to get into heavy touring is to join a society or organization. You get a planned tour, the benefit of a group leader who will set a pace within your capacity, and lots of free friendly help and advice. Ride with and get information from:

American Youth Hostels, Inc.

20 West 17th Street,

New York, New York 10011.

A somewhat strait-laced but nevertheless very good outfit with over 4000 hostels in 47 countries, about 100 in the U.S. of A. Good equipment and books. Hostels are sometimes spartan but always serviceable, with fees up to $2. Tours in the U.S. of A. and abroad. Inexpensive.

International Bicycle Touring Society,

846 Prospect Street,

La Jolla, California. 92037.

An easy going outfit for adults only. Tours are volunteer organized and fairly luxurious. A sag wagon follows each tour and carries baggage and repair parts. Overnight stays at inns and motels at moderate rates.

League of American Wheelmen,
3582 Sunnyview Avenue N.E.
Salem, Ore. 97303.
An organization founded in 1880 which faded into obscurity but was revived in the 1960s and has been growing ever since. LAW members are nation-wide, and will give you information about local conditions to aid you in planning a tour. LAW is also into influencing legislative activity, and will give you information on bikeways.

Bicycle Institute of America,
122 East 42nd Street,
New York, New York 10017.
A trade organization which gives out a lot of free information on all aspects of bicycling from car top carriers to bikeways.

Where

Where you go depends on your own temperament, interests, physical conditions, and available equipment. I would suggest that you make your initial rides about 20 miles or so, and work up to longer hours and overnight stays as you get used to it. If you favor back roads off the beaten track and camping, you are going to have to deal with equipment for both you and the bike; touring on better roads and sleeping in inns means less and lighter equipment.

Riding

Safety
I recommend taking the smallest, least travelled roads practicably possible. Not only are they almost always more interesting, but the fewer cars there are around the more comfortable you will be. Cars in the country are a serious hazard because a bicycle rider is a completely unexpected phenomenon for most drivers, and they are not prepared to drive in a fashion safe for you, the cyclist.

Safe country riding is largely a matter of common sense. Most of the rules for traffic riding apply here also.

* Always carry identification and your health insurance card if you have one. Leave a motor vehicle operator's license at home, as it can be endorsed with traffic offenses committed on a bicycle.

A CLUB RIDE IN THE COUNTRY

* The cardinal rule is "what if?" Look and think ahead. Don't, for example, time your riding so that you and an overtaking car reach a curve at the same time. If a car – or worse yet a truck – comes the other way there just isn't going to be enough room.

* Bear in mind the tremendous relative velocity of cars. In traffic you can pretty much keep up, but in the country cars will have up to 70 mph over your 5 to 15. If you crest a hill for example, and there is no oncoming traffic, move over into the opposite lane for a while. This avoids the hazard of overtaking cars who cannot see you over the crest.

* Try to have a hole to duck into should everything go wrong. Where will you go if that tractor pulls out? If a car comes around the corner on your side of the road are you going to try for the ditch or a tree? You may wreck a bike going off into a field, but this is a lot better than colliding with a car. Think about this as much as you can and try to make it an automatic process. This way when an emergency arises instead of freezing in panic you may be able to save your life.

* Be particularly wary, when you have speed up, of people doing odd things. Cannonballing down a hill you may be doing 40 m.p.h., a fact that many motorists and pedestrians do not com-

prehend. They see a bicycle, and automatically class it is as slow and unimportant, dismissing it from mind (as you can be sure they would not do for a large truck), and step or drive out onto the road, or pass, or whatever. This capacity for visual recognition with no subsequent cognitive comprehension may seem bizarre, but I assure you it is so. Never trust other road users.

* After running through puddles or wet grass, dry your brakes off by applying them lightly as you ride. Running down steep hills do not hold the brakes steady, which can cause overheating, but pump on and off. This also tells you if you have stopping power in reserve – which you always should.

* Run to the right, but leave room to manuver in case you encounter road litter, potholes, or whatever.

* On two lane roads watch out for overtaking motorists coming towards you. They often do not see or just plain ignore a bicycle coming towards them. If you move out to the center of your lane most motorists will return to their lane. Some will not and you must be prepared to stop on the shoulder of the road. You might care to have a few rotten tomatoes handy for such moments.

* Beware the Hun in the Sun. At sunrise and sunset motorists with the sun in their eyes may not see you.

* Rural farm traffic is a law unto itself. Many farmers operate machinery on local public roads as if they were in the middle of a field.

* Watch for loose gravel, dirt, or sand, and especially at driveway and side road entrances.

* Bridge gratings, cattle guards, railroad tracks, etc. can all swallow up a bicycle wheel and send you flying.

* Dogs. Dogs and other creatures of the field and air are a menace to the cyclist. I was once attacked by a determined and large goose. Dogs are the main problem though, and you need to keep a constant lookout for old Towser.

There are many theories about why dogs attack two-wheeled vehicles. I think that the spokes make a noise which drives them nuts. There are also a number of dog owners who take a not-so-secret pleasure in having vicious attack-prone animals, and others who should not even try to take responsibility for a cockroach. One couple expressed puzzlement to me after their dog bit my riding companion: every time the dog was disobedient they said, they

beat it until their arms hurt. Why wouldn't it obey? With treatment like that, any dog will become vicious and irrational.

Understanding that old Poochie may not be directly at fault does not make being bitten more fun. Dogs are livestock, fully the responsibility of the owner, and excepting dogs crazed by disease, can be trained to leave cyclists bloody well alone. I like dogs very much and accept that some adjustment to their particular natures and quirks is necessary if they are to be around. I do not accept being knocked off my bike by some giant hound. If the owner will not control the dog, I will, and with brute force if necessary.

Most dogs attack according to a pattern. They circle to the rear of the cyclist and come up from behind. So sometimes you can outrun a dog. Often this is not possible, but 99 times out of a 100 there is still no serious problem. Many cyclists become hysterical on the subject of dog defense, and recommend whips, car aerials, clubs, and other weapons that will really hurt a dog. This is not necessary. It really isn't the dog's fault. Nine times out of ten he is normally friendly. All you have to do is stop, dismount, and face him directly. That's all. Simply stop. Often he will come up wagging his tail. When you leave, walk away like all "normal" (to the dog) people do, and the matter will be forgotten.

The tenth time, when a dog still threatens attack: the main thing when dealing with a vicious dog is to have *confidence*. As a human being you are one of the largest mammals on earth and a formidable contender in a fight. Suppress your fears and radiate the notion that any dog that messes with you will regret it for the rest of his days, if he lives that long. It is only the rarest of dogs that will attack a human obviously prepared for self-defense. Speak to the dog in firm tones, keep your bike between you, and slowly walk away.

If the dog attacks: one defense are aerosol pepper sprays (hardware stores) made for exactly this purpose. They have a range of about 10 feet and are light enough to clip to the handlebars or your belt. A water pistol loaded with a water ammonia solution will also work, but is a good deal less convenient. If you have neither of these and can't or won't climb a tree get a stick or large rock. No? The bicycle pump. In any event, don't cower or cover up, because the dog will only chew you to ribbons. *Attack.* Any small dog can simply be hoisted up by the legs and his brains dashed out. With a big dog you are fighting for your life. If you are weaponless try to tangle him up in your bike and then strangle him. Kicks to the balls and which break ribs are effective. If you have got a pump or stick hold it at both ends and offer it up to the dog horizontally. Often the dog will bite the stick/pump and hang on. Immediately lift the dog up and deliver a very solid kick to the genitals. Follow up with breaking the dog's ribs or crushing its head with' a rock. If worst comes to worst, ram your entire arm down his throat. He will choke and die. Better your arm than your throat.

If you are bitten and the dog gets away, make every effort to find the dog and owner. If the dog cannot be quarantined you will have to get a long series of painful rabies shots. Ask around the area, check with local gas stations, stores, etc. In any event, get immediate medical treatment, even for a light bite. Then notify the dog warden or police of the incident. If the dog owner is unco-operative about paying for the doctor and any other related expenses, just get a lawyer. The law is completely and absolutely on your side.

If you successfully fend off an attack, notify the dog owner and dog warden or police. This is a very real responsibility because the next person might not be as well prepared as you. A little girl for example, like the one three dogs down the road from my parents' place pulled down and killed a few summers ago.

The affluent may care to try an electronic sounder which emits a noise painful to dog ears. This is the Dog Chaser, $44.50 from Spencer Aircraft, 8410 Dallas Avenue South, Seattle, Washington 98108. I do not know if it works or not.

Technique

Cadence plays an extremely significant part in the technique of long-distance touring. In short sprint you can drain your body's resources and strength, but on a long tour output must not exceed ability to continuously replenish fuel and oxygen. Which makes it sound simple: just take it easy and have something in reserve. Not quite.

If you are interested in covering a lot of ground (not everybody is) and in feeling comfortable, then you must strive for an exact balance between energy output and the body's ability to synthesize and store energy. There is a *pace* which works best. Go too fast and the result will be fatigue and possibly strained muscles that will dog you throughout the tour. But go too slow, and you will become sluggish and lethargic, and mistake this for genuine tiredness.

A rough indicator of pace is respiration and heartbeat. You simply cannot sustain for long periods effort which noticeably increases either. Thus, the exact pace you can maintain depends on your physical condition, not on your strength.

I particularly recommend that you take it easy at first, sticking to the lower gears and not pushing hard against the pedals. This will help you to find your own cadence and pace, and perhaps avoid

excessive initial effort. Most people tend to lean into it hard the first day. The result is strained and sore muscles, and the next day they can hardly move. You'll go farther and faster if you take it easy at the start.

Riding position can make a tremendous difference. Going into the wind try to get low down. With a strong tail wind straighten up and get a free push. In Europe many riders use home-made "sails" resembling kites strapped to their backs. These are effective even with a quartering wind. Position determines the muscle groups in use: hands high on the bars eases the back, stomach, arms, and hands; down positions do exactly the opposite and are best for hill climbing.

Equipment

Bike: Choice of bike depends on the kind of touring you do. A 3-speed is good for durability and off-road riding, but heavy weight and an inefficient gear train make it a poor choice for distance work. For all around use, the 10-speed is best by far. It can be set up to favor durability, and thus be usable off-road, or to favor performance, for fast road riding. Experienced tourists often prefer 15-speed bikes with ultra wide gear ranges, but for the tyro these bikes can be a mechanical headache. Tourists who mix transportation modes frequently, going by bus, train, plane, or auto from one place to the next, may find a portable folding bike such as the Bickerton the most convenient.

Chapter 2, Choosing Mounts, gives capsule reviews on the characteristics of various bikes now available, and the discussions of luggage, lights, etc. below will suggest what bits and pieces are necessary for your needs. Whatever bike you use, be sure that it is geared right for the terrain you will encounter (chapter 5).

One touring/sport variant is off-road riding along trails, and through woods and fields. The scenery is great, there are no cars, and the riding is exciting. The going can get muddy and rough, and even on smooth sections there are concealed rocks, limbs, and other debris. Machines for this sort of use need heavy-duty tires and should have a minimum of equipment to rattle off or get damaged. Fenders are both a curse and a boon, protecting against water spray and flying stones and mud, but also jamming up tight with mud and litter.

Cyclo-cross bikes are made especially for this sort of riding, but as they are competition bikes, are light and can get bent easily. They also have derailleur gears which require constant servicing. My own choice for an off-road bike is a stock 3-speed with an extra large rear sprocket, cut down alloy fenders, cage pedals, and knobby speedway tires. It cannot be jumped and bashed like a BMX racer, but it is also still perfectly usable as a road bike.

Tires: The development of narrow profile high pressure clincher tires precludes the use of tubulars by all but a handful of affluent fanatics. For poor roads and/or very heavy loads use a $1\frac{1}{4}''$ heavy-weight tire, or at the ultimate, a 650-B $1\frac{3}{4}''$ tire. For more performance, use a lighter $1\frac{1}{4}''$ high pressure gumwall, and if you really want to blast along, then use a $1\frac{1}{8}''$ high pressure (90 psi) tire.

Remember: the narrower and harder, the faster, and the more punctures.

Tool kit: What you need depends on how far you go and how you maintain your bike. I keep basic toolkits for each type of bike (3-speed or 10-speed, clincher or tubular tires), and expand the toolkit with extra tools and parts when necessary. At the minimum, have:

  Tire repair kit including levers and spare valve
  Dog bone or 4″ adjustable wrench
  Screwdriver
  Chain tool and spare links
  Any special allen wrenches required for your bike.

For longer journeys add:

  A few assorted nuts, bolts, and screws
  Brake and shift cables
  Spokes and nipples
  Brake pads
  Do-all wrench to fit hub cones, brake locknuts, etc., *or* hub cone
    wrenches and assorted small wrenches as necessary
  Spare tube
  Spoke wrench
  Wire cutters
  Freewheel remover
  Cotterless crank extractor
  Lubricants, including grease
  Any special gizmo you'll be the needing of.

Sounds like a lot, but it can all be packed into a compact bundle. On group rides cut down on the number of spare parts per rider, and share one set of tools. Your lighting system as a matter of course should carry spare bulbs. Include a bit of wire and tape for longer runs.

For mending you, a basic first aid kit. I generally also carry: a multi-purpose pocketknife, compass, waterproofed matches, button thread for clothing repairs, game snares, or fishing line, and when appropriate, a snake bite kit.

Lights: A requirement at night. Most tourists prefer generator lights as they are consistently bright and less expensive than battery lights. However, some people do not care to pedal against the resistance of a wheel or hub generator, and wiring tends to snag and break at inconvenient moments. Unless fitted with a storage battery adding 14-16 ounces weight, generator lights go out when the bike stops.

Battery lights are simple, can be used off the bike for map reading or roadside repairs, and left off the bike altogether on a fast daytime run. They are best for off-road riding, as they do not dim if you go slowly, and there are no wires to snag.

What is best for you depends on how you ride. Generator lights are about the only sensible answer for strong lights and extended night runs. However, if you are riding when the days are long, and need lights only for an hour or so at a time, then lightweight battery lights will do. In either case, have a spare light in case the main system fails.

I strongly suggest using a warning flasher unit such as the Belt Beacon (see Accessories). Another good item is the Matex flashlight, which straps on the arm or leg and shows a white light to the front, red light to the rear. It will also do as a camp light or for roadside repairs.

Fenders: A great pleasure in wet going and on rough back roads. Plastic models are light and easily removed when not needed, but eventually warp. Alloy and stainless steel models are sturdier, and offer mounting points for lights and other knick-knacks. They tend to transmit sound, but this can be cured with a coat of undercovering paint from an auto shop.

Bicycle shoes and cleats: Used in conjunction with toe clips these are essential for any long distance travelling, unless you plan to be on and off the bike frequently. Pack along shoes for walking as bicycle shoes are very unsuitable for this. Do not use soft soled shoes such as sneakers as these do not provide sufficient support for the foot.

Baggage: Loading a touring bike is an art. The cardinal principle is to load low, toward the centerline of the bike, and evenly. Piling gear up in a high stack or all in one place creates tremendous instability for the bike. Bicycle carriers are designed to distribute loads properly. There are 3 basic kinds: handlebar bags, saddlebags, and panniers, each available in a variety of sizes and models. People travelling light can get by with a saddlebag. These fasten to the seat and seat post and can hold a lot of gear. The next addition would be a handlebar bag. This makes for good fore and aft weight distribution, and is handy for food, cameras, rain capes, and other things you need often. Get one with a transparent map case and that opens forward for easy accessibility.

Panniers hang alongside the wheels on special racks. Most often used are rear panniers. Front panniers stiffen steering and do not have much carrying capacity. For a tourist who will be very heavily laden however, they allow a better distribution of weight.

Panniers come in one of two basic designs: single bag, which allows maximum cramming in of gear, and multi-compartment bag, which separates gear for easy access. Most panniers made today are quick on or off the bike, and some can be converted into backpacks.

Good brand names are Karrimore, Kirtland, Bellwether, Eclipse, Cannondale, Recreation Equipment, Gerry, Kangaroo, and Touring Cyclist Shop. Recommending one over another would not be fair as different models suit different uses. You really need to go to a bike shop and inspect the merchandise personally. For those of you not near a shop, herewith some addresses for catalogs and mail order:

Bellwether
1161 Mission St.
San Francisco, CA 94103

Recreation Equipment
1525 11th Ave.
Seattle, WA 98122

Kangaroo Baggs
306 E. Cota
Santa Barbara, CA 93101

Gerry
5450 N. Valley Hwy
Denver, CO 80216

Cannondale
35 Pulaski St.
Stamford, CT 06902

Touring Cyclist Shop
P.O. Box 4009
Boulder, CO 80306

Kirtland
Box 4059 FN
Boulder, CO 80306

Eclipse
P.O. Box 372 B-7
Ann Arbor, Mich 48107

Bikecology
2910 Nebraska Ave.
P.O. Box 1880
Santa Monica, CA 90406

Frostline Kits – sew it yourself
Dept BY077
Frostline Circle
Denver, CO 80241

Handlebar bags should be used in conjunction with a rack which prevents the bag from fouling the wheel, brake mechanism, or brake levers. Rear panniers require a stout rack which will not sway under load. Karrimore's is a proven performer.

When you load, put heavy gear at the bottom of the bags, light bulky stuff like sleeping bags at the top. Give yourself a few local shakedown trial runs. The extra weight takes getting used to, and nothing is quite so irritating as rebuilding a luggage rack in the middle of a tour. After the rack bolts and screws have bedded in, use a locking material such as Loctite to hold them firmly in place.

Maps: A compass is not only useful in conjunction with a map, but can itself guide you in the general direction you want to go without strict routing. Sometimes it is fun to dispose of maps altogether. Just go where fancy takes you, and ask directions along the way. You get to meet people, and often they can suggest really interesting routes, scenic attractions, swimming holes, and the like. But have a map in reserve.

As well as keeping you on a desired route, maps have the vital function of keeping you off main travelled roads and out of industrial areas. Of gas station maps I have found Esso's to be the most detailed, but even these do not meet the needs of the cyclist. The best source is the U.S. Geological Service, who publish contour maps for each state. If you know the exact area you'll be in, they also have local maps down to 1:24,000, a scale which shows walls, foot-paths, tiny streams, etc. These are too detailed for any but the most local use, but are extremely interesting. Many map stores carry the U.S.G.S. maps, or you can order them direct (for local maps ask first for free state index map):

East of the Mississippi	West of the Mississippi
U.S. Geologic Survey	U.S. Geologic Survey
Washington District Section	District Section
1200 South Eads Street	Federal Center
Arlington, Virginia 22202	Denver, Colorado 80225

Clothing: Wash and wear is a must for long jaunts. A nylon windshirt is very useful, as are cycling jerseys with big pockets for stashing gear. A poncho can serve also as a groundsheet and/or a tent.

A DANGER BOARD

Camping gear: Personal preferences and abilities can completely determine choices here. Some people need a tent and a prepared campsite with running water. Others insist on portable stoves, radios, etc. There are many good books on camping equipment and woods lore, and if you are unfamiliar with this craft you should get one. There is space here for only the most generalized suggestions.

1. Sleeping bag. Tents and stoves, etc. can always be improvised with fair success, but only the most skilled can keep warm in a bad bag. A poor bag weighs more, and if you freeze and can't sleep, this will give you ample time to brood on the economic and practical merits of having gotten something that would do the job in the first place. Get the best bag you can afford. Also, although your bike has carrying capacity and most of your touring is apt to be in warm weather, I suggest you keep other possibilities such as backpacking, or tours in the autumn (fantastic!) in mind.

The best bags, pound-for-pound, are of down. Down has the greatest range (temperatures at which the bag will work), resiliency (bag packs small), recovery (gets loft back when unpacked), wicking properties (carries moisture away from body), and moral character. Down bags run from $50 to $125 and the less expensive, lighter (filled with $1\frac{1}{2}$–$2\frac{1}{2}$ pounds of down) models are OK for warm weather. I suggest a multi-layered and/or openable bag that will also take a flannel insert. This gives optimum range and comfort.

An interesting new insulative material is poly foam, used in Ocaté bags. These are only fractionally heavier ($4\frac{1}{2}$ pounds overall) than lightweight down bags ($3\frac{1}{2}$ pounds), and the manufacturer claims a degree range down to $-5°$, about that of a middleweight down bag (4-$4\frac{1}{2}$ pounds). The advantage is that it will keep you warm wet or dry.

The least expensive bags contain synthetic fillers such as "Dacron 88" and "Astrofill." These run from $15 to $40, weigh about 6 pounds, and are OK for warm weather and low altitudes.

2. A ground sheet such as a triple-purpose (raincape, tent) poncho.

The remaining equipment listed here can always be improvised. The trouble with this is that garnering boughs for a bed or building fires is rather wasteful and ecologically unsound. There are enough campers now so that the total destruction can be devastating. In many areas you are not allowed to do these things. So, drag that it may be, it is both practical and considerate to be as self-sufficient as possible.

3. Sleeping mattress or pad. Air mattresses (avoid plastic ones) are comfortable but bulky. Pads such as ensolite are fine.

4. Tents come in all shapes, sizes and grades. Conditions and personal preference dictate choice. Tents are good for protection against bugs, rain, and to ensure privacy. For myself I see no point in hieing to the Great Outdoors and then sleeping in a dark hole. Polyethylene fly sheets can be rigged into a decent shelter with only a little effort and are extremely cheap and light. A poncho is just as good. In tents the Gerry "Pioneer" is well thought of by everybody. This makes up as a one-man tent with floor and mosquito netting, or as a two-man tent without a floor.

Gerry
5450 North Valley Highway
Denver, Colorado 80306

5. Cooking stove and utensils. You should have, but I don't know anything about them. Four skewers can be used to form a grid for a pot, a grill, to skewer food, or as tent pegs. Heavy-duty aluminium foil will make a flat-folding re-usable pot.

6. Food. Freeze-dried light-weight foods are extremely convenient and quite palatable. I suggest carrying enough for emergencies only however, and trying for fresh food along the route. Stock up on breakfast and dinner at about 4 o'clock. Mixtures of dried fruit, nuts, grains, dried milk, yeast, etc. are nourishing, tasty, and easy to carry.

Most any city has a camping equipment store. Mail order outfits I have done business with to complete satisfaction are:

L. L. Bean
Freeport, Maine 04032
Not deadly cheap, but always quality equipment which *works*.

Herter's
Route 1
Waseca, Minnesota 56093
Catalog – $1.
My favorite. Chest-thumpers, but sound equipment at very low cost.

Recreational Co-op 1525 11th Ave.
Seattle, Washington 98122
Excellent equipment at good prices, with a 10% dividend at the end of the year. Nice knapsacks. Costs $1 to join.

Gerry
5450 North Valley Highway, Denver, Colorado 80306
Expensive, but first-rate equipment which works really well.

Bikecology
2910 Nebraska Ave.
P.O. Box 1880
Santa Monica, CA 90406
Good equipment selected with the cyclist in mind.

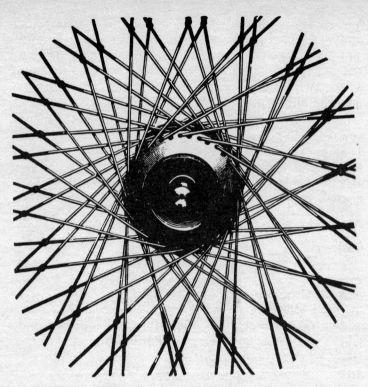

NEW RAPID TANGENT WHEEL.

Getting There

Other forms of locomotion complement bicycles very well.

Cars. A 10-speed with the wheels off will fit in the trunk of many economy cars and certainly on the back seat. For carrying several bikes you can buy or make a car carrier. There are two types, rear end and top. The rear end version holds 2 bikes and is easy to load. It is hard to get at the trunk however, and the bikes get a lot of road grit and scratch each other. A popular model is Bike Toter, about $16 in bike stores or direct from:

Bike Toter
Box 888
Santa Monica, California 90406

Top mounted carriers hold 4 to 5 bikes, and require that each bike be strapped down. But machines are kept clean, separate, and out of harm's way. A deluxe model is available from

JC-1 Industries
904 Nogales Street
Industry, California 91744

Most any auto store has luggage racks for about $15 which can easily be adapted for bikes. Or you can make your own, and have something exactly suited for the job. *Bicycle Camping and Touring* (Dell, $4.95) has plans, and so does

Bicycle Institute of America
122 East 42nd St.,
New York, New York 10017
(free)

When loading, alternate direction for 3 or more bikes. Seat on one cross-bar, handlebars on the other. Careful of brake and shift cables. Lash down with toe straps or elastic luggage straps at contact points, and especially the handlebars, since these hold the bike upright. Guying, running straps from the side of the car to high points on the bike (like with a sailboat mast), is a *good idea*.

Mixing up a tour with public transportation, or even just complementing a trip with a bicycle, is a great way to travel. You get the benefits of mobility and covering a lot of ground, but at the same time a bike lets you examine interesting areas in detail. Preparation of your bike for travel depends on the kind of carrier you will use.

Airlines: These handle bikes routinely and some, like United, provide special bike boxes. Remove the rear derailleur if you have one, and loosen stem and twist handlebars parallel with front wheel. They may ask you to remove or reverse the pedals. I myself would protect the frame and chainwheel with a broken-up cardboard box. Deflate tires to $\frac{1}{2}$ pressure. Airlines sometimes let bikes on free, and sometimes charge.

Buses: Here your bike lies flat on its side in a luggage compartment with a lot of other junk that can bang into it. I strongly recommend picking up a box from a local bike dealer and stuffing yours inside. If you are leap-frogging, send the box on ahead.

Railroads: In Europe you can load a bike into the baggage compartment yourself. In the U.S. of A. the make-work contingent has rigged it so a baggage handler must do the job – badly. Stories of bikes mangled into oblivion by baggage handlers are legion. Insist on personally supervising loading or don't go. Hang the bike from the ceiling or side of the baggage car if possible, and in any case see that it is lashed down securely and that no heavy stuff can fall on it.

Boats: Same story. One boat-loading crew broke an internal gear on a motorcycle of mine. I still haven't figured out how.

TOURING ABROAD

"Going foreign" with a bike is a particularly satisfying way of travelling, as it allows you to explore and savor a country to a degree not otherwise possible. In most places people admire and respect cyclists, and are exceptionally helpful and friendly. For uninteresting or arduous sections of the journey you simply use public transport. In Europe, if you buy a quality bike, you can usually save enough money to substantially reduce the air fare from and to America. One general over-view book is *International Bicycle Touring* (World Publications, P.O. Box 366, Mountain View, CA 94040, $2.95).

Great Britain

Where

Explore the Cotswolds by Bicycle by Suzanne Ebel and Doreen Imprey (available from the British Cycling Bureau, address below) gives historical background and notes places and events of interest as well as listing specific routes. Written with the cyclist in mind is *The Roadfaring Guide, South-West England* by Reginald Wellby (Cyclists Touring Club, Cotterell House, 69 Meadrow ,Godalming, Surrey, GU7 3HS).

Information is available from

British Cycling Bureau
Greater London House
Hampstead Road
London NW1

which distributes leaflets on various aspects of cycling, a list of equipment-hire shops, detailed itineraries for a number of tours, and comments on good touring areas. Other organizations providing general information are:

British Tourist Authority   Scottish Tourist Board
Tourist Information Centre   23 Ravelston Terrace
64 St. James Street   Edinburgh
London SW1 1NF   Scotland EH4 3EU

First and foremost of the touring organizations is:
Cyclists Touring Club
Cotterell House
69 Meadrow
Godalming, Surrey GU7 3HS

I commend this organization to every cyclist, tourist or not. Membership (write for cost) includes the *Cycle Touring Club Handbook*, a thick list of 3,000 recommended accommodation addresses, places to eat, cycle repairers, and CTC local information officers for Great Britain; a list of overseas touring correspondents; information about touring areas, equipment, and travel by air, rail, and sea, including ferries, tunnels, and bridges; a catalog of the books and maps for Great Britain, the Continent, and Morocco available through the bookstore; and a complete exposition of club services. For the tourist, the most important of these is the touring department, which has available a large library of comprehensive, personally researched tours complete with maps, such as this one:

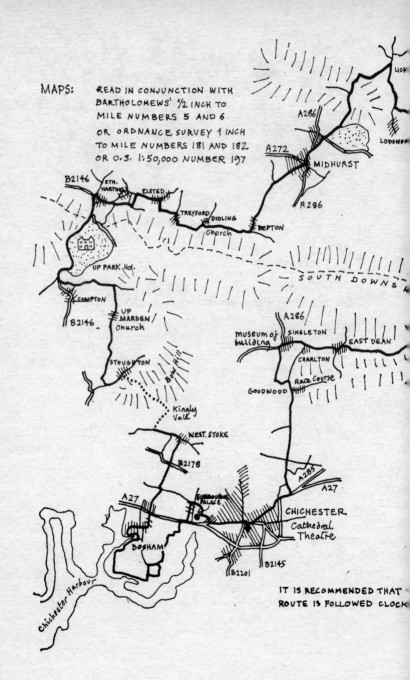

MAPS: READ IN CONJUNCTION WITH
BARTHOLOMEWS' ½ INCH TO
MILE NUMBERS 5 AND 6
OR ORDNANCE SURVEY 1 INCH
TO MILE NUMBERS 181 AND 182
OR O.S. 1:50,000 NUMBER 197

LICK

A286

LODSWOR

A272

MIDHURST

A286

B2146   STH. HARTING   ELSTED

TREYFORD   DIDLING
Church   BEPTON

UP PARK Ho.

SOUTH DOWNS

COMPTON

B2146   UP MARDEN Church

A286   SINGLETON

Museum of building

EAST DEAN

CHARLTON

STOUGHTON

Bow Hi.

Race Course

GOODWOOD

Kingly Vale

WEST STOKE

B2178

A285

A27

A27

A27   FISHBOURNE PALACE

CHICHESTER
Cathedral
Theatre

BOSHAM

B2201   B2145

Chichester Harbour

IT IS RECOMMENDED THAT
ROUTE IS FOLLOWED CLOCK

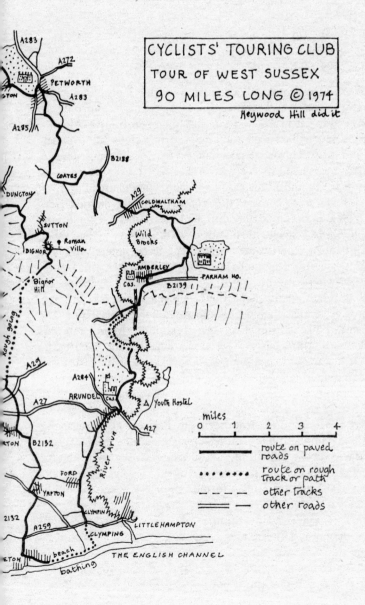

CYCLISTS' TOURING CLUB
TOUR OF WEST SUSSEX
90 MILES LONG © 1974

Heywood Hill did it

miles

route on paved roads
route on rough track or path
other tracks
other roads

THE ENGLISH CHANNEL

155

The touring department will also plan and suggest tours for routes and areas you request, and will advise on cycle and personal equipment, gears, maps, and travel books. In addition, the CTC London office,

CTC Travel Ltd.,
13 Spring Street
London, W2 3RA

will make bookings for all air, sea, and rail journeys abroad, and has information sheets on most European countries. In this connection, CTC is a founding member of the Alliance Internationale de Tourisme, linking touring clubs all over the world, and provides on request an AIT cycle-touring card as introduction for requests for advice and assistance. There is an International Camping Carnet, and CTC members are allowed to take cycles via cross-channel hovercraft, normally banned from April to September. Membership includes subscription to the bimonthly *Cycle Touring*, filled with news of interest to the cyclist, articles on touring and tours, equipment tests, letters, ads, and useful information. Insurance services include free third-party liability anywhere in the world, and policies are available for personal accident, ·damage or theft to cycle, cameras, luggage, and inclusive, which include all the foregoing, cancellation and curtailment, and additional personal liability. Membership is worth it for the third party cover alone, even for the cyclist who goes only to the station and back. The CTC also provides free legal aid in obtaining compensation for members in road accidents ranging from encounters with motor vehicles to dog bites to damages caused by bad road surfaces. The CTC will make representation from appropriate local authority to Parliament in regard to any justified complaint by members on such matters as: dangerous road surfaces, traffic difficulties, and unfair restrictions on the use of cycles; discourtesy and poor service in the conveyance of cycles by public transport; and misinformed or biased press or public criticism of cyclists.

The CTC organizes any number of rallies, tours, and competitions on both national and regional levels; and district associations and sections organize local cycling tours and events and social occasions. Tours vary in difficulty, with accommodation at Youth Hostels, guest houses, and inexpensive hotels.

Another organization providing an accommodations handbook, maps, and touring and insurance services for members, is

British Cycling Federation
70 Brompton Road
London SW3 1EX

BCF is also the internationally recognized controlling body for cycle racing in Great Britain, and is affiliated with the Union Cyclist International, the world governing body of the sport.

THE YOUTH HOSTEL ASSOCIATION
Headquarters:

Trevelyan House
8 St. Stephen's Hill
St. Albans, Hertfordshire

Offices and shops:

29 John Adam Street
London, WC2 6JE

35 Cannon Street
Birmingham B25 EE

36/38 Faintain Street
Manchester M2 2BE

Scottish Youth Hostels
Association
7 Glebe Crescent
Stirling, Stirlingshire
Scotland SK8 2AJ

Irish Youth Hostels
Association
39 Mountjoy Square
Dublin
Irish Republic

Youth Hostel Association
of Northern Ireland
28 Bedford Street
Belfast BT 27FE
Northern Ireland

Hostels are sometimes spartan, but always serviceable. You provide your own sleeping bag, and help a bit with the chores. Inexpensive, and you can cook your own food. The association stores sell camping and touring equipment, have a tourist service, and run guided tours. An essential organization for the economy minded.

Riding

The word on British roads is take the smallest you can find. These reduce automobile speeds down to a level where a cyclist can co-exist with autos in relative comfort. On the main through routes (called "A" class roads), vehicle speeds are high, and there is often no room for a cyclist to maneuver. There will be no shoulder for example, only a solid earthen embankment. Anyway, the smaller roads ("B" class and under) are far more scenic and interesting. The British are a nation of social drinkers, and on Friday and Saturday nights after 9 o'clock the roads are full of tipsy drivers going home from pubs. Don't be out on a bike at that time.

In Britain you are required by law to obey the rules of the road and all traffic regulations. You must have lights front and rear at night, and a reflector. These rules are enforced with fines. Pick up a copy of the *Highway Code* at any (British) newsagent or book shop to familiarize yourself with the regulations. The British drive on the left side of the road. This can be terrifying in prospect for some people, but in actuality it is quite easy.

Equipment

Fenders are pretty much a requirement for British and Continental touring. The weather tends not to steady downpours that last all day (in which case fenders make no difference since you are soaked anyhow), but to a bit of wet here or there.

Although not alpine, many hills in Britain are steeply pitched. Gear low. For a 5-speed, the Cyclists Touring Club recommends a 13-15-18-23-31 to 40 front, and for a 10-speed, 15-17-19-21-23 to 28 × 46 front (read up on gearing in Chapter 5 if you do not understand what these numbers mean). These combinations concentrate the gears in a low range, without large gaps. I myself prefer to have more top end, and obtain a low gear by running a large back sprocket, 14-16-19-23-28 to 36 × 52 front for example. A very heavily laden bike can go to a 30, 32, or even 34 tooth back sprocket.

If you want to buy a bike in Britain, best value for money will probably be a British product, although certain French and Austrian models are also good buys. Off-the-shelf touring bikes include the longtime favorite Dawes Galaxy, now available in three different models with successively better specification; the British Eagle, probably the best value in a 531 plain gauge frame all alloy component specification bike; the Falcon Olympic, as British Eagle above but with steel wheels and vinyl saddle; and the Falcon Black Diamond, as Falcon Olympic but with frame of plain tubing. Depending on specification, expect to spend about what you would stateside – $130 to $250.

In the price range of $300 and up are the offerings of small manufacturers and custom shops. Most have stock hand built frame bikes in touring, road racing, time trials, hill climb, and cyclo-cross models. Specification is basic good quality, and can be altered to suit the customer. For a fully custom "bespoke" frame made to your order allow a month to several months for delivery. Herewith a list of bike shops and/or builders noted for high class machinery. Those marked * have particular experience with touring bikes.

*F. W. Evans Ltd.
77-79 The Cut
London SE1

Hetchin's Bike Shop
117/119 Hamstel Road
Southend-on-Sea

*Condor Cycles
90 Gray's Inn Road
London W C1

Harry Quinn Ltd.
17/19 Walton Road
Liverpool 4

*W. F. Holdsworth Ltd.
132 Lower Richmond Road
Putney, London SW15

David Rattray & Co. Ltd.
261 Alexandra Parade
Glasgow G31 3AD

Bob Jackson
148 Harehills Lane
Leeds LS8 5BD

Tommy Godwin
10/12 Silver Street
King's Heath
Birmingham, 14

*Jack Taylor Cycles
Church Road
Stockton-on-Tees
Teesside, TS18 2LY

Woodrup Cycles
345 Kirkstall Road
Leeds 4

Roy Swinnerton
69/71 Victoria Road
Fenton, Stoke-on-Trent

Fred Baker
144 Cheltenham Road
Bristol, 6

Mercian Cycles Ltd.
28 Stenson Road
Cavendish, Derby DE3 7JB

Major Nichols
48 Durban Road
Smethwick, Birmingham

Norman Fay Cycles Ltd.
109 South Eldon St.
South Shields, Tyne & Wear

Ron Kitching
Hookstone Park
Harrogate, Yorks.

*Cliff Pratt Ltd.
84 Spring Bank
Hull, Yorks.

Beta Bikes
275 West End Lane
London NW6 1QS

An alternative to buying is renting. Two firms that rent touring bikes and equipment are:

Rent-a-Bike Ltd.   Beta Bikes
Kensington Student Centre   275 West End Lane
Kensington Church Street   London NW6 1QS
London

Two firms with baggage equipment available in bike shops are:

Karrimore Products Ltd.   Carradice of Nelson Ltd.
Avenue Parade   North St.
Accrington, Lancs.   Nelson, Lancs. BB9 7NF

Catalogs available on request. Also available in bike shops are the American Eclipse bags, of course at a higher price than stateside.

Maps

Ordnance Survey maps are the best. A catalog is available from:

Director General
Ordnance Survey
Romsey Road
Maybush, Southampton SO9 4DH

The maps are obtainable in many bookstores, and from Ordnance Survey Agents, a list of which is obtainable from:

Cook, Hammond & Kell Ltd.
22-24 Caxton Street   *for England and Wales*
London SW1

Thomas Nelson & Sons
18 Dalkeith Road   *for Scotland*
Edinburgh EH16 5BS

The 1:25,000 scale maps are extremely detailed, showing individual buildings, walls, tiny streams, and the like, and give an endless amount of information about the area covered. They are wonderful for detailed exploring; but for overall route planning, $\frac{1}{2}''$ or $1''$ scale maps are better. These still show virtually all roads, footpaths, villages, rivers, and other stuff, like youth hostels, inns, national trust properties, windmills, public rights of way, and more. There are also a number of tourist maps made up especially for popular and scenic areas, and archaeological and historical maps.

Bartholomew's $\frac{1}{2}''$ series, probably the most useful size, is obtainable in bookstores or from:

John Bartholomew
12 Duncan Street
Edinburgh, Scotland EH9 1TA

Both Ordnance and Bartholomew's maps are available from the Cyclists Touring Club at a reduced price for members.

Camping

The Camping Club of Great Britain and Ireland, Ltd.
11 Lower Grosvenor Place
London SW1

Membership includes an International Camping Carnet, insurance services, a handbook on camping, and a guide to 1,500 sites in Great Britain and Ireland. Another organization is:

Cycling Section
Association of Cycling and Lightweight Campers
30 Napier Way
Wembley, Middlesex

and site lists are also available from:

British Tourist Authority
239 Old Marylebone Road
London NW1

Camping equipment can be hired from:

Crystal Palace Camping
11 Church Road
London SE19

Eaton's of Wimbledon
1003 106 Haydons Road
London SW19

The British rail system is extremely comprehensive, and is great for getting to a particular area, or for skipping over uninteresting sections on a long tour. On most trains the bike goes for free. Load and unload the bike from the luggage car yourself, and use elastic straps to hold it upright. Note: never ship a bike alone via British Rail unless it is insured against any possible disaster – even then, be prepared for the worst.

AWHEEL IN FRANCE.

The Continent

An excellent book is *Bicycle Touring in Europe* by Karen and Gary Hawkins (Pantheon Books, 201 East 50th Street, New York, N.Y., USA, $2.95), which has much useful information on technique and places to go, including nine complete, mapped tours. A similar book is *International Bicycle Touring* (World Publications, P.O. Box 366, Mountain View, CA 94040, $2.95). There are cycling clubs, associations, federations, and organizations to which you can write for information. Those marked * are specifically concerned with touring, others sometimes operate touring services, and will usually assist with information.

ALBANIA

Federata Sportive Shaiptare-Bruga
Abdi Toptani, 3, Tirana

AUSTRIA

Osterreischiche Radsport Kommission
Prinz Eugenstrasse 12
Vienna IV

* Osterreichischer Automobil, Motorrad
and Touring Club
Schubertring 3
Vienna I

BELGIUM

* Touring Club Royal de Belgique
Rue de la Loi 44
Brussels

* Royale Ligue Vélocipédique Belge
49 Avenue du Globe
1190 Brussels

Lique Velocipedique Belge
8 Place des Martyrs
Brussels

BULGARIA

Federation Bulgare de Cyclisme
Boulevard Tolbouk hine 18
Sofia

　　　　　　　　　　　* Automobil and Touring Club
　　　　　　　　　　　Rue Sv. Sofia 6
　　　　　　　　　　　Sofia

CZECHOSLOVAKIA　　 * Ustredni Automotoklub
　　　　　　　　　　　CSSR
　　　　　　　　　　　Opletalova 29
　　　　　　　　　　　Prague 1

　　　　　　　　　　　Ceskoslovenska Sekce Cyklistiky
　　　　　　　　　　　Na Porici 12
　　　　　　　　　　　Prague 1

DENMARK　　　　　　 Danmarks Cykle Union
　　　　　　　　　　　Gronneraenge 21
　　　　　　　　　　　2920 Charlottenlund
　　　　　　　　　　　Copenhagen

　　　　　　　　　　　Danmarks Professionelt Cykle Forbund
　　　　　　　　　　　Grambyvei 56
　　　　　　　　　　　2610 Rodovre

　　　　　　　　　　　* Dansk Cyklist Forbund
　　　　　　　　　　　Avedøre Traervej 15,
　　　　　　　　　　　2650 Hvidovre

EAST GERMANY　　　 Deutscher Radsport Verband
　　　　　　　　　　　Kochhannstrasse 1
　　　　　　　　　　　1034 Berlin

FINLAND　　　　　　 Suomen Pyorailyliitto
　　　　　　　　　　　Yrjonkato 21b
　　　　　　　　　　　Helsinki

　　　　　　　　　　　* Suomi Touring Club
　　　　　　　　　　　Unioninkatu 45H
　　　　　　　　　　　Helsinki 17

FRANCE　　　　　　　 * Touring Club de France (TCF)
　　　　　　　　　　　65 Avenue de la Grande-Armée
　　　　　　　　　　　Paris 16

* Fédération Francaise de Cyclotourisme (FFCT)
66 Rue René Boulanger
Paris 10

GERMANY

* Allgemeiner Deutscher Automobil-Club (ADAC)
Königinstrasse 9-11a
Munich 22

GREECE

* Automobil and Touring Club de Greece
6 Rue Amerikis
Athens

Hellenic Amateur Athletic Association
4 Rue Kapsali
Athens

HUNGARY

Magyar Kerekparos Szoveteg Millenaris Sporttelep
Szabo Jozsef u3
Budapest XIV

ICELAND

* Felag Islenzkra Bifreidaegenda (FIB)
Eiriksgata 5
Reykjavik

IRISH REPUBLIC

Irish Cycling Federation
72 Prospect Avenue
Glasnevin
Dublin, 9

ITALY

Federazione Ciclistica Italiana
Palazzo delle Federazione Viale Tiziano 70
Rome

* Touring Club Italiano (TCI)
Corso Italia 10
Milan

LUXEMBOURG	Federation du Sport Cycliste
	Luxembourgeois
	Case Postale 145
	Luxembourg City
NETHERLANDS	* Netherlands Cycletouring Union
	(NRTU)
	Ambachtsherenlaan 487
	Zoetermeer
	Alphen-a-d-Rijn
	Koninklijke Nederlandsche Wielren Unie
	15 Nieuwe Uitleg
	The Hague
	* Royal Dutch Touring Club
	A N W B
	Wassenaarsewg 220
	Den Haag
	* Stichting Fiets
	Europaplein 2
	Amsterdam
NORTHERN	Northern Ireland Cycling Federation
IRELAND	S. Martin
	13 Premier Drive
	Belfast 15
NORWAY	Norges Cykleforbund
	Youngstorget 1
	Oslo
	* Norges Automobil-Forbund (NAF)
	Bertrand Narvesens Vel 2
	Etterstad
	Oslo 6
POLAND	Polska Zwiazek Kolarska
	1 Plac Xelaznej Bramy
	Warsaw

* Polskie Towarzystwo
Turystyczno-Krajoznawcze (PTTK)
Senatorska II
Warsaw 40

PORTUGAL

Federacao Portuguesa de Ciclismo
Rua Barros Queiroz 29-1,
Lisbon

* Automovel Club de Portugal (ACP)
Rua Rosa Araujo 24 & 26
Lisbon

RUMANIA

Federatia Romina de Ciclismo
Vasile Conta, 16,
Bucharest

* Association Des Automobilistes (AAR)
Stradan Beloianis 27
Bucharest 1

RUSSIA

Federation Cycliste U.S.S.R.
Skatertnyi Pereoulok 4
Moscow 69

SPAIN

Federacion Espanola de Ciclismo
Alfonso XII 36, 1st Dacha
Madrid 14

* Real Automobil Club de España
(RACE)
General Sanjurjo 10
Madrid 3

SWEDEN

Svenska Cykelforbundet
Stora Nygatan 41–43
Stockholm C

* Svenska Turistföreningen (STF)
Stureplan 2
Stockholm 7

SWITZERLAND	(German-speaking Cantons) Schweiz Radfahrer-u-Motofahrer-Bund Schaffhauserstrasse 272 Zurich 57
	(French-speaking Cantons) Union Cycliste Suisse 4 Rue du Vieux-College 1211 Geneva, 3
	* Touring Club Suisse (TCS) Rue Pierre-Fatio 9 Geneva
TURKEY	* Turkiye Turing ve Otomobil Kurumu Sisli Meydani 364 Istanbul
WEST GERMANY	Bund Deutscher Radfahrer Westanlage 56 B.P. 263 Giessen-Lahn (Hessen.)
YUGOSLAVIA	Federation Yougoslave de Cyclisme Hilendarska 6 Belgrade
	* Auto-Moto Savez Jugoslavije Ruzveltova 18 Belgrade

Many national tourist offices have developed information especially for the cyclist, with preplanned tours, information on roads, places to rent bicycles, cycling areas, and other relevant data.

The Cyclists Touring Club has information sheets, preplanned tours, maps, and insurance and travel services which are an unbeatable value for the tourist. They also conduct tours. So do the Youth Hostel Associations, and membership includes a number of useful guides and handbooks. The British Cycling

Federation does not conduct tours, but does offer insurance services and some 50-odd preplanned tours. The

International Bicycle Touring Society
846 Prospect Street
La Jolla, California 92037

also runs tours in Europe. These tend to be at an easy pace, with a following "sag wagon" car for carrying all but members' personal clothing; accommodations are in inexpensive hotels and meals in restaurants. Higher in cost than hosteling of course, but preselection of hotels keeps expenses moderate.

And then there are always the traditional aids to travel – the Michelin guides and various sight-seeing tomes. One of the nicest things about cycle touring is that you are not obligated to make a plan and stick to a schedule. Even in crowded holiday areas you should not have much difficulty in finding accommodations if you just veer off the beaten track – which a bike makes easy.

Africa

Bicycles are a common form of transport for Africans, but their machines are of course extremely stout and sturdy, as often there is simply no road at all. In Morocco, for example, south of the Atlas Mountains and into the Sahara Desert, the roads are dirt tracks resembling streambeds. Most of the locals simply cycle over the desert itself. However, in Northern Morocco the roads are quite negotiable, and there are not many cars. I should imagine that similar varied conditions prevail throughout Africa.

Parts are a problem, and in many areas so is thievery. Cyclists in Africa have been trapped in disease quarantine areas. There are all kinds of wars, revolutions, famines, and other excitements to interest the tourist. Life is less than cheap. Still, I would say that the prospects for cycle touring were good. A lot depends on your own attitudes and how you get on with people. In any case, few enough people have cycled in Africa so that there is little annotated information. If you go it will be as something of a pioneer. The magazines *Bike World* and *Bicycling!* carry articles on African touring from time to time. The Cyclists Touring Club has correspondents in Africa, and if you are seriously interested you might try corresponding with Walter Stolle, c/o P.O.B. 728, Lagos, Nigeria, who has cycled extensively throughout Africa.

Asia and the Pacific

A chronicle of cycling conditions in Asia is to be found in *Sting in the Tail*, Peter Duker's account of his around-the-world ride (Pelham, 52 Bedford Square, London WC1, £2.60). Duker battled sandstorms and government officials, crashed, ran endless gauntlets of rock-throwing men and boys, was clouted viciously by three men who tore limbs off a tree and attacked him, and in general had a Hard Time. By his own account Duker seems a unique enough individual so that his experience is not necessarily the norm, but it would be foolish not to anticipate some difficulties. Both the Cyclists Touring Club and the Youth Hostels have information on Asia.

Australia

Duker's ride covers this area, and you should be able to get information from:

Amateur Cyclists' Association of Australia
W. S. Young
34 Wardell Road
Earlswood
Sydney, New South Wales

Australian Cycling Council
153 The Ringway
Cronulla, 2230
Sydney, New South Wales

Japanese Cycling Federation
Kishi Memorial Hall
25 Kannami-Cho-Shipuyaku
Tokyo

New Zealand Amateur Cycling Association
C.P.O. Box 30459
Lower Hutt

Philippine Cycling Association
Rizal Memorial Track-Football Stadium
Dakota Street
Manila
as well as the Cyclists Touring Club and the Youth Hostels.

The Americas

Canada

The Canadian Bicycle Book (D. C. Heath Ltd., Toronto, $3.95) is mostly an introduction to cycling but has some touring information. Organizations are:

Canadian Cycling Association   also at
3737 rue Monselet   333 River Road
Montreal Nord, P.Q.   Vanier, Ontario

Canadian Youth Hostels Association
268 First Avenue
Ottawa, Ontario

Mexico

Federacion Mexicana de Ciclismo
Confederation Sportive Mexicaine
Avenue Juarez Num 64-311
Mexico City 1

The Cyclists Touring Club has correspondents in Mexico.

South America

Organizations are:

Federacion Ciclista Argentina
Av. Pte. Figueroa
Alcoeta 4600
Buenos Aires, Argentina

Brazilian Confederation
    of Sports
Rue da Quitanda 3
2nd Andar
Case Postale 1078
Rio-de-Janeiro, Brazil

The Cyclists Touring Club and Youth Hostels may have information. I'm headed that way myself with a boat and bicycles and will be happy to let you know how it goes, but this won't be for a while yet.

10. Racing

Bicycle racing is quite specialized and involved. Space and my own limited knowledge of the subject permit only the briefest comments and descriptions. For further information I suggest the chapter on racing in Eugene Sloane's *The Complete Book of Bicycling* (Trident Press $9.95); *Cycling*, edited by David Saunders (Wolfe Publishing, available from Foyles, 119 Charing Cross Road, London WC2, England); and *Cycle Racing* by Bowden and Matthews (Temple Press, 42 Russell Square, London WC1, England).

John Forester's *Effective Cycling* (Custom Cycle Fitments, 782 Allen Court, Palo Alto, CA 94303) contains much information of value to the racer. *All About Bicycle Racing* and *Bicycle Track Racing* (World Publications, P.O. Box 366, Mountain View, CA 94040, respectively $2.50 and $3.95) are very good. *Winning Bicycle Racing*, by Jack Simes (Henry Regnery Co., Chicago, $4.95) is written with the novice in mind. A classic is *Cycling*, published by the C.O.N.I., Central Sports School, Rome (available in a few cycle shops). A monthly publication is *Competitive Cycling* (P.O. Box 2066, Carson City, NV 89701). William Sanders does a regular column for *Bike World Magazine* on racing which is particularly good.

To participate in organized racing you must join a club. Ask at your local bike shop for the one nearest you, or write

U.S.C.F.
Box 669
Wall Street Station
New York, N.Y. 10005

and they will advise you. Club level racing does not require a license, but sanctioned races require a U.S.C.F. license. You compete according to age, sex, and ability, so if you are a beginner do not worry about being trounced first time out – most of the riders will be fairly evenly matched. Some of the greatest bike riders in the world are little shrimps. The less weight to lug around the better. Big people are not excluded either – on downhills they generally have the edge. What counts in the end is heart. Bike racing is an extremely rigorous sport. In skiing, running, football, and most other sports, when you are finished you drop. On a bike a lot of your weight is supported by the machine and only a small amount of energy is required to maintain balance. It is quite possible to run your body to the finish and beyond, so that when you stop you are unable to stand on your feet. Any serious racer has to keep fit with a year round physical conditioning program.

The three basic types of races are road, track, and cyclo-cross.

Road

Time trial – Individual or team rides against the clock over 10, 25, 30, 50, and 100 mile courses, or rides for the greatest distance covered in 12 or 24 hours. Pure riding ability and stamina count the most.

Massed start – Everybody starts together, first human over the finish line wins. The course can be 10 miles, or 2,600, as in the Tour de France. Most single day events are between 50 and 100 miles for amateurs, and 80 to 180 for professionals. Races lasting two days or more are called stage races.

In road racing riders are pitted against each other, and the resulting shenanigans are sometimes incredible. Intelligence, strategy, trickiness, and psychology play an equal role with riding ability and strength. Teams work together to launch a strong teammate ahead of the pack to victory, and block opposition riders. In big races like the Tour de France bicycles collide and pedals jam into spokes. In Europe these races go on despite wars, revolutions, or anything else, and are the subject of intense popular interest. Bikes are of a conventional design, with freewheels and brakes.

A type of road race popular in America is the criterium. It is usually held on a closed circuit measuring less than two miles around, with sharp and narrow corners, over distances ranging from 25 to 62 miles. Very precise riding is needed to cope with the corners, and the dense pack of riders created by the narrowness of the streets or road. Criterium bikes tend to have very stiff frames for quick handling, and a high bottom bracket so that pedalling can continue through the corners.

Cyclo-cross

Cross-country races from point to point or around a course, from 1 to 16 miles in length, run either as a time trial or with a massed start. These are typically through steep climbs and descents, mud, thick woods, streams, and hurdles. Some sections are negotiated on foot. It is a rough sport, physically very demanding, with plenty of spills.

Track

The machine common to a wide variety of track events is the greyhound of bikes: an ultra-light frame with a short wheelbase; a fierce position with the saddle high and handlebars low; a single fixed wheel gear, with no brakes; and tires bonded to the rims with shellac, to withstand the stresses of violent track maneuvers. There are no quick release hubs, gears, pumps, cables, etc., making these among the most lovely and functional of bikes.

There are many different kinds of track events. Here are a few:

Sprint – Usually a 1000 meter course with only the last 200 meters timed. Involves all kinds of tricky tactics and scheming.

There are times when racers hold their bikes stock still while jockeying for position. *Behind* the leader and in his slipstream until the final dash is the favored winning position.

Pursuit – Two riders or teams start on opposite sides of the track and try to catch each other.

Time Trials – Against the clock, as in road racing.

Devil Take the Hindmost – Last man over the line every 2 or 3 laps is out.

Paced racing – Motorcycles are used as pace-setters for the riders, who stay as close as possible to the pacer's rear wheel so as to minimize wind resistance. Speeds up to 60 mph

Madison – Two man teams run in relays. Events run from 50 kilometers or one hour to six day races. Each team member runs one or two laps and then hands over to a teammate, literally throwing him by the seat of his pants or by a hand-sling. A very spectacular form of racing.

11. Accessories

Most accessories are unnecessary. Whenever possible try to peel weight off your bike. Streamers, doodads, and various decorative garp are out, unless they are of such incredibly redeeming character as to make them worth carrying at any cost. I had a Bombay Taxi Driver's Horn like that once, a great gleaming diesel-like trumpet, but it went when the Golden Flash was stolen.

Pump – A necessity for tubular tires, an excellent idea for clinchers. What use is a tire repair kit if you don't have a pump?

Toe clips – These nearly double pedalling efficiency and with smooth-soled shoes the feet can be slipped out easily in an emergency.

Bicycle shoes and cleats – Bike shoes are cut for ankling and have a steel shank for even foot pressure on the pedal. Cleats will give you tremendous get up and go and are a must for long tours and racing, but not advisable in traffic.

Lights – These present a whole series of problems. There are two basic types of lighting systems: battery and generator. Generator types take power off the wheel or hub, thus increasing pedalling resistance. There is more hardware, wires can snag and break, and the system is permanently attached to the bike. Under way the lights are bright and strong, but when you stop they go out.

Battery lights stay on when you stop, but gradually fade. They can be got on and off the bike easily. This means you can eliminate dead weight when you want to. Battery lights are useful for map reading and roadside repairs. They are easily stolen off a parked bike. They can be misplaced and difficult to find just before a ride.

Either a generator or battery light is capable of failing at any time. A second back-up light of some sort is essential.

The choice of main system type is up to you and the conditions you encounter. If you ride a lot at night and/or frequently lock up on the street and/or just want lights on the bike there, when you need them, then a generator system is probably best. You can complement it with a voltage regulator and battery charger unit such as the BVR (cycle shops) which will keep the lights on when you stop and add 14 ounces weight to the bike, or a battery light (5 to 16 ounces).

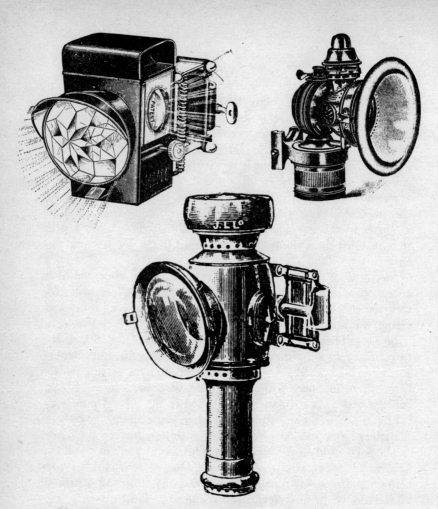

If you have a performance bike which cannot be lumbered with additional weight when not needed and/or ride mostly in the daytime, battery lights will probably be the most convenient. You will want still another back-up light.

Lights are not so much that you see, as you are seen. This is where the back-up light can serve a vital function. The French Matex light has a white front and red rear, weighs only 5 ounces, and straps to an arm or leg. Because it is moved about it is very visible. Every rider should have, at the minimum, the Matex light (bike shops, about $2.50).

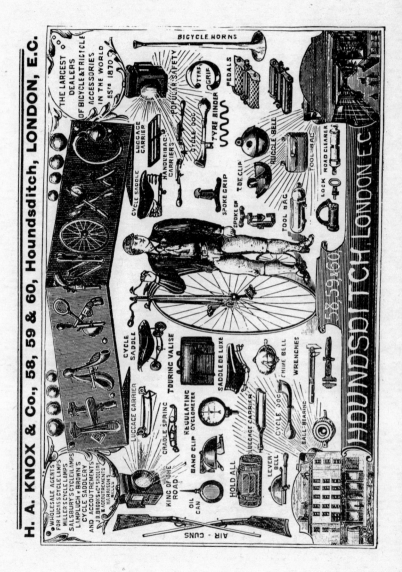

A still more eye-catching device is the Belt Beacon. This is an amber high intensity light which flashes on and off at between 40 and 60 times a minute. It can be attached to the belt or to the bike. Anybody riding regularly at night would be well advised to use one or even two (front and back) Belt Beacons (bike shops, about $7.00). It may all seem like a little bit much – main light system, Belt Beacon, and Matex or other spare light. The problem at night is to survive. Bicycle lights are diminutive. In cities and towns they are easily lost in the welter of traffic lights, street lights, and neon signs. In the country the car coming up from behind may be doing

70 mph to your 10 mph. That's an 88 foot per second speed differential, and if the visible range of your rear lights is 300 feet or less, it is under the distance required for a car to stop (315 feet). In short, if the driver blinks his eyes, or turns for a casual quick glance at a passenger, you can be wiped out.

The Belt Beacon is visible for at least 600 feet in cities and towns, and for far greater distances in the country. The rapid blinking action draws immediate attention. And that is what you want.

Another safety light which I have not yet tested is the Mighty Lite, which uses a fluorescent tube to cast a green tinted light in a 25′ circle around the cyclist. Power by generator. Sounds weird

but might be good. Write Maxon Co., 20630 Harper Ave., Harper Woods, Mich. 48225 for details.

Whatever type of system you use, carry spare bulbs. Room to store these can often be found inside the lamp, or you can wrap them in a bit of plastic and stuff them in the ends of the handlebars.

Reflectors – By law, bikes sold today must have reflectors front and rear, on the pedals, and on the wheels. Wheel reflectors are not very useful, since they are usually visible only when the cyclist is already broadside on to the motorist. Front, rear, and pedal reflectors must be regarded only as an added precaution. What makes a cyclist visible at night are good lights. If you use panniers dress them up with a reflecting tape such as Scotchlite. It adds virtually no weight and does a lot for your visibility. Reflecting tape is also good for your helmet, the back of your jacket, and the backs of your gloves so that turn signals are more clearly indicated.

Electric turn signals – These are silly. A blinking turn signal is useful only on a vehicle wide enough and with sufficient other lights so that the blinker is clearly on one side of the vehicle. Bike turn signals are too close together for a motorist to tell from a distance what is going on.

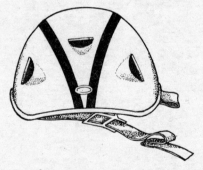

Helmet – In most fatal bicycle accidents the injury is to the head. Even a drop of two feet onto a hard surface is enough to fracture the skull. Wear a helmet whenever you cycle. It's inconvenient. So is not being able to think or talk because your head has been pounded into jelly.

The classic cycling helmet consists of padded strips of leather with spaces in between for ventilation. It is better than nothing but far from good enough. The best protection is provided by a hard shell helmet with a shock absorbing liner or suspension system. Two on the market are Bell and MSR (about $30, at bike shops). I personally prefer the Bell, which has large ventilation air scoops, and very precise individual fitting through the use of interchangeable velcro backed foam pads of varying thicknesses.

One problem with the Bell and MSR helmets is that when climbing hills in hot weather there is not enough air flow to keep the head cool. You can get fairly drenched in sweat. A helmet that attempts to beat this problem is the Skid-Lid, which concentrates on protecting the front, back, and sides of the head. It is lighter and more well ventilated and comfortable than the Bell or MSR helmets, but does not give anything like as much protection. Skid-Lid adherents agree that protection is less, but say that comfort and convenience make one more likely to actually use a Skid-Lid.

Well, there is a very effective poster shown on billboards throughout England. It shows a man in a wheelchair. The caption reads, "I didn't wear a seatbelt because it was inconvenient." Get a Bell or MSR helmet. Use it always.

Gloves – Cycling gloves are fingerless, with ventilated mesh backs and padded leather palms. The padding can help a lot to prevent numb hands from pinched nerves, and affords some protection in the event of a spill.

Handlebar tapes – Standard tapes of plastic or cloth are quite thin. If your hands numb easily you may want to use something thicker. The Tape is vinyl backed and suede finished and feels very nice. Eight washable colors, about $2 a set. Thicker is the Bailey III cushioned tape, with a soft center and tapered edges, also eight colors and about $3.50 a set. Cyclegrip tape is also soft center tapered edge, but is made of real leather. It feels really good. Black or tan and about $7 a set from bike shops, or $7.50 direct from Cyclegrip, P.O. Box 1494, Highland Park, NJ 08904. For the ultimate in thickness try contoured foam handlebar sheaths. Sets are made by Pro Tour and Grab On and cost $7 to $10.

Bullseys pulleys – People interested in tuning a bike up for maximum performance might consider these sealed bearing chain roller wheels for derailleur units. They reduce friction by one-sixth. $12.50 from Durham Bicycles, 3944 Marathon Street, Los Angeles, CA 90029.

Junior pedalling attachment – This device fits onto the rear seat tube of a tandem bike, and consists of a bottom bracket and chainwheel which drive a freewheel fitted to the main bottom bracket below. It allows very small children to ride the back seat of the tandem and contribute to the pedalling when they feel so inclined. It is more interesting than sitting around doing nothing, and the position is safer. Obtainable from Andrew Hague Cycle Engineering, 1 Kipling Grove, Anstey Lane, Leicester LE4 0PF, England, for £15 plus postage.

Saddle bag clamp – Many racing saddles do not have the necessary loops for attaching a saddle or tool bag. This gizmo solves the problem and is quick release as well. From Andrew Hague, address above, for £1 plus postage.

Tool bag – Small and compact, these will hold a tire repair kit, chain tool and chainlinks, and a few tools. Almost in the carrier class is the Bike Pocket tire bag also fitting under the saddle, but able to hold 2 tubular tires, tools, lamps, and other gear. Good for fast day rides. About $14 from Synergy Works, 255 4th Street, Oakland, CA 94607.

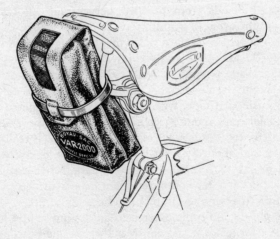

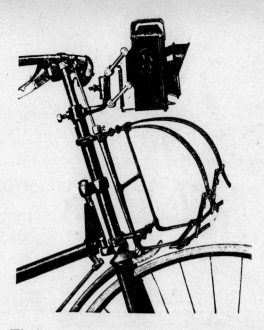

Carrier – The best sort of carrier depends on your needs. A cloth slingbag or rucksack can go with you on and off the bike and is handy while shopping. So are the quick release front baskets, and rear panniers. For around town use the lightweight alloy racks fitting over the rear wheel and clamping to the back seat stays are quite adequate. For heavier going a steel rack designed for use with panniers is much better. See the baggage section in chapter 9 for more information.

Child carriers – The only kind worth considering put the child behind the rider and have full leg shields to prevent feet from tangling in spokes. The Kiddie Rider by American Products (about $18) works very well. The Troxel Model 1 (about $18) features a quick release for the seat. An alternative to a rear mounted carrier is a trailer.

Trailers – For hauling heavy loads of laundry, groceries, camping gear, etc., trailers are excellent. Usual capacity is up to 80 pounds. They attach and detach from the bike in seconds and free you of the need for racks and panniers. One good brand has the name Bugger, and comes in closed, open, and child carrier models. About $100 at bike shops. An open big basket model is the byKart, about $80 at bike shops.

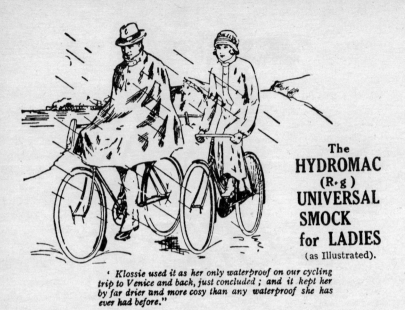

The
HYDROMAC
(R·g)
UNIVERSAL
SMOCK
for LADIES
(as Illustrated).

' *Klossie used it as her only waterproof on our cycling
trip to Venice and back, just concluded ; and it kept her
by far drier and more cosy than any waterproof she has
ever had before.*"

Rear view mirrors – Bicycle mounted rear view mirrors wiggle
about too much to be reliable. Wrist mounted mirrors such as the
See-Bak and eyeglasses mounting mirrors such as the Golden
View Mirror are useful accessories once you learn how to use them,
and providing that you always take what you see with a grain of
salt. The field of view of these mirrors is very small and limited
to possibly warning you of upcoming traffic. To check and see
if the way is clear for you to pull out farther onto the road, duck
your head and look directly.

Nail pullers or *flint catchers* – These are small half loops of wire
that ride along just above the tire and brush off shards of broken
glass, pebbles, etc. For tubulars and narrow profile clinchers.

Fenders – In very wet conditions you and the bike are going to
get soaked anyhow. You might as well save yourself the extra
weight and wind resistance. In sometime wet conditions, or if
you regularly ride wearing good clothing, fenders will help
prevent you and the bike from being sprayed with wet and dirt.
Plastic fenders can be got on and off the bike easily if yours is a
dual use machine.

Locks – see chapter 4.

Horns and bells – Yelling is quick, reliable, and the most expressive. Little bells and horns are forever failing or being stolen. Freon horns are wonderfully loud – excessively so.

Water bottle – On longer tours and races it is quite easy to become dehydrated. This raises body temperature. It is a good idea to carry your own supply of liquid and a bit of high energy food.

Spoke guard – This is a thin plate designed to prevent the rear derailleur from catching in the spokes of the rear wheel. With a properly adjusted derailleur it should never happen, but should the derailleur malfunction or break (as has happened to me) then down you go, and with the back of the bike twisted into spaghetti.

Chain guard – These are designed to help prevent the soiling of clothes by dirty chains, and are probably worthwhile on a commuting bike. I find them a needless amount of extra weight and trouble on a racing bike.

Kickstand – Adds a lot of weight for very little useful function. There is almost always something against which a bike can be leaned.

Odometer or *velometer* – Tells how far you have gone. Not important.

Speedometer – Tire drive models are generally inaccurate and increase drag. Electronic models are expensive (about $80) but also include a pedal rpm counter. This can be useful when trying to determine maximum power power points in various gears. A club could share one unit among several members.

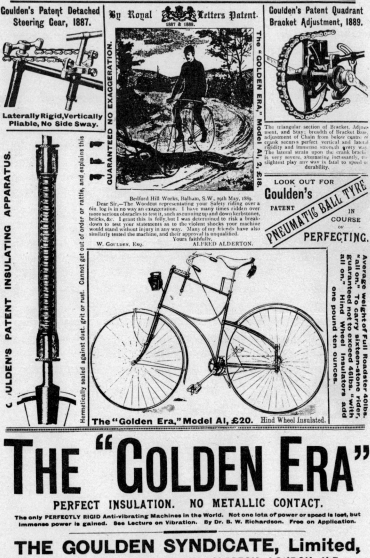

12. Old Bikes

If you have a little spare space, antique cycles are a dandy item to collect and restore. Early models were largely a blacksmith's creation, and bringing them "up to snuff" is well within the capacity of a competent handyman. The last part of the nineteenth century was the heyday of innovation and experimentation in cycles, and many wacky and wonderful machines were produced. Some are illustrated in this book. Because they are unique they can command high prices, and even a plain ordinary penny-farthing in good nick can fetch $450 to $675. By 1910 or so cycle designs had fairly well settled down, and machines from this date onwards can be had for a more reasonable sum. From my own point of view this is fortunate, as I collect (when I can) on the basis of aesthetic appeal, and on this count find the machines of the '20s, '30s, and even '40s very attractive.

The best source for old bikes is grandfather's attic. Most machines already on the market are wildly expensive. The thing to do is find some old wreck moldering in a field or root around in the old junk shed of friendly Uncle Fred the bicycle dealer who unexpectedly kicked the bucket two decades ago. Often what you find is a disheartening pile of rust, but it is surprising what some elbow grease and rust remover can do. And listen, if you do know of such a wreck or old shed and aren't interested . . . drop me a line, hm?

There are any number of books on old cycles, and a nice inexpensive one is *Discovering Old Bicycles* by T. E. Crowley (Shire Publications, Ltd., 12B Temple Square, Aylesbury, Bucks, 35p). A real winner is *King of the Road* by Andrew Ritchie (Ten Speed Press, Berkeley, CA).

Organizations in America:

Antique Bicycle Club of America
Roland C. Geist
260 West 260th Street
New York, New York

A.D. 1879. Jan. 18. No 208.
BRUTON'S Provisional Specification.

Veteran Wheelmen's Association
Franklin Institute
Philadelphia, Pa.

The Wheelmen
Robert McNair
32 Dartmouth Circle
Swarthmore, Pa. 19801

The Wheelmen Antique
Bicycle Club
214 Maywinn Road
Defiance, Ohio

The Wheelmen Newsletter (has ads)
Keith Larzelere
P.O. Box 38
Petersburg, Michigan 49270

In England:
Southern Veteran Cycle Club
Iain Cowan
Woodbine Cottage
8 Shrubbery Road
Gravesend, Kent

Boston Veteran Cycle Club
P. Bates
15 Rosebery Avenue
Boston, Lincolnshire

Publishes *The Boneshaker*, a wonderfully interesting magazine, and a newsletter, *News and Views*.

Bygone Bikes Yorkshire Club
J. W. Auty
85 Priory Road
Featherstone
Pontefract, Yorkshire

Peterborough Vintage
Cycle Club
Ms. Young
48 Newark Avenue
Peterborough

Long Sutton and District
Veteran Cycle Club
P. Shirtcliffe
Hillcrest
Crowhall
Denver
Downham Market, Norfolk

Roadfarers Veteran Cycle Club
A. C. Mundy
22 High Street
Caister, Peterborough

National Association
of Veteran Cycle Clubs
Ray Heeley
124 Southfields Avenue
Stanground, Peterborough

Benson Veteran Cycle Club
C. N. Passey
61 The Bungalow
Brook Street
Benson, Oxfordshire

Between four small wheels is one large wheel, with a crank & steering handle, which is connected by a Hooke's joint to the axles of the four small wheels, and when it is moved to turn a corner the small wheels track exactly as the skate rollers do when the rider leans over.

A flexible frame consisting of two jointed fork bars surround the main wheel, and pivot on the crank axle. This frame being composed of two forks jointed near the crank, the hind or fore wheels may be lifted off the ground as desired, or may be set so that all the wheels run.

ELLIOTT QUADRICYCLE.

BOOK TWO

1. Maintenance and Repair

Maintenance Program

The subject of maintenance and repair of bicycles is usually clouded with negative feelings. It is regarded as something in the "must be done" category and approached as a chore. Bicycle repair books are fond of saying that any cretin can understand how to fix his machine, or that the book itself has the answer to any problem that might conceivably come up. Both approaches underestimate the reader's intelligence and compartmentalize maintenance and repair, keeping it separate from "riding". This is a basic mistake. The extent to which you get involved in working on your bike should be a direct function of how you ride. One follows the other like night and day. The awareness that riding a bike precipitates usually includes an awareness and interest in the bike itself. How the bike responds is very much a function of maintenance. Ideally, you are going to work on your own bike because you want a together, tight machine under you, i.e., you will do it because *you want to*.

As with all things, you get back in proportion to what you put in. It is essentially a question of fineness. It is the nature of bikes that they are at their best when well-lubricated and carefully adjusted. A sensitivity to this sort of refinement does not happen the instant you mount a bike. Give it time. As you ride you will become increasingly aware of your bike's mechanical characteristics. A well set-up bike fits you like a suit of clothes, and you will soon develop an "ear" for the sound of bearings and a 'feel" for other parts, such as the brakes. The development of this sensitivity – the result of personal and direct participation – is part of the reason for owning a bike in the first place. Eventually, you will find that increased riding pleasure is not just a reward for doing your own maintenance, the mechanical sensitivity itself becomes part of the riding pleasure.

As I say, this is all something that you should grow into. The idea of having a bike is to have fun. A fair amount of latitude is possible in servicing bikes and you have hopefully chosen a machine suited to your level of interest. So you can minimize or maximize maintenance as per your own inclinations. But bear in mind that most machines, and certainly bicycles, need a certain amount of lubrication and adjustment if they are to function at all. Without it, they rust away, and because the parts are unlubricated and out of kilter, they slowly chew themselves to bits when ridden. I have seen "old dependables" that have been left out in the rain for years and have never seen an oil can or a mechanic. They make it for years – and then snap a chain in the middle of a tour or a brake cable at the start of a long hill. Or eventually the rust destroys them. There is no need for this. A properly maintained bike will easily last a lifetime (one of mine was made in 1935 and has seen plenty of hard service to boot). For reasons of simple economy and safety, if you can't be bothered to do routine maintenance then take your machine to a bike shop for servicing at least twice a year.

Bike shops. Alas! There are good ones and bad ones. An excellent reason for doing your own work is that you are apt to do a better and quicker job than the shop. Over 10 million bikes were sold in the U.S. of A. last year. Many stores are so busy selling new machines that service programs are minimal. Customers therefore find service time-consuming, expensive, and frequently not very good. It's a real drag to call for your bike a couple of times and be told it's not ready, the part didn't come, it rained, etc. etc.

The other side of the coin is that some stores have recognized the need for decent service programs and sell their bikes with service guarantees for one to three years. This means that you can bring the bike in for routine servicing and any breakage not due to normal wear and tear is covered, parts and labor both. The stores that offer this feature are usually large, and with a high volume of sales, so that their prices are perfectly competitive with other stores. Even if you do your own work their guarantee is a nice insurance to have. A good bike store needn't be fancy either. There is a tiny, one-man bike/locksmith shop around the corner from me that does perfectly good work at devastatingly reasonable rates. So look around. You may have one or two bad experiences but should eventually find a reliable shop.

No matter if the shop is good or bad, you can't expect the mechanic to have as much interest in getting things just right as you do. Once you learn the drill you will almost always do a better job. Also, it is time-consuming to leave your bike at the store for three days for work that takes ten minutes to do.

Another important reason for doing your own work is that it makes preventive maintenance almost automatic. Preventive maintenance is replacing parts before they wear out and break,

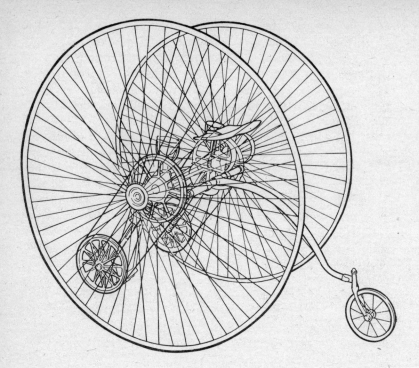

usually at an inopportune time and miles from any bike store. If you are paying attention to the various parts of your bike and keeping it in tune this is pretty much going to happen as a matter of course. In turn, breakdowns and repairs will also be fairly well obviated.

I think this approach is the easiest and the most efficient. I have studied every repair manual I could find. Most stress fixing something *after* it has broken. Even though I know how to fix bicycles most of them lose me right away. Either they are filled with long passages of incomprehensible jargon, or they have computer-programming style directions ("If A, go to page 28 C; if not A, go to B, page 34, then to page 28 D.") designed to reduce you to a mindless automaton.

Here is my approach: each major component system of the bicycle such as brakes, wheels, gears, etc. is broken down into four areas –

How It Works
Routine Adjustments
Replacing Parts
Troubleshooting

The idea is to give you a basic understanding of what is happening – and make you a mechanic! How It Works for each section is required reading. It does no good for you to diddle with this or adjust that if you have no idea of how it works. And if something is broken it is impossible for you to fix unless you know how it works in the first place.

It will help a lot if as you read, you look at and feel the corresponding parts of your bike.

I don't cover everything. One wheel is pretty much the same as another. I have tried to include representative types of equipment currently in use but there are bound to be exceptions. If this happens to you try to find the item in this book which most closely resembles the part you are servicing or fixing. Pay particular attention to *function* and then analyze your own part the same way. This should get you through most anything.

There are also some tasks which are just not worth doing. Getting into the innards of a coaster brake multi-speed hub is one of these. It takes a long, long time and isn't fun at all. Some people may resent these omissions. They want to do everything for themselves. Well, the point of diminishing returns is reached with attempts to service the coaster brake 3-speed hubs. Even most bike shops refuse to overhaul these units and simply replace them – it's actually cheaper this way. If you insist on doing this sort of work, detailed instructions are available from the bicycle manufacturer or from the hub manufacturer.

Tools

You can get by with amazingly little in the way of tools. However, for some kinds of work there are a few you will just have to get. Also, what you need depends on what kind of bike you have.

Before going into particulars a word on tool quality: do yourself a favor and buy good ones. Dime stores, supermarkets, and even hardware stores carry cheap bargains like 29c screwdrivers and $1.00 wrenches. These are a false economy, for they are made of inferior metals that will break or bend under stress, or they are made badly enough so that they don't even work. In the long run good tools are well worth the investment.

Many bike shops sell pre-assembled tool kits such as the Cycle Pro. Be sure your tools are the correct size. Foreign made bikes, and American bikes with foreign components, use metric system nuts and bolts. If you have an all-American bike make the substitutions indicated on the following lists.

For both 3- and 10-speed bikes:
Hardware store
8″ or 6″ Adjustable end wrench.
Pliers.
Hammer.
$\frac{1}{4}$″ tip, 4-5″ shank screwdriver.
$\frac{1}{8}$″ tip, 2-3″ shank screwdriver.
Wire clippers.
6″ File, mill bastard.
Bike store
Mafac tool kit – contains tire irons, wrenches, other gear, including tire patching kit.
All-purpose tool like Raleigh give-away.
Thin hub wrenches, 13 × 14 and 15 × 16.
Spoke wrench.
Pedal wingnut wrench (for pedals with outside dustcap only).
Note: For all of above, substitute U.S. equivalent if you have an American bike.
Tire gauge: for Schrader valve if you have clincher tires.
for Presta valve if you have tubulars.
Tire patch kit for your tires.

10-speed bikes:
Bike store
Chain rivet remover.
Freewheel remover. There are two basic types:

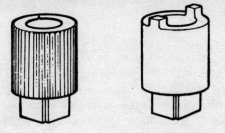

Look at your freewheel and see if it is splined or not on the interior to see what kind you need.

Set metric allen wrenches (Sears also sells these).

If you have a Campagnolo derailleur, a special Campagnolo combination allen and socket wrench.

If you have cotterless cranks you will need a special crank removing tool as per your brand of crank.

Other useful tools:
Set of wrenches.
Vise-grip pliers.
Channel lock pliers.
Small portable vise.

As you can see from studying the list, many of the tools are for specialized jobs so you do not have to acquire them all at once. Absolutely essential, and especially for trips, is the Mafac toolkit, a screwdriver, and an all-purpose combination tool like the Raleigh give-away.

If you have difficulty obtaining tools from local shops, or would just like to read over an amusing tool catalog, write to The Third Hand, 3945 High St., Eugene, Ore. 97405.

You will need some means of holding the bike steady. One method is to simply turn the bike upside down. With downswept handlebars use a narrow cardboard or wood box with slots cut in the side to support the handlebars and keep the brake cables from being bent against the ground. A nail driven into a doorjam with a rope to hang the bike by will also suffice. Best of all is a proper work stand. These are rather expensive ($25 and up) but perhaps you could share one with friends. Bikecology (2910 Nebraska Ave., P.O. Box 1880, Santa Monica, CA 90406) sells a folding stand that is easy to store and carry about.

Lubrication

This is a general discussion of lubrication. For details look under the part in question, e.g. brakes, gears, hubs, etc.

There are a number of different types and forms of lubricants. Oil is the old standby. Be sure to use a good grade, such as motorist's SAE 30, or Sturmey-Archer cycle oil. Do not use household oils as these have a vegetable gum base which ultimately creates a hard residue.

Grease is used for bearings. Ordinary grease from a motorist's shop will work well enough. Lithium greases such as Filtrate and Cycle Pro are less likely to be washed away by water. Also good in this respect is Bardahl Multi-purpose grease. Best of all is Phil Wood Waterproof Bicycle Grease. The very, very expensive Campagnolo Special Grease is, in English vernacular, a load of old cod.

For the ultimate in slipperiness add a small quantity of Moly-Slip to your grease and oil. This contains molybdenum disulfide, a sub-microscopic substance that fills in microscopic irregularities on metal surfaces, reducing friction and wear.

Your bicycle has upwards of 200 ball bearings held in place by cups and cones:

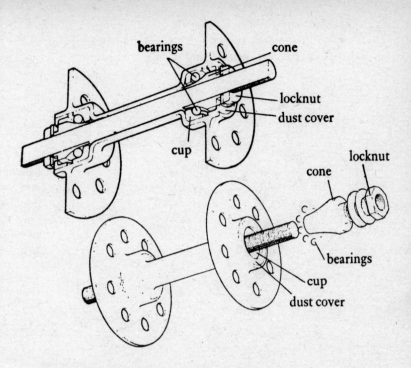

The cone remains stationary while the cup, and whatever part is attached to it – in this example it would be a wheel – rides on the ball bearings and spins around. The distance between the cone and the cup is adjustable and must not be too tight or too loose. Sometimes the ball bearings are held in a clip called a *race:*

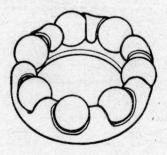

Typically, this is positioned so that the open side through which the balls stick is against the cup. You will find bearings at the headset, bottom bracket, wheels, and pedals:

These bearings are usually disassembled, cleaned thoroughly in kerosene or other solvent, packed with grease and reassembled, every six months. See under relevant section for disassembly technique. Some bearings are both greased and oiled, and in particular, 2- and 3-speed hubs and hubs on ultra-fancy racing bikes. You can tell these by the fact that the hub has a small oil cap or clip:

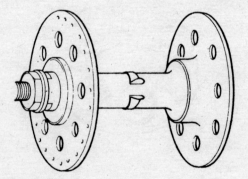

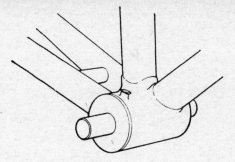

These need oil once a month: multi-speed internal gear hubs a tablespoonful, regular hubs about ½ teaspoonful, and coaster brake hubs 2 tablespoonfuls. Some bottom brackets are set up to use oil. A teaspoonful once a month. Use oil wherever you find oil caps or clips. Too little is better than too much. If oil leaks out of the sides of the bearings and dribbles all over your crankset or wheels, you are using too much.

I prefer the use of a dry lubricant for the chain, freewheel, derailleur, brake pivots, cables, and any other parts which do not use grease:

Dry lubricants usually come in spray form and contain an exotic and sometimes secret blend of ingredients. Often included is molybdenum disulfide. Dry lubricants can be used as a substitute for oil. They are not as long lasting, but ease of application makes more frequent servicing relatively painless. The important thing is that the lubricants are dry. The trouble with oil is that it attracts dirt which then mixes with the oil and forms a gooey abrasive mess, greatly increasing mechanical wear. Everything gets dirty, including you. In the case of the chain, for example, this means that once a month you have to remove it, soak it clean in kerosene or other solvent, dry it, oil it, and then reinstall it. It's time consuming and messy. If you use a dry lubricant you need do this job only once every two or three months. You must lubricate more often – bi-weekly in normal service, weekly in hard service – but with a spray this job takes only a few seconds. The same rationale applies for the freewheel and derailleur. The spray is particularly useful for the brake pivots and all cables. Oil has a tendency to leak out onto the brake levers and handlebars, and brake shoes. Once a month is sufficient.

At this writing the best dry lubricant is LPS, which comes in three grades of thickness (LPS-1, -2, -3) and also as a paste which can be used as a grease for cables. I have not yet tested the suitability of the paste as a bearing grease.

Note: Dry lubricants will usually dissolve ordinary greases and oils. Do not mix the two types!

Another dry lubricant is paraffin wax, available in grocery stores. It is extremely good for prolonging chain life. Clean your chain in the conventional manner with kerosene or other solvent. Melt the paraffin in a coffee can over the stove. Dump the chain in and then hang to dry so that drippings fall back into can. Use oil or spray for the brake pivot points, freewheel and derailleur. The paraffin will not work well on these parts because it cools and hardens too quickly on contact with the metal to penetrate effectively. It is excellent for brake cables, however. Just run the cable through a block of paraffin a few times until it is well impregnated. Save and re-use the old paraffin. Paraffin, like spray, does not attract dirt.

Note: New bikes fresh from the dealer and bikes that have been standing around for a long time may be dry as a bone. *Oil Evaporates!* Be sure to lubricate such machines before using.

General Words

There are a number of things to keep in mind when servicing bikes:

1. Do not use a great deal of force when assembling or disassembling parts. Bicycle components are frequently made of alloys for light weight. These are not as strong as steel and it is not hard to strip threads or otherwise damage parts. Always be sure that things fit. Be careful and delicate. Snug down bolts, nuts, and screws firmly, not with all your might.

2. Most parts tighten *clockwise* and come apart turning *counterclockwise*. This is called a right-hand thread. A left-hand thread tightens *counterclockwise*, and loosens *clockwise*. Left-hand threads are not used often.

3. When fitting together threaded parts hold them as perfectly aligned as you can, and turn one backwards (loosen) until you hear and feel a slight click. Then reverse and tighten. If this is new to you, practice on a nut and bolt until you have the feel of it perfectly.

4. If you get stuck with a rust-frozen bolt or nut, soak it in penetrating oil, give it a few light taps to help the oil work in, and then try to undo it again with a tool that fits exactly. If this fails try a cold chisel and hammer:

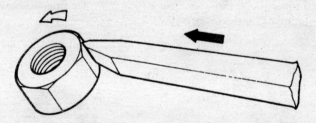

Go at this carefully since if you slip you may gouge a chunk out of your bicycle. If this fails, hacksaw or file the nut or bolt off. How did it get this rusty in the first place?

5. When assembling or disassembling try to be neat and organized. Lay parts out in the order which they came apart or go together. Put tiny parts in boxes or jars.

6. There are a number of little nuts and bolts on your bike for cable clamps, racks, brake lever mounts, gear shift lever mounts, and the like. These tend to get loose and need tightening about once a month.

7. The left side of the bike is as if you and the bike both point forward.

8. Solvents: kerosene and paint thinner are good. Gasoline is very dangerous. Another way of cleaning greasy parts is with a degreaser such as Spray Away or Gunk.

9. Finish: a good quality auto paste wax will preserve your paint job and make it easier to keep clean. Wipe the bike down once a week and after major journeys. Do not wax wheel rims where brake shoes contact.

10. Wire cable is used for brake and gear controls. If you need to trim a new cable to size, do so with wire snips for a clean cut. Pliers will fray the cable end so that it will not pass through the cable housing. After snipping, solder the cable end to prevent fraying, or alternatively, dip it in epoxy glue. File away excess solder or glue.

Ordinary cables and housings work very well but when replacement time comes consider using Ultra-Glide cables. These are extra strong cables running through a housing lined with teflon, perform excellently, and do not require lubrication.

11. Sealed bearing hubs, bottom brackets, and pedals are not covered in this manual. By definition, sealed bearing units are maintenance free. When servicing or repair is needed, usually special tools and techniques are required for each particular make of unit, and often the work is done by the factory.

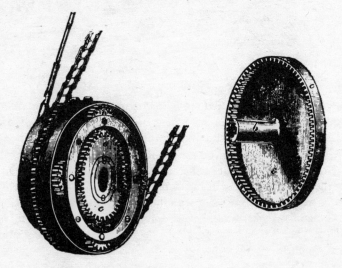

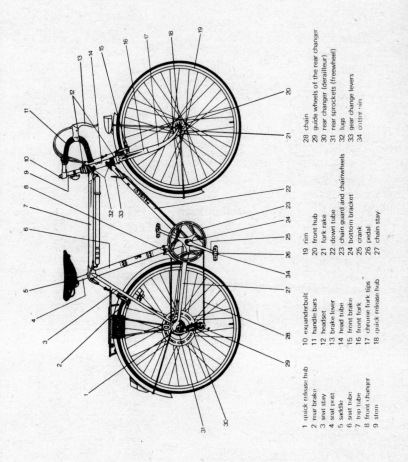

1 quick release hub
2 rear brake
3 seat stay
4 seat post
5 saddle
6 seat tube
7 top tube
8 front changer
9 stem

10 expander bolt
11 handle bars
12 headset
13 brake lever
14 head tube
15 front brake
16 front fork
17 chrome fork tips
18 quick release hub

19 rim
20 front hub
21 fork rake
22 down tube
23 chain guard and chainwheels
24 bottom bracket
25 crank
26 pedal
27 chain stay

28 chain
29 guide wheels of the rear changer
30 rear changer (derailleur)
31 rear sprockets (freewheel)
32 lugs
33 gear change levers
34 cotter pin

2. Brakes

Contents

General   209

How Caliper Brakes Work   210

Lubrication   214

Routine Adjustments   215
Caliper Brakes   215
  Shoes   219
  Cables   219
  Pivot Bolt   222
Roller Lever Brakes   222

Replacing and Disassembling Parts   224
Brake Shoes   218
Cables   224
Handles   228
Brake Mechanism   230

Trouble-shooting   231
Category 1 — No or very weak brakes   231
Category 2 — Uneven or noisy brakes   233
Category 3 — Sticky or dragging brakes   234

Disc Brakes   239
How It Works   239
Lubrication   240
Adjustment   240
Replacing Parts   241
Trouble-shooting   241

General

Bicycle brakes come in three basic types: hub coaster pedal operated, disc hand operated, and caliper hand operated. The coaster brake is inferior on several counts. Under conditions requiring a quick stop it tends to lock the rear wheel, causing the bike to skid rather than slow down.* It has poor heat dissipating qualities and can burn out on a long downhill. It is difficult to service. It is for the rear wheel only, thus cutting braking efficiency below 50%, since it is at the front wheel that the greatest braking power can be attained. In fact, on dry pavement it is difficult if not impossible to lock up a front wheel. This is because braking throws the weight forward, increasing traction. If you have a bike which has only a coaster brake equip it with a caliper brake for the front wheel. Only children without the necessary strength to operate caliper brakes should have a coaster brake, and they should not ride in any situation requiring quick stops or sustained braking.

If something goes wrong with your coaster brake, simply remove the entire rear wheel and take it to a bicycle shop for overhaul or replacement. It is complicated to fix, and infinitely more trouble than it is worth.

Disc brakes are heavy, but offer good stopping power under both wet and dry conditions. They are a logical choice for tandems and tricycles, but are a bit finicky to adjust and service.

Caliper brakes offer a good balance between weight and stopping power. Modern brake shoes give an at least reasonable performance under wet conditions, and very good performance under dry conditions. They are relatively simple to service.

Caliper and disc systems are fairly well identical in operation and principle. All of the operations on brake levers and cables described in the section on caliper brakes below apply equally well to disc brakes. I therefore carry caliper brakes right the way through the chapter, with a section on adjustment and maintenance of disc brakes at the end.

* A screeching tire-smoking stop is not the quickest. When the wheel is locked, the rubber literally melts into the road, providing a *liquid* point of contact between the tire and road surface, and greatly increasing stopping distance. The quickest stops are done by slowing the wheel to the point just before locking. Skidding also means a loss of directional control and often results in a fall.

How Caliper Brakes Work

Caliper brake systems all work on the same basic principle. There is a hollow, flexible tube called a cable housing between the brake lever mount and the cable hanger:

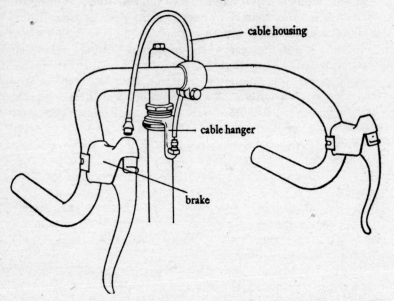

The cable housing is flexible so that the handlebars can turn back and forth. Through the cable housing passes a cable which is attached to the brake lever at one end:

And to the brake mechanism at the other. This is in turn attached to the bicycle frame and functions like a pair of complicated ice tongs with double pivot points. When the brake lever is operated, it pulls the cable through the cable housing and pinches together

the arms (called *yokes*) of the brake mechanism, causing the two
rubber brake shoes attached to the yokes to press against the wheel
rim and stop the wheel:

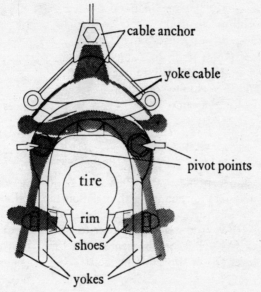

When the lever is released, a spring forces the yoke arms away
from the wheel rim:

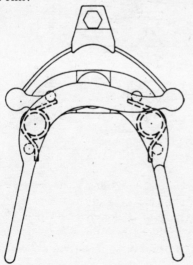

This in turn returns the brake
lever to an off position, and keeps
continuous tension on the entire
brake assembly. This is the basic
center-pull mechanism.

The side-pull brake uses only
one pivot point, with the cable
housing attached directly to one
yoke, and the cable to the other.
The effect is the same:

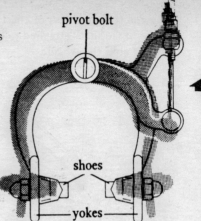

All caliper brake systems have an adjusting screw (called a
barrel adjustor) for changing the relationship of the cable housing
length to the length of the brake cable. On the side-pull brake this
is almost always found on the yoke to which the cable housing is
attached (A), while on the center-pull brake it is usually at the
brake lever (B) or the cable hanger (C):

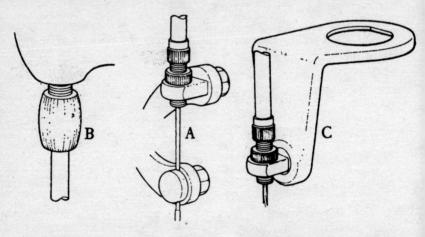

Properly adjusted brake shoes are so close to the wheel rim that
the tire will not slide between them when removing the wheel.
Accordingly, better grade brake systems have a means for creating
a little extra slack in the brake cable. This is usually a small button
which allows the brake lever to open more:

button

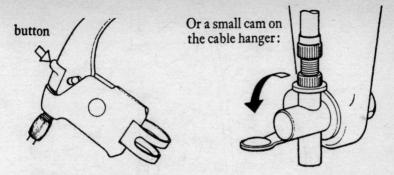

Or a small cam on
the cable hanger:

These are the basics of any caliper brake system: a brake lever, a brake cable and housing with adjustor barrel, a cable hanger for center-pull systems, and the brake mechanism, including yokes, springs, and brake shoes. Better systems include either a button or cam to provide extra slack in the cable when removing the wheel or servicing the brakes:

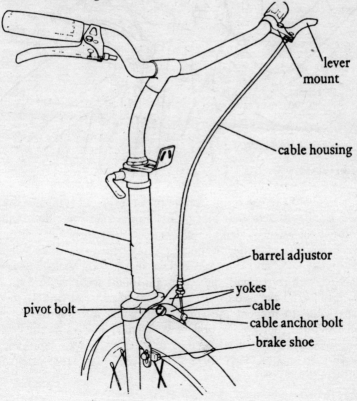

lever
mount

cable housing

barrel adjustor

yokes

cable

pivot bolt

cable anchor bolt

brake shoe

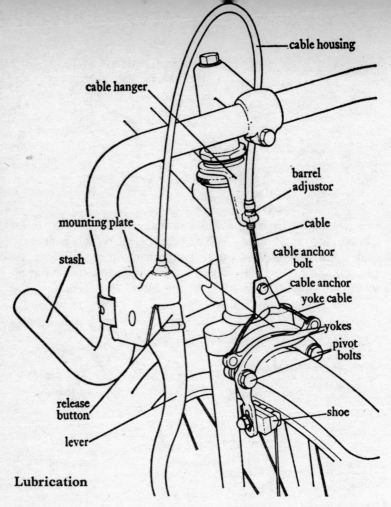

cable housing

cable hanger

barrel
adjustor

mounting plate

cable

cable anchor
bolt

stash

cable anchor

yoke cable

yokes

pivot
bolts

release
button

shoe

lever

Lubrication

Try to avoid the use of oil. At the brake levers it works out over
everything and gets your hands dirty every time you ride. At the
brake mechanism it dribbles down to the brake shoes, cutting
braking power. A better product is a spray such as LPS-1, which
displaces water and does not attract dirt. Use the little plastic
nozzle which comes with the can for pin-point accuracy, and spray
pivot bolts, all exposed cable (use a piece of paper or cardboard as
a backstop to prevent the spray from going all over the bike),
yoke cable anchor points, brake lever pivots, and inside the cable
housings. Machines used once or twice a week need lubrication
every two months, those in daily use, monthly. More often on
tours.

Routine Adjustments

Caliper Brakes

Whatever kind of caliper brake system you have, there are two basic kinds of adjustments: (1) seeing that the brake shoe hits the wheel rim properly, and (2) keeping slack out of the cable between the brake lever and mechanism, so that the lever travels the shortest possible distance when putting on the brakes.

First check to see that the wheel is true by spinning it and seeing that the rim, not the tire, stays about the same distance from the brake shoe all the way around. If play is greater than approximately $\frac{1}{8}''$ the wheel should be trued (see p. 278) before any brake adjustments are attempted. Check also that the wheel is reasonably centred between the fork arms, and that the rim is free of major dents and abrasions. If off center, take the bike to a shop to have the forks checked, and if the rim is badly banged up, get a new one.

Brake shoes: These need to be aligned so that the shoe hits the rim squarely:

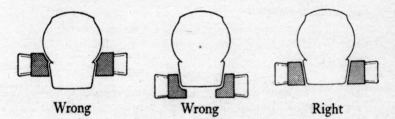

Wrong   Wrong   Right

Brake shoes are held on either by a conventional bolt:

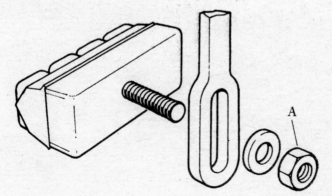

A

or an eyebolt:

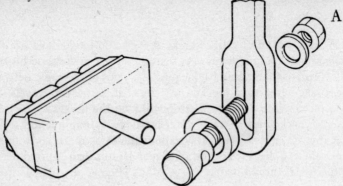

In either case, loosen nut *A*, adjust brake shoe to meet rim, and tighten. One method is to loosen nut *A* just a little bit and gently tap the shoe into the proper position with the wrench handle. With conventional bolts you'll find that the brake shoe twists to the right when you tighten the nut back down. A good trick is to set it slightly counter-clockwise so that the final tightening brings it perfectly into position. Do not use too much force. Brake bolt screws strip easily.

Eyebolt-type shoes are easy to adjust so that the face of the shoe is flush with the rim. Achieving this effect with a conventional-bolt brake shoe sometimes requires bending the yoke. Remove the brake shoe altogether and fit an adjustable end wrench snugly over the end of the yoke:

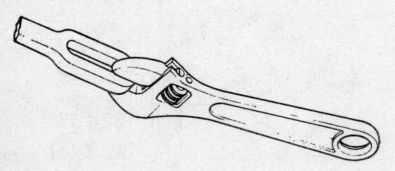

If the yoke needs to be bent outward, simply pull on the handle of the wrench. *Go Slow* – if you break or mangle the yoke you will probably have to get a whole new (expensive) brake mechanism. If the yoke needs to be bent inward, provide a pivot point by wedging another wrench, screwdriver handle, or other object between the yoke and tire, and push on the wrench handle:

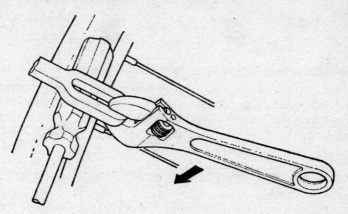

If you don't have a suitable wrench, use a screwdriver:

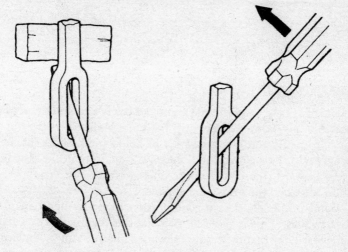

Do not be especially keen to start bending things. New brake shoes, for example, will frequently wear into correct alignment with a few days' use:

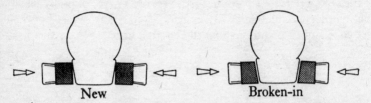

New   Broken-in

Use soft rubber racing-type brake shoes (usually colored red) rather than the hard rubber (usually black) kind typically supplied with side-pull brakes. The soft shoes wear out faster but work a lot better and cost only a few cents each. You can buy the shoes separately from the metal holder and bolt. The holder is open at one end. Slide the old shoe out and the new one in:

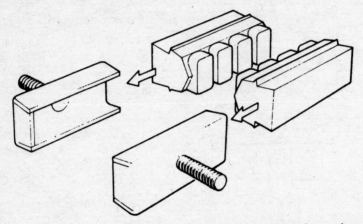

If the old brake shoe will not come out easily and you do not have access to a vise to securely grip the holder while you tap out the shoe, forget it and buy a new set of holders and shoes (about 50 cents each). Be sure to install the new units so that the closed end faces forward (the direction the bike goes), or else the shoes will slide out when the brakes are applied.

Some people consider it good practice to toe-in the fronts of the brake shoes. This is done by twisting the yoke with a wrench or screwdriver so that the front of the shoe hits the rim $\frac{1}{32}$" before the back. Under hard braking however, the whole shoe is flush to the rim. If you have squealing brakes this may cure the problem. Do not toe-in modern soft composition shoes such as Mathauser's, as this can cause severe grabbing and snatching – hard braking when you do not want it.

Cables: Once the brake shoes have been properly aligned they should be placed as close to the rim as possible without rubbing when the wheel is spun, $\frac{1}{8}''$ or less. This is done, for both side- and center-pull brakes, with the barrel adjustor and locknut, and the cable anchor nut and bolt:

Barrel adjustor

Cable Anchor Bolt

The idea is to screw in the barrel adjustor, take up as much slack as possible at the anchor nut, and then use the barrel adjustor to take up slack every few days. The cable is always stretching. When the barrel adjustor reaches the limit of its travel, the process is repeated. There are a number of different methods for doing this job, depending on the number and type of tools that you have. A very handy gadget is called a "third hand" and is a spring-like affair for compressing brake shoes together. Bike stores have them. The reason for this tool, or substitute, is that if you just loosen the anchor cable nut the spring tension of the brake yoke arms will pull the cable through and you will have a hard time getting it back in. With or without a third hand:

Undo locknut and screw adjustor barrel all the way in:

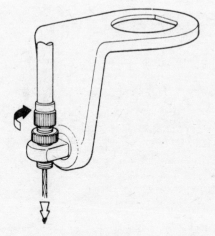

Check and see that the brake release button or cam is set for normal operation (not on all bikes). If you have a third hand, mount it. Or use a C-clamp. Or even string. If you have none of these things, squeeze the brake yoke arms together with your hand. With the other hand, pull the cable at the brake mechanism out so the brake lever is fully home, as it would be if the brakes were not on. Make sure the cable housing has not caught on the outside lip of the barrel adjustor. Now look at the amount of slack in the cable. For center-pull brakes this is the distance between the yoke cable and the cable anchor A:

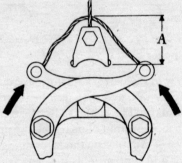

And for side-pull systems, it is the amount of new cable protruding beneath the yoke A:

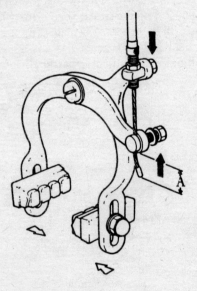

Estimate the amount of slack to be taken up with a ruler, tool handle, or finger. Disengage the yoke cable from the cable anchor (center-pulls) or the cable end from the yoke (side-pulls). Eliminate this step if you have a third hand or similar device. Use two wrenches to slacken the cable anchor nut. Avoid twisting the cable. Pass the cable the required distance through the hole in the cable anchor bolt:

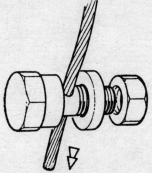

If it is sticky use a pair of pliers to pull it. Tighten cable anchor nut. If no third hand, hold brake yoke arms together again and slip yoke cable back over cable anchor, or cable back into yoke. If you have the feature, now is the time to use the brake button or cam to give you that little bit of extra slack you need. Release the second or third hand, as the case may be. Only one or two turns of the barrel adjustor should bring the brake shoes as close as possible to the wheel rim without actually touching when the wheel is spun. If you have gotten it right (it usually takes a couple of tries), use wire-cutters to snip off the excess cable for a neat job. Frayed cable ends have a habit of snagging fingers and clothing.

SANGER RACER.   **AAP**

Pivot bolt adjustment
Side-pull brakes:

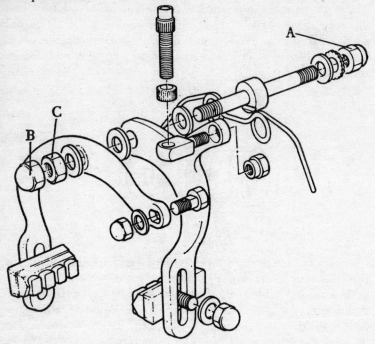

Make sure nut A is tight. Turn in locknut C one half turn while holding acorn adjusting nut B still with another wrench. Turn both B and C in flush against brake yoke arm. Back B off one half turn, hold in place, and lock locknut C against it.
Center-pull brakes: see p. 236.

Roller Lever Brakes

As with caliper brakes, roller lever brake shoes must be aligned to hit the inside of the rim squarely. This is done by means of a metal guide (A) clamped to the fork blade or chainstay:

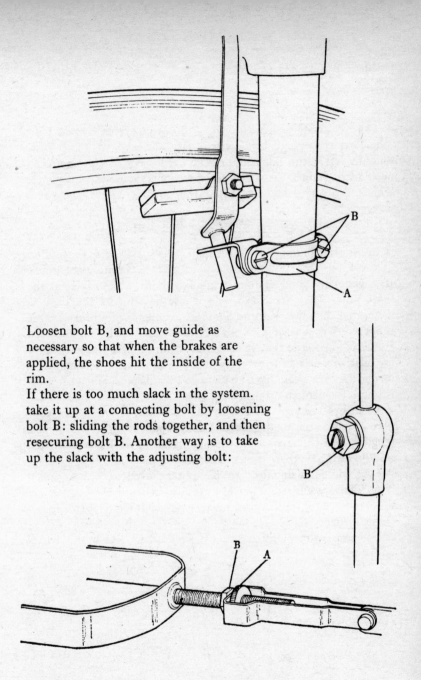

Loosen bolt B, and move guide as
necessary so that when the brakes are
applied, the shoes hit the inside of the
rim.
If there is too much slack in the system.
take it up at a connecting bolt by loosening
bolt B: sliding the rods together, and then
resecuring bolt B. Another way is to take
up the slack with the adjusting bolt:

by first undoing locknut B, and then tightening nut A.

Replacing and Disassembling Parts

Brake shoes: See p. 218.

Cables:

The frequency with which you will need to replace brake (and other) cables depends on how you use your bike. Machines consistently left out in the rain, or used hard every day, are going to need them sooner than well-cared-for or average-use machines. There is no hard and fast rule. Any obvious defect, such as a frayed cable:

is immediate grounds for replacement, as is stickiness in the motion of the cable through the cable housing (see Trouble-shooting). It is generally good practice to replace both brake cables at the same time. They are cheap, and if one has run its course, it is likely that the other has too. The inconvenience of a broken cable is not worth the gain of a month's extra use. If you have purchased a used bike I would replace cables all around unless you know they are relatively new and obviously in good condition. Good condition means they are clean, have no kinks or frayed spots, and pass easily through the cable housings.

Unless you can specify the brand and model of brake, take your bike or old cable to the store. Cables come in different shapes, lengths, and thicknesses. It is very irritating to discover in the middle of things that you have the wrong part.

I recommend using the right hand brake lever for the rear brake. This follows standard practice, and since the rear brake is generally more favored for routine braking, leaves the left hand free for cross-traffic signals.

For any caliper brake system, first screw home the barrel adjustor:

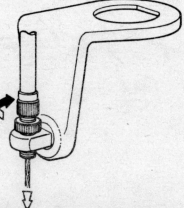

Center-pulls: push together brake yoke arms (use third hand or similar device if available) and slip yoke cable off brake anchor. Undo cable anchor bolt and nut and slide same off cable:

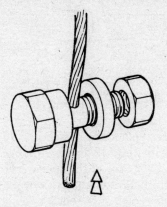

Side-pulls: One kind of side-pull brake uses a cable anchor bolt and nut at the yoke. Slack it off and pull out the cable the same way as with a center-pull. Another type of unit has a ball or nipple on the cable which slips into a slot on the brake yoke arm. You will have to replace both the cable and cable housing as a single unit. Compress brake yoke arms and release ball or nipple from yoke:

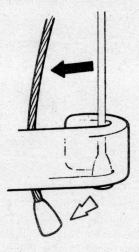

Center-pulls and Side-pulls:
Front brakes: Slide the cable housing off the cable, If yours has ferrules:

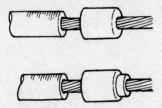

keep track of where they go.

    Rear brakes: Leave the housing attached to the frame and pull the cable out of the housing. If you have a one-piece cable and housing (nipples on both ends of the cable), loosen the clamps on the frame and draw the unit through. Examine the cable housings to see if they need replacement. Are they kinked or broken?

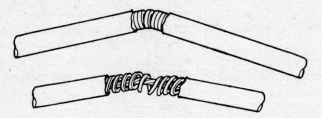

Are the ends free from burrs?

wrong   right

You can eliminate a burr by
(1) snipping off the cable housing end with a strong pair of wire cutters (pliers are not good enough);
(2) clamping the cable housing end in a vise and filing it down; or
(3) by using a tool called a taper ream, which you insert in the cable housing end and twist until the burr is gone.

If you use wire cutters be sure to get the cutting edges in between the coils of the housing or else you will mash the ends flat:

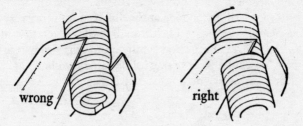

Use this opportunity to lubricate the inside of the cable housing.

Fully depress brake lever. Side-pulls: move cable until it is aligned with the slot on the side of the brake handle and then slide it out sideways:

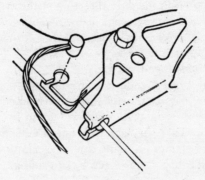

On center-pulls the process is exactly the same, or the slot may be parallel to the cable, as on the Weinmann:

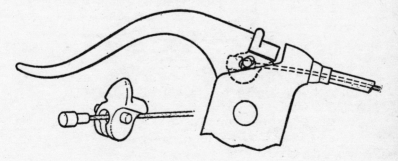

When installing the new cable, save any cutting for last. Cutting invariably frays the cable end and makes it hard to slide through the housing and cable anchor bolt. Installation is the reverse of removal, and for clarification look at the illustrations for that section.

One-nipple cable: Slip cable through brake lever mount and attach to brake lever. Front brakes: including ferrules where used, slip housing on cable. Rear brakes: slide cable into housing. Twist the cable or housing as you do this to avoid catching the cable:

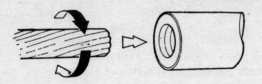

and be sure to do it in the right direction or the cable will unravel. Push free cable end through cable hanger (center-pulls), or through barrel adjustor at yoke (side-pulls), and then through cable anchor bolt hole. To adjust see pp. 219 – 21 .

Two-nipple cable (one-piece housing and cable): Attach to brake lever. For rear brakes, slide housing through clamps on frame. Front and rear, pass cable end through barrel adjustor on brake yoke arm and fix to opposite brake yoke arm by slipping ball or nipple into slot. Take up slack with barrel adjustor. Rear brakes, tighten housing clamps on frame, and take care that they are set so clothing will not snag on the screws when riding.

Handles

Outside bolt type:

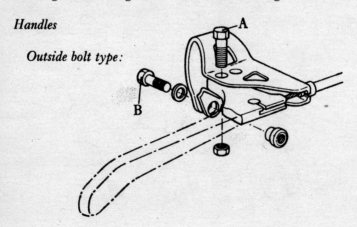

To adjust, slacken A and move. To remove, take off bolt B. May have to be slid back off handlebar in which case grip must be removed. If your brake lever mount has a slot in the bottom:

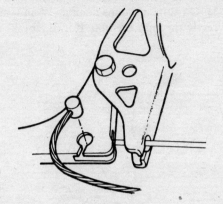

or if the cable ball or nipple will pass through the hole in the mount, then create enough slack by screwing home the barrel adjustor and clamping together the brake shoes, and disconnect the cable from the lever. If this is not possible, then disconnect the cable anchor bolt at the brake mechanism and take the cable out altogether.

Inside bolt type:

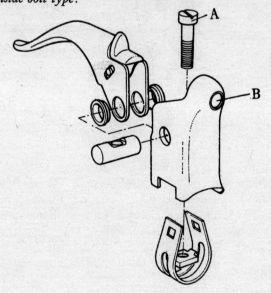

Disconnect yoke cable from cable anchor. Fully depress brake lever and use screwdriver or socket wrench on bolt A. If you are replacing the brake lever, you may need to take out the brake cable (see p. 224). On some systems such as Weinmann the cable end will pass directly through the hole B in the brake mount.

Brake Mechanism

First disconnect brake cable.
 Side-pull systems:

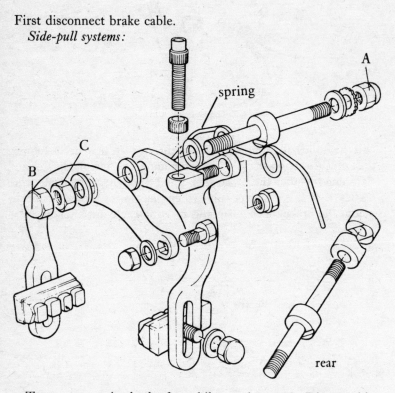

To remove entire brake from bike, undo nut A. Disassembly should be done only to replace a specific part if it won't work. Start with brake mechanism on bike. Undo the brake spring by prising it off with a screwdriver. Careful of fingers. Separate nut B from nut C, and take them both off the pivot bolt. Then the rest of the stuff. Keep the parts lined up in the order which you remove them. If you are replacing the pivot bolt, undo nut A and take off bolt. Reverse procedure for re-assembly.

Center-pull systems:

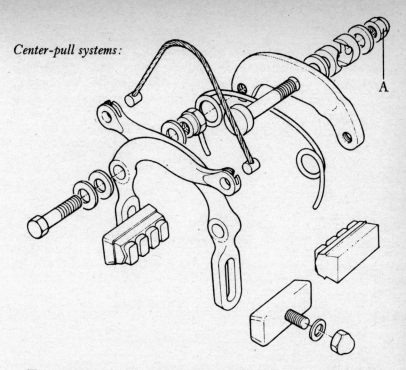

A

To remove unit from bike, undo nut A, remove washers and seating pads, and then brake mechanism. Disassembly: there's no good reason for this. Any badly busted up parts needing replacement probably cannot be obtained, and you will need a new mechanism. You insist? See pp. 236

Trouble-shooting

Before using this section please read How It Works and Adjustments. You have to know how it works in the first place in order to figure out what's wrong. brake problems come in 3 broad categories. In each category there are three possible areas in which the trouble may be: brake lever, cable, or mechanism. The first thing is to find in which of these the problem originates, and this is done by isolating and actuating each unit separately.

Category 1 – No or very weak brakes.
  * Is rim oily?
  * Are shoes hitting rim?
  * Will brake mechanism compress when you squeeze it with your hand? If no, go to Category 3, sticky brakes, below. If yes,

* Does lever move freely? Yes? Broken cable. Replace.
* Lever will not move. Disconnect cable at brake mechanism end. Will cable housing slide off cable? No? Cable is frozen inside housing. Get it off somehow and replace. If cable and housing separate easily then,
   * Lever is frozen. First see if your unit has an adjustable bolt (B)

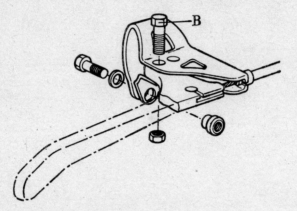

for the lever: and if so give it a try. No? A major bash may have pinched together the sides of the brake lever mount housing. examine it carefully and bend out dented parts with a big screw-driver:

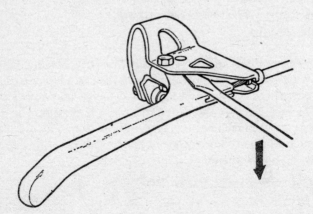

Or the lever itself may be bent. Bend it back. If the bend has been severe replace the lever or unit. Metal which has been bent a lot may look perfectly OK but it is fatigued and weak, and may well snap under the pressure of an emergency stop.

Category 2 – Brakes work, but unevenly or make noises.

* Juddering. Can be caused by a loose brake mechanism, uneven rims, or sometimes by a very loose headset. To fix the brake mechanism:

Side-pulls. Make sure nut A is tight. Undo locknut C from acorn adjusting nut B and screw both in flush against brake yoke arm. Back off B one half turn and lock in place with locknut C. (see next page)

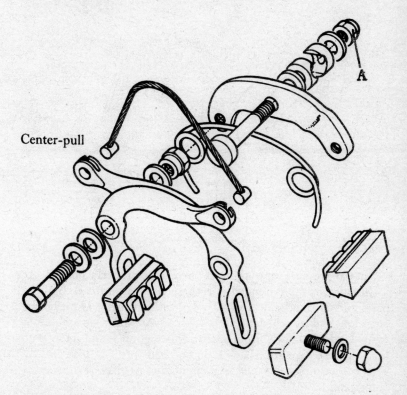

Center-pull

Center-pulls. Tighten up nut A on the mounting bolt.

* Squealing. Brake shoes may be old and hard. Sometimes rubber from shoes has streaked rim. Clean with a strong solvent like benzene or cleaning fluid in a WELL VENTILATED AREA. Squealing brakes can sometimes be fixed by toeing in the brake shoes (see p. 218), and sometimes this problem just can't·be eliminated.

Category 3 – Sticky or dragging brakes.

This is the most common problem. First determine if it is the lever, cable, or mechanism which is at fault.

* If it is the lever, see Frozen lever (p. 232).
* If it is the cable, replace it (pp. 224–228).
* Brake mechanism.

Side-pulls:

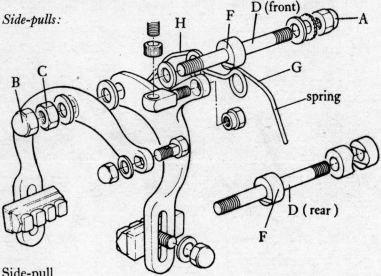

Side-pull

First make sure everything is there and properly hooked up. This sounds simple-minded, but there is a reason for each of the parts and the mechanism won't work without them. Is the spring complete and attached to both yoke arms? Make sure nut A is tight. Undo locknut C from acorn adjusting nut B and screw both flush against yoke arm. Back B off one half turn and lock with C. Check that pivot bolt D is straight and replace if necessary. Lubricate.

If one shoe drags against rim: loosen the mounting nut A, hold brake yokes in correct position, and re-tighten. No soap? Examine brake seating pad F. If it has a slot for the spring you will have to try bending the spring. There are two ways to do this. One is to prise the spring arm off the brake yoke which is dragging and bend it outward using pliers or similar tool. The second is to take a big screwdriver and poise the end against point G or H, whichever is *opposite* the dragging shoe, and give it a sharp bash with a hammer. This second method is quicker, but of course a little riskier.

Still no soap? Check to see that the brake yokes are not rubbing against each other. If so, bend them apart with a screwdriver:

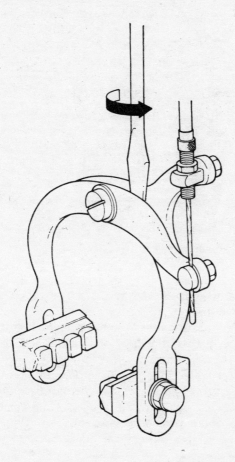

or slide in a piece of fine emery cloth (like sandpaper) and file it down.

If this is not the problem and you have tried everything else a complete disassembly (see p. 230) is necessary. Study each part to see if it obviously needs replacing (like a washer bent out of shape). It may be that the yokes cannot rotate on the pivot bolt. File down and polish the bolt, or enlarge the holes in the yokes (with a taper ream, or emery cloth wrapped around a nail). If none of these things work get a new brake mechanism.

Center-pulls:

Is cable adjusted correctly?

Are all parts there? Is spring intact and properly mounted?

Is mounting nut A tight?

If one shoe is dragging against rim, slack off A, center brake mechanism, and re-tighten A.

If both shoes stick try lubricating the pivot bolts B while wiggling the yokes back and forth. No? You will have to get into the pivot bolts.

First disconnect the spring. Study the bolts to see if they are type 1, where the pivot bolt screws into the brake arm bridge H; type 2, where the pivot bolt screws into a post which comes off the brake arm bridge and on which the yoke rotates; or type 3, where the pivot bolt simply goes through the brake arm bridge and the yoke rotates on a bushing.

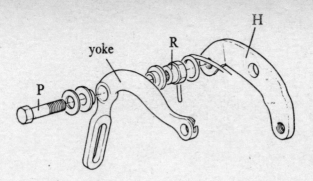

Type 1:

First try slacking off the locknut R and undoing the pivot bolt P one quarter to one half turn. On some models the locknut R is on the other side of the brake arm bridge H. If yoke will now pivot, retighten locknut R. If not, remove pivot bolt P altogether. Keep track of all the washers. Is the pivot bolt P straight? Look for dirt or scarred surfaces on the pivot bolt P and inside the yoke. Clean and polish. If yoke will not turn freely on pivot bolt, enlarge yoke hole with a taper file or ream, drill, or emery cloth wrapped around a nail. Or sand down the pivot bolt. Lubricate and reassemble.

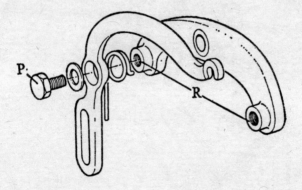

Type 2:

Undo spring and remove pivot bolt P. Remove yoke and keep track of washers. Check for grit and clean. Is post R scarred? Polish with fine sandpaper or steel wool until yoke will rotate freely on it. Lubricate and reassemble.

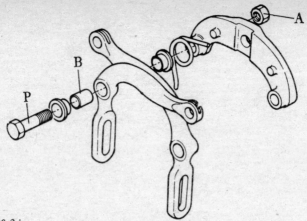

Type 3:

Undo nut A and remove pivot bolt P. Keep track of bushings and washers. Is pivot bolt straight? Is bushing B in good condition? Check for grit and clean. If yoke still sticks, try polishing pivot bolt with steel wool. Lubricate and reassemble.

Disc Brakes

How It Works

The operation of a disc brake is very similar to that of a caliper brake. Actuating the brake lever causes a cable to pull a cam mounted brake arm which then compresses two brake shoes or pads against opposite sides of a revolving metal disc attached to the wheel.

Lubrication

Only a tiny bit of LPS spray inside the brake arm mounting point 23. Avoid at all cost oil or LPS on the disc or pads 28 and 32.

Adjustment

Unlike the caliper system, the cable adjustor bolt 17 and cable anchor bolt 24 are not used to adjust pad clearances, only to keep slack out of the brake levers.

To adjust pad clearances: Remove bracket cover 2 by undoing screws 1. Undo locknut 6 and slacken setting bolt 5. Use pliers to turn brake adjustor 15 clockwise until pads meet disc and wheel will not turn. Reverse brake adjustor counterclockwise ½ turn. Turn in setting bolt 5 until it touches holder 16 lightly and secure in place with locknut 6.

Check that the pads and disc are parallel (see opposite page). If not, again slack off setting bolt 5. Slack off adjusting bolts 3, 3A, and 4. Diddle with these adjusting bolts until pad A is parallel with disc. Tighten each adjusting bolt an even number of turns until pads almost touch disc. You've done it. Turn in setting bolt 5 and lock into position. Replace cover.

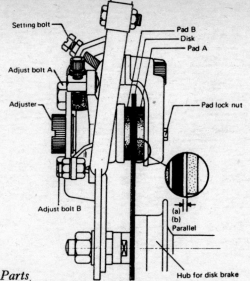

Setting bolt
Pad B
Disk
Pad A
Adjust bolt A
Adjuster
Pad lock nut
Adjust bolt B
(a)
(b)
Parallel
Hub for disk brake

Replacing Parts

Cables – Procedure is exactly the same as for a caliper brake so refer to that section for instructions.

Pads – Remove rear wheel. With a 6 mm allen wrench undo through bolts 34 and remove holder 33. Take off locknut 40 and undo screw 31. Remove pad 32 and replace.

Next, undo screw 30 *carefully*, as there is a spring lurking underneath it. Remove pad 28 and replace. After tightening down screw 30, back it off ½ turn. Restore holder 33 to mate and make sure bolts 34 are done up good. Follow procedure for adjustment, above.

Trouble-shooting

Brakes slip or are weak

Grease or oil on discs and pads. Clean disc with solvent, rub pad surfaces with No. 60 emery paper.

Brakes don't work

Pull up on brake arm lever 23. If it moves and the pads are hitting the disc it is a cable or brake problem. Turn to caliper brakes, trouble-shooting, for instructions.

If it is the unit itself that is frozen up, try removing the pads and dunking the whole unit in solvent. No? Your guess is as good as mine. Have at it and see if you can figure out what has gone wrong. If you can't, take it to your friendly bicycle dealer and see if he wants to play with it.

3. Staying Aboard

Contents

Saddle 243
  Adjustments 244
  Trouble-shooting 245
Handlebars 247
  Adjustments 247
  Trouble-shooting 249
Stem 251
  How It Works 251
  Adjust or Remove 251
  Trouble-shooting 252
Headset 254
  How It Works 254
  Routine Adjustments 256
  Lubrication and Disassembly 257
  Trouble-shooting 260
Forks 261
  How They Work 261
  Lubrication and Dismantling 262
  Trouble-shooting 262

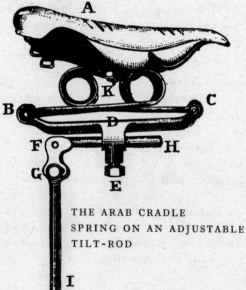

THE ARAB CRADLE
SPRING ON AN ADJUSTABLE
TILT-ROD

Saddle

There are two important factors in bicycle saddle design: supporting weight, and reducing friction between the legs. The mattress saddle used on bikes with level handlebars has to support all of the weight of the rider, and is therefore usually wide, and equipped with coil springs:

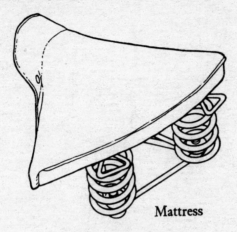

Mattress

Bikes with dropped handlebars support part of the rider's weight on the bars, and can use a long, narrow seat which minimizes friction between the legs:

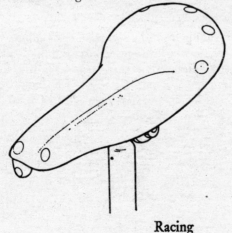

Racing

Springiness in the narrow racing saddle should be kept to a comfortable minimum as it adversely effects pedalling power. If yours is too tight or loose, adjust it by turning nut *A*:

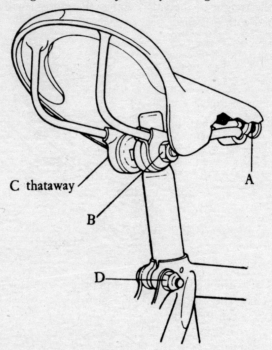

C thataway

A

B

D

To remove the saddle from the seat post, or to adjust its position backward, forward, or to tilt it, loosen nuts *B* and *C*. This applies also to mattress saddles. Some seat posts have micro-adjusting bolts or allen screws:

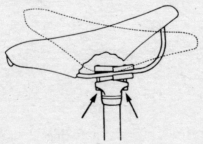

Loosen bolt or screw on end to be raised, tighten bolt or screw on end to be lowered. Loosen both an identical number of turns to slide saddle forward or backward. For proper saddle position refer to Fitting, pp. 93–95.

To raise or lower the saddle, loosen the binder bolt D.

Be sure to use a wrench which fits the nut exactly. It has to be tight, and the wrong tool can tear up the nut.

Only leather saddles need special care. A new leather saddle should be thoroughly saturated with neatsfoot oil from *underneath*.

Then, depending on how much you ride and how much you sweat, the saddle should be cleaned periodically with saddle soap and lightly dressed with neatsfoot oil. The idea is to keep the leather clean, nourished, and comfortably pliable. Once a year should be enough. You can avoid this bother by using a plastic saddle, but in warm weather you will slide about in your own sweat.

Trouble-shooting

Seat tilts or swivels unnecessarily. Tighten binding bolt nuts *B* and *C* (see opposite page).

If the seat bottoms harshly on bumps and you have a mattress type saddle – too bad. If you have a racing saddle, tighten nut *A*.

The seat post sinks slowly into the frame while you ride. This can be a real stinker. First see if the seat post is the correct diameter by checking that the lips of the seat tube do not meet at the binder bolt:

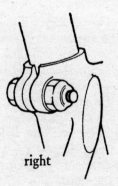
right

wrong

If the post is the right size and is greasy, try cleaning it and the inside of the seat tube thoroughly. On no account try the use of shims or abrasive material like emery paper between the seat tube and the seat post. The chances are excellent that some of the material will fall down the seat tube and get into the bottom bracket, where it will make mincemeat of your crankset bearings (thought seats were simple, hah?). The only sure-fire solution is to install a thin bolt through the seat post and seat tube at point *P*:

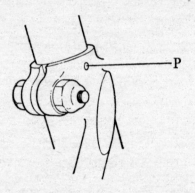

To do this you need a drill, hand or electric, a bolt, nut, and washer, and a drill bit. *Do all drilling with the bike upside down so that shavings do not fall down the seat tube into the bottom bracket.* If you are having a shop do the job make sure that they do this. Position seat at desired height. Make an initial dent with a center punch or with a hammer and sharp nail at point *P*. Then put a couple of drops of oil on the end of the drill bit and drill through. Go slowly to avoid heat build-up. Use single-speed electric drills in short bursts. You will want more than one saddle height position. To do this, loosen the binder bolt and rotate the seat post one eighth of a turn at the same time that you raise or lower it a little bit. Now use the already existing holes in the seat tube as a guide for drilling a new set of holes in the seat post. Repeat 3 or 4 times. The idea is to be able to make fine adjustments in saddle height without weakening the seat post. At the finish, the job should look like this:

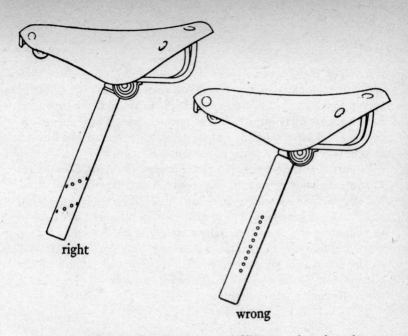

right

wrong

Be sure to clean up all shavings and filings so that they do not fall down into the bottom bracket.

If your seat post is the micro-adjusting type the holes will have to be in a straight line.

Handlebars

Adjustments

To change handlebar position loosen binder bolt *A* on stem and reset bars:

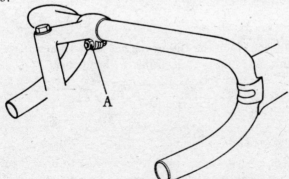

A

Height adjustments are made with the *stem* (next section).

Taping

I prefer non-adhesive tapes. Adhesive tapes gum everything up with a sticky residue which ultimately leaks out all over everything. Plastic tape is cheap and easy to clean. Cloth tape feels good but gets dirty quickly and is hard to clean. The Tape, suede finished and vinyl backed, and washable, is probably the best all around tape. See Accessories for more information.

Be sure that the brakes are in the position you want. Start about 2″ from the stem. Use a small piece of scotch tape to hold down the end of the tape where you start. Work directly from the roll to minimize confusion, and maintain a continuous light tension as you apply the tape. First take a couple of turns at the starting point and then start down the bar, overlapping $\frac{1}{2}$ to $\frac{1}{3}$ of the tape. At the bends you will have to overlap more on the inside than the outside. For a neat job, loosen the brake lever mount (see p. 228), tape underneath, and retighten:

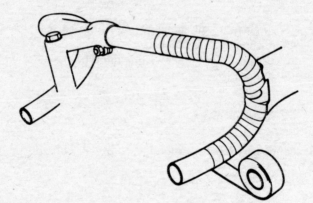

When you reach the end of the bar leave an extra 2–3″ of tape. Fold this over and push it inside the handlebar:

Finish off with a bar plug (bike stores) to hold tape securely. If plug is difficult to insert, rub some soap on and tap it in with a hammer. Bar plugs can also be made from champagne corks.

Use something – if you spill, an open bar end can make a hole in you.

Trouble-shooting

* Bar spins around on stem: tighten binder bolt *A*:

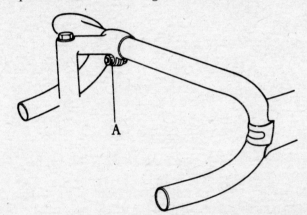

A

If binder bolt spins uselessly remove it and see if the little protrusion on it has been worn off, or if the corresponding slot on the stem into which it fits has been damaged. If the problem is the bolt, get a new one. If it is the stem, get a proper bolt with a hex nut that you can grip with a wrench. In a pinch, you can use pliers or vise-grips to hold the round part of the old bolt.

If binder bolt is in working order check and see that the clips of the stem do not meet:

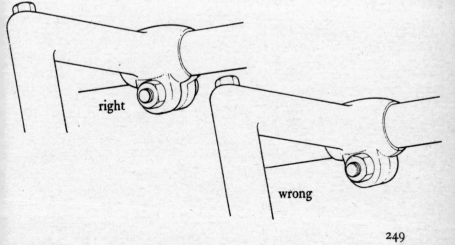

right

wrong

If they do, new bars (expensive) or a shim (cheap). Shimming: find a small piece of flat metal slightly longer than the width of the stem lips. Something that won't rust, like aluminum, is preferable (hardware stores, machine shop litter, junk lying around), but part of a tin can or a finishing nail will do. Remove binder bolt. Using a screwdriver, prise apart the lips of the stem:

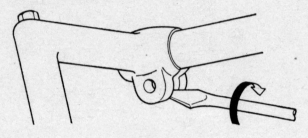

Slip the shim into the gap between the handlebar and the stem, and reinstall binder bolt.

* Bent bars: steel ones are hard to bend, alloy a lot easier. Lay the bike on its side. If the ends of the handlebars have been bent in, place your foot on the end resting on the ground (watch out for the brake lever) and pull up on the other end. If the ends have been bent out, lean your weight on the upright bar:

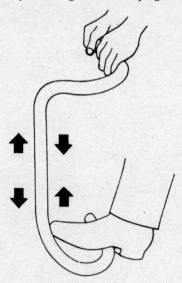

Stem

How It Works

The stem is a tube which holds the handlebar in position, and fits down inside the headset. The tube is split at the end, and down its length runs a bolt, called an expander bolt, which is attached to a wedge nut (A):

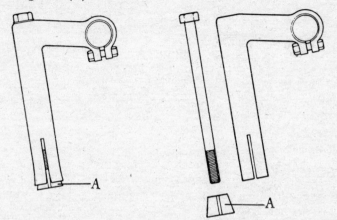

When the expander bolt is tightened, it draws the wedge nut into the tube, and this in turn forces apart the split sides of the stem, pressing them against the sides of the headset and holding everything in place.

Adjust or Remove

Undo expander bolt two turns. Using a wooden block or piece of cardboard held against the expander bolt to protect the finish, tap it with a hammer or heavy object:

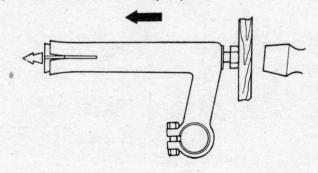

Repeat as necessary to get stem loose. Adjust height or remove. If you remove altogether and reassemble note that some wedge nuts have a dog guide which must fit into a corresponding slot on the stem:

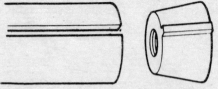

Keep at least 2½″ of the stem tube in the headset.

Retighten expander bolt so that when you stand in front of the bike with the wheel clasped between your legs you can twist the handlebar and stem in the headset. This way, if you take a spill the bars will give instead of bending or breaking.

Trouble-shooting

* Stem is loose and expander bolt comes out freely: wedge nut has come off. Take out stem, turn bike upside down, and shake wedge nut out. Reassemble.

* Stem is frozen in place and expander bolt spins uselessly: threads on wedge nut have stripped (1), or expander bolt has snapped (2).

(1) Separate expander bolt from wedge nut by grasping it with pliers or vise-grips and maintaining a continuous upward pressure while twisting it. If it is obstinate, help it along by wedging a screwdriver between the expander bolt head and the stem:

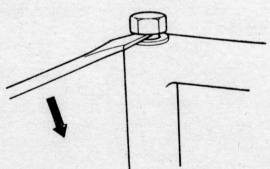

Once the expander bolt is free of wedge nut leave it inside the stem.

(2) Remove top half of snapped expander bolt. Find a rod or bolt which will fit inside stem and touch wedge nut while still protruding an inch or two above the stem.

(1) and (2): Use a hammer to lightly tap the expander bolt or rod, working the end inside the stem around the edges of the wedge nut:

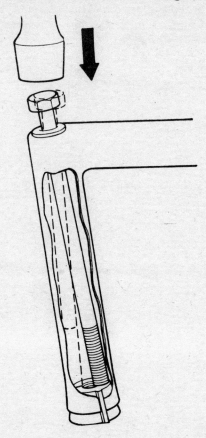

Work firmly but gently; too hard a blow will jam the whole thing. When stem comes loose, turn bike upside down and shake out wedge nut.

* Stem tube cracked. Replace it.

Headset

How It Works

The headset connects the front forks to the head tube of the bicycle frame and, through the stem, to the handlebars. The fork is held solidly to the bicycle but allowed to turn freely by using ball bearing sets at the top and bottom of the head tube. Starting at the bottom, the crown of the fork has a fork crown bearing race (A), then come the ball bearings (B),

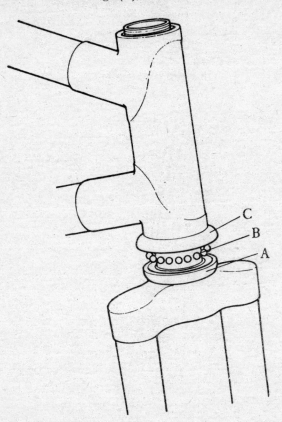

and next is the bottom set race (C), screwed or force-fitted into the head tube.

Put together, it looks like this:

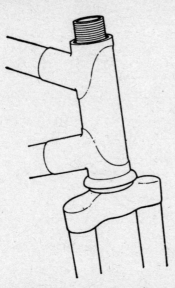

To keep the forks inside the head tube and evenly positioned, a second set of races is used at the top of the head tube. There is a top set race, screwed or force-fitted into the head tube, more ball bearings, and what actually keeps the forks in position is the top race, which is threaded onto the fork tube:

top race ⎯⎯⎯⎯⎯⎯

top set race ⎯⎯⎯

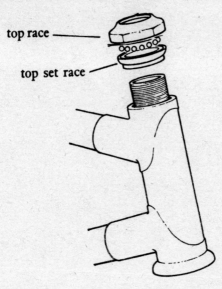

This is capped by a washer, the cable hanger and/or other accessory mounts, if used, and a locknut to keep the top threaded race exactly in place:

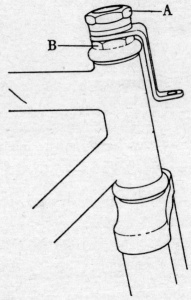

Routine Adjustments

Forks should turn freely but without excessive up and down play. A simple test for looseness is to lock the front brake and rock the bike forward and backward. A clicking noise from the headset indicates loose bearings. To adjust, loosen locknut *A* (above).

Sometimes this locknut is designed with notches. Loosen with a hammer and center punch or screwdriver:

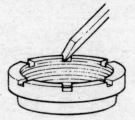

If you are using big wrenches or pliers be careful not to bend nuts or races.

Now turn down the threaded top race B handtight against the bearings, and then back it off one quarter turn.

Snug down locknut A, being careful to keep threaded top race B in position. Check play again.

Lubrication and Disassembly

The headset should be dismantled, cleaned, and regreased about once a year. Remove stem (p. 251) and front wheel (p. 264). Lay bike down on side with newspaper or white rag under the headset. This is to catch falling ball bearings. There are many different headsets, and no way for me to tell you how many are in yours. So don't lose any.

Undo and remove the locknut, washer, cable clamp (if you have one), and anything else necessary to get to the threaded top race. Secure the fork to the frame. You can do this with rubber bands, elastic carrier straps, shoelaces, etc., but the simplest way is to hold it with your hand. Be sure to do something, or what you do next will cause the fork to fall out along with a rain of ball bearings. Next: undo the threaded top race A:

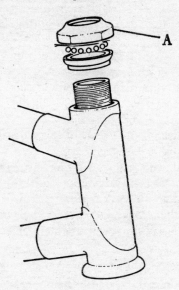

You will have loose ball bearings and are to follow instructions for (1), or bearings in a clip in which case follow (2).

(1) A few may stick to the threaded race, a few may fall on the newspaper, and most will probably stay in the top set race. Get them all together, count them, and put bearings and race into a box or jar. Next: make sure head tube is positioned over newspaper or rag. Slowly draw out fork tube. Ball bearings will fall out. Get and count them, including any that are still stuck to the bottom set race, the fork tube, or whatever, and put them in a jar.

(2) Clipped bearings: Lucky you. Remove clip, noting carefully which side goes down against the top set race, and put in a jar or box. Now draw out fork tube and lift out clip for bottom race.

Further disassembly for routine lubrication is not necessary.

(1) & (2) Soak and clean thoroughly all parts in solvent. Use a rag to clean out the top and bottom set races, and the fork crown race. Ball bearings should be smooth and unpitted. Clipped bearings should be securely in place. Races should be evenly colored all the way around where the balls run. Place them on a glass surface to see if they are bent or warped. Replace any defective parts.

Reassembly: pack fresh grease in the top and bottom set races. Just fill the grooves; excessive grease will attract dirt.

(1) Push ball bearings into grease on bottom set race. Grease will hold them in place.

(2) Put some grease inside the clip. Slip it down over the fork tube to rest on the fork crown race.

(1) & (2) Carefully insert fork tube into head tube. Keeping it snug against the bearings, check that it turns freely. Hang onto fork so that it does not fall back out.

(1) Stick ball bearings into grease of top set race.

(2) Grease and slip on clipped bearings.

(1) & (2) Screw down top threaded race. These threads are fine, so do it carefully (see General Notes, p. 205, for best technique). Set it hand tight, and then back it off one quarter turn. Pile on washer, cable anchor mount, etc., and locknut. Be careful to keep threaded top race in position when tightening locknut. Check for play.

Complete Disassembly

If the bike has been in a smash-up or if rust has got to the bearings, it may be necessary to do a complete disassembly.

Take fork and ball bearings out as per for lubrication. Remove crown fork race from fork. If it is stuck, pry it up *gently* with a screwdriver, working around the edges a little at a time. Be careful, it is easy to bend:

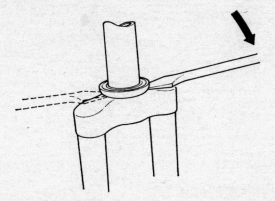

Remove top and bottom set races. You may possibly have threaded set races, in which case simply unscrew them. For force set races, insert a large screwdriver, piece of pipe, or stiff rod into the head tube and tap around the edges of the race:

Clean all parts with solvent. Test races for uniformity by seeing if they lie flat on glass or other smooth surface.

Reassembly: screw in threaded set races. For force set races use a wooden block (to avoid denting or bending the race) and hammer:

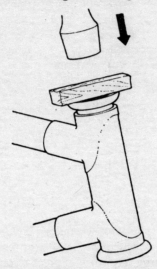

Make sure that it is seated fully into the frame. Use a wooden block also on the fork crown race if it is balky but be very delicate, and tap evenly all the way around the race.

Trouble-shooting

* Fork tube is extremely loose in the head tube. May just need adjustment (p. 256), but if things have come to this pass I suggest dismantling and checking condition of parts.

Adjustment does not work: top threaded race or fork is stripped. Dismantle and see. It is unlikely that this is the result of excessive tightening, and likely the top threaded race was screwed down off center. When you have your new parts review General Notes, Threading, p. 205, before starting.

* Fork binds or catches, or makes grating and rasping noises when you turn handlebars. Adjust as per p. 256. No go? Something is broken or bent, completely worn out, or there are too many or too few ball bearings. Review the possibilities. Has fork or headset been whacked severely lately? A couple of months ago? Did you

or someone else service the headset and lose a bearing or two, or place too many in one race and not enough in the other? Or perhaps the bike is simply ancient, and needs new races? In any case, disassemble (p. 257), clean, and check all parts. Are bearings evenly distributed (ask your bike shop how many should be in your headset), and free of dents, cracks, and pitting? Do races lie flat on a glass surface? Replace defective parts and reassemble. If you can find nothing wrong take the parts down to your bike shop and see what they say.

Forks

How They Work

The fork holds the front wheel in place and allows the bike to be steered. The fork arms are curved, giving the axle drop-outs rake or trail from a line drawn through the fork tube:

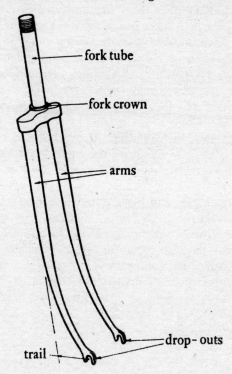

This rake or trail has two purposes: it makes the bike handle better, and it helps the bike to absorb bumps and other road shocks. The amount of trail varies as according to the purpose of the bike. Touring bikes have a slightly longer trail for a softer, more comfortable ride. Racing and track machines have a shorter trail for greater efficiency in transmitting rider effort to the wheels. Additionally, the forks may be solid or tubular, the latter lighter and more flexible.

Lubrication and Dismantling

Covered under Headset, p.257.

Trouble-shooting

* All problems with turning, grating noises, etc. are covered under Headset, p.260.

* Bent forks: replace them. Bending fatigues metal and makes it weak. The weakness does not show. What happens is that the fork suddenly gives up while you are tearing along at 30 m.p.h. This does not happen very often, but once is enough. Bicycle shops do have special tools for straightening bent forks and if the bend in yours is slight, you may want to try it. Be aware that you are taking a calculated risk, however small.

Tests for bent forks: the bike will ride funny. If forks are bent to one side, the bike will always want to turn to the left or right. Test by taking your hands off the handlebars. Any decently set-up bike can be ridden hands off for miles. Forks which have been bent in, usually through a head-on collision, make the bike's ride choppy and harsh, and make it feel like it wants to dive in the corners. A sure sign of bent-in forks is wrinkled paint on the upper fork arms, or at the join of the fork tube and fork crown. Forks which have been bent out (rare) manifest themselves in a sloppy, mushy ride, and curious, long arcing turns. Again, there will probably be paint wrinkles at the bend point.

4. Wheels

Contents

Wheel Removal and Replacement   263

Tires   266
   How They Work   266
   Routine Adjustments   267
    Pressure   268
    Riding   268
    Storage   269
    Flats   269
     Clinchers   270
     Tubulars   275

Rims and Spokes   278
   How They Work   278
   Adjustments   278
   Replacing Spokes   279
   Trouble-shooting   280
   Wheel Building   281

Hubs   282
   How They Work   282
   Adjustments   282
   Lubrication   284
   Disassembly and Replacement   284
   Trouble-shooting   285

Wheel Removal and Replacement

Wheels need to be removed often, for a variety of reasons, and sometimes on the road. So you can and will do this with a free-standing bike, but it is much easier if it is hung up. Most 3-speeds and some 10-speeds can simply be turned upside down on handlebars and seat, as long as cables or shift selectors are not damaged. Bikes with caliper brakes in proper adjustment should require some slacking of the brakes (see pp. 212–13) so that the tire will pass between the brake shoes.

Wheel will be held to fork by hex nuts, wing nuts, or a quick-release lever:

For nuts, undo both simultaneously (counter-clockwise) and unwind a turn or two. Levers, flip it. Remove wheel. Note washers go outside fork drop-outs.

Rear wheel

10-*speed bikes:*

Run chain to smallest sprocket. Undo nuts or lever as for front wheel, and push wheel down and out. If you have a free hand hold back the derailleur so that the freewheel clears it easily, otherwise just gently wiggle it by.

3-*speed bikes:*

Shift to 3rd gear. Disconnect shift cable at rear hub by undoing locknut A and unscrewing adjustor sleeve B from pole:

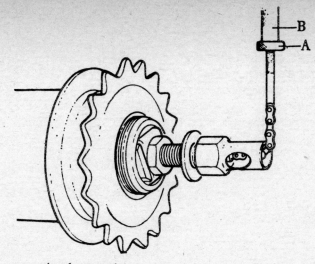

Undo nuts simultaneously) (counter-clockwise). Remove wheel, and note washers are outside drop-outs.

Single-speed coaster-brake bikes:

Disconnect coaster-brake bracket from bike frame (metal arm at left end of rear axle), undo nuts (counter-clockwise), and remove wheel.

Replacing Wheels

Front, any bike

Axle with nuts: back off nuts a few turns and slip axle onto drop-outs. Washers go outside drop-outs. Set nuts finger tight and check that rim is centered between fork arms before snugging them down. Re-set caliper brakes if you have them.

Levers: Slip axle onto drop-outs with lever on left side of bike. If this is difficult, hold knurled cone with one hand and unwind lever a couple of turns with the other. Slip axle on drop-outs and wind lever down just short of finger tight. Check that wheel rim is centered between fork arms, and close lever so that it points upwards and backwards. It should be firmly shut but not hysterically so. Re-set caliper brakes.

Rear wheels

10-speed bikes:

Work axle into drop-outs, slipping chain over smallest sprocket on freewheel. Set nuts or lever for light tension. Pull wheel toward rear of bike until right end of axle hits the back of the drop-out.

Use this as a pivot point to center the rim between the chain stays, and tighten nuts or lever. Re-set caliper brake.

3- and 1-speed bikes:

Work axle into drop-outs, slipping chain over sprocket. Lightly tighten nuts (washers are outside drop-outs), and pull back wheel so chain has ½″ play up and down:

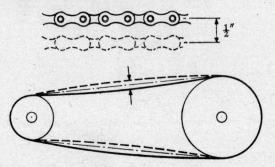

Center rim between chain stays and tighten down nuts. Check chain tension. 1-speed bikes, reconnect coaster brake bracket to frame. 3-speed bikes, with gear selector in 3rd, reconnect barrel sleeve to hub gear chain, and set locknut with cable slightly slack. Test gears and adjust if necessary (p 308). Re-set caliper brake.

Tires

How They Work

Any pneumatic tire works by supporting a casing, the part touching the road, with an inside tube which is filled with air like a balloon. With tubular tires the tube is fully encased by the casing; with clincher tires the tube is held in place by a combination of two wire beads which run around the outside edges of the tire, and the rim sides:

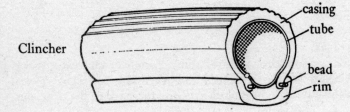

Clincher — casing, tube, bead, rim

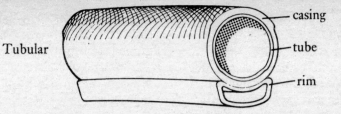

Tubular

casing

tube

rim

Air is pumped into the tube through a valve which comes in two types. Almost all clincher tires have Schraeder valves, the kind typically found on cars. A few clinchers and all tubulars have 'Presta' type valves, which require either a bicycle pump, or a special adaptor for gas station air pumps:

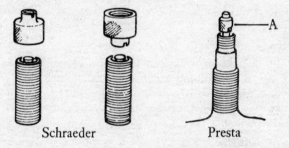

A

Schraeder   Presta

'Presta' valves need to have the locknut A undone in order to be pumped up.

Tire Selection

There are tires for nearly every purpose and condition: rain, mud, racing, touring, and carrying heavy loads. In tubulars heavy-duty 15–16 ounce tires are about the only practical choice for touring and general use. Racers use lighter tires which run 7 to 11 ounces. In clincher tires I suggest you explain your needs to a shop and try their recommendation.

Generally, 3-speeds are fitted with an all-purpose coarse-thread heavy-duty tire, and 10-speeds with a lighter road pattern tire. Better tires cost only a little more and are worth it in the long run.

Routine Adjustments

Tire pressure

Use your own tire pressure gauge (bike shops). Gas station gauges are unreliable. When filling your tires at a gas station do it yourself. The proper pressure for your tire may be as high as

100 pounds per square inch, but the total volume of air is small, and it takes only seconds to blow a tire out. Some air pumps take a few moments to fill the tire; others will do it instantaneously. Jab the air hose down on the valve for just a second, then release and test. Tires should be hard enough so you can barely dent them with a finger, and bulge only very slightly when ridden. Consult chart below for proper pressure.

Bicycle pump and Schraeder valve: draw hose fitting out of pump handle and fit to pump and valve. Check connections periodically and as you pump. 'Presta' valve: undo valve locknut, push pump on valve, hold firmly to tire with one hand, and pump with the other. Keep pump perpendicular to valve. Disengage with a sharp downward knock of the hand; wiggling will lose air and possibly bend valve.

Recommended Pressures

Note: for heavier loads increase pressure. The difference between pressure for a 125 pound rider and 200 pound rider is about 15 to 20 pounds per square inch.

> Tubular 27″ – Rear, 85 to 100; front, 75–90.
> Clincher 27″ – 75 to 90
> Clincher 26″ x $1\frac{1}{4}$″ – 45 to 60.
>   x $1\frac{1}{2}$″ – 40 to 55.
>   x $1\frac{3}{8}$″ – 40 to 55.
>   x $1\frac{3}{4}$″ – 35 to 45.
>   24″   – 35 to 45.
>   20″   – 45 to 50.
>   18″   – 35 to 45.
>   16″   – 30 to 40.
>   12″   – 30 to 40.

Check tire pressure often. Tubular tires "breathe" air through the sides and need filling frequently. Hot weather in the 80's and up may require that you bleed some air from the tire to avoid over-inflation and a possible blow-out.

Riding

Most tire problems are the result of picked-up debris working into the casing as you ride. Going over rocks, through pot-holes, and on and off the curbs will cause ruptures. Cultivate an eye for these hazards, and if you are forced to go through a patch of broken glass, for example, check and see that the tire has not picked any up. A useful gadget for tubular tires is a nail-catcher (bike shops) which rides lightly over the tire and brushes off particles before they can cause damage:

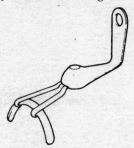

Keep oil away from tires. It rots rubber. Grease, do not oil bicycle pumps. Oiled bicycle pumps can vaporize and blow oil inside the tube. Check cement on tubulars about once a week.

Care and Storage

Keep clincher spares in a dry place. Tubular spares should be carried folded so the tread is on the outside and not folded back on itself. Under the seat is a dandy place. Secure with straps or rubber bands:

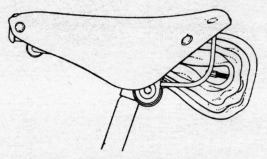

Every two weeks or so inflate a folded spare and let it stand for a while. Refold in the opposite direction.

Flats

Flats take the form of violent blow outs (rare), or punctures (common) which leak air with varying degrees of speed. Blow outs are usually terminal, doing so much damage that the tube and sometimes the tire must be replaced. Punctures which are not gaping wounds can be repaired. There is debate as to proper policy for this and some bike shops maintain that any patching is "temporary" and prefer to install a new tube. I suggest that you patch newish tubes and throw out older ones.

Clincher tires

You will need a tube patch kit containing patches, glue, an abrasive surface, tire irons (the kind which hook onto spokes are handiest), and chalk.

First check valve by inflating tire slightly and placing a drop of spit on the end of the valve stem. A leaky valve will bubble or spit back. Tighten valve if necessary with valve cap or suitable part of pressure gauge:

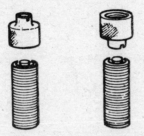

Hooray if the problem was a loose or defective valve. If not, spin the wheel and look for an obvious cause like a nail or piece of glass. Yes? Dig it out and mark the spot.

What you do next depends on circumstances. It is easier to work on a puncture with the wheel off the bike (see p. 263). However, you may not have the tools to accomplish this feat, or perhaps you know exactly where the puncture is. At any rate, the basic procedure is the same.

Deflate tire and remove valve stem locknut if you have one. Work the tire back and forth with your hands to get the bead free of the rim. If the tire is a loose fit on the rim you may be able to get it off with your hands. This is best, because tire irons may pinch the tube and cause additional punctures. To do this make sure that the bead is free of the rim all the way around. Take a healthy grip on the tire with both hands and pull it up and off-center so that one bead comes over the rim:

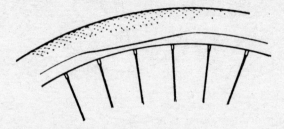

Then go around the rim working the bead completely off.

You will probably need to use tire irons. Use tire irons, not screwdrivers, as these are likely to cut the tube. Free bead from rim. Insert tire iron under bead, being careful not to pinch the tube, and lever it over the side:

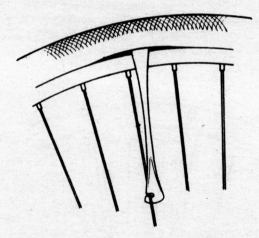

Insert second iron 2″ or 3″ away from first iron, and past where bead is over side of rim. Lever iron. For most tires this will do the job. No? A third iron. If this doesn't work, use the now free 2nd iron for a fourth attempt:

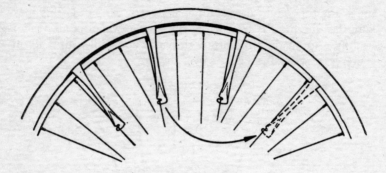

and repeat process as often as necessary.

If you don't have tire irons which hook onto the spokes, then you will need to use elbows, knees, etc. to hold down the irons as you work away. Be careful not to inadvertently crush a spoke, and keep your face away in case something slips and tire irons start jumping about.

If you have only two tire irons and need a third, scrounge something up. In the country a flat rock or a stick. In the city a pencil, a beer can opener, or something from the garbage. Look around. At any hour there will be *something*. Prise up bead with a tire iron. Insert foraged tool between bead and rim and wiggle iron out:

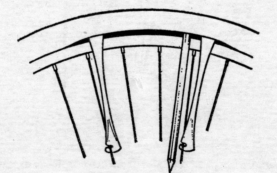

Use tire irons to make two prises on either side of foraged tool.

One bead is off rim. Push valve stem up into tire, and remove tube. Use chalk or eidetic memory to make note of which way tube was in the tire. Inflate tube and rotate it past your ear. If you can locate the puncture through the hiss of escaping air mark it with chalk. No? Immerse tube in water and look for escaping air bubbles. Dry tube with a rag while holding finger over puncture, then mark with chalk.

Take sandpaper or metal abrader supplied with patch kit and rough up the area around the puncture. Spread a layer of cement over this area and let dry tacky. Peel the paper backing off a patch without touching the surface thus exposed, and press it firmly on the puncture. Hold for a moment next to tire and valve stem alongside valve hole and note where puncture occurred. Set tube aside to dry.

If puncture was on inside of tube probably a protruding spoke caused it:

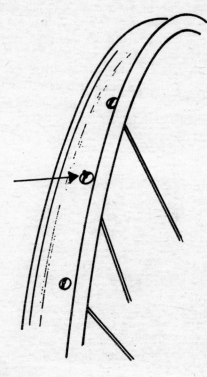

File the spoke flush with the rim. Check other spokes.

If the puncture was on the outside of the tube find what caused it by rubbing your fingers around inside the casing. Check the rest of the casing for embedded particles, and for ruptures or breaks:

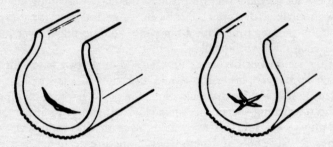

Replace the tire at the first opportunity if it has these.

To install the tube, first inflate it slightly to prevent it from folding and pinching itself. Push the part of the tube with the valve stem into the tire, and the valve stem through its hole on the rim. Fit valve stem locknut loosely. Stuff rest of tube into tire being careful not to pinch or tear it. Check that valve stem is still straight.

Push valve stem partway out, and slip bead of tire at that point back over the rim. It is important that you hold the base of the valve stem clear of the rim as you do this, or the bead may catch on it, creating a bulge in the tire:

Work around the rim replacing the bead and always taking care not to pinch the tube. Ideally you can do the entire job with your hands. Check that the valve stem is still straight. The last bit will be hard. Just keep working at it with your thumbs, first from one side, then from the other. When about 2″ of bead remains give it the grand mal effort. Don't wonder if it will go over; decide that it will. If you have to use a tire iron, be very careful not to pinch the tube.

Tubular tires

You will need:
Patches
Needle
Thread
Rubber cement
Sandpaper
Talcum powder
Chalk
Screwdriver
Sharp knife or razor blade

Remove wheel (p. 263). Deflate tire completely by opening locknut A on valve and holding down:

Presta

Remove tire from rim with your hands. Inflate and immerse in water a little at a time. Do not be misled by air bubbles coming out by the valve. Since the tire is sewn, the valve hole and puncture hole are the only places air can escape. Hold finger over puncture when located, dry tire, and mark puncture with chalk.

With a screwdriver or similar implement pry away about 5″ to 6″ of the tape on the inner side of the tire at the puncture area:

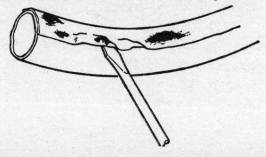

Next cut stitching about 2″ to either side of puncture. Make only two cuts to avoid numerous bits and pieces of thread, and cut upwards to miss tire:

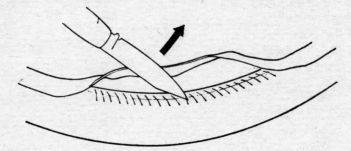

Gently remove tube and locate leak. A misture of soap and water will pin-point elusive ones. Dry tube if wet. Abrade area around puncture with sandpaper. Apply cement and let dry. Peel protective paper from patch without touching surface thus exposed and apply to puncture. Dust with talc to prevent tube from sticking to casing. Get whatever caused puncture out of casing. Insert tube, inflate, and check for leaks. Do this carefully. You are going to be mad if you get it all back together only to discover it still leaks.

Thread the needle and knot the two loose ends of thread. In a pinch 12 pound linen thread or silk fishing line will do. Using the old holes, start with an overlap of about $\frac{1}{2}$″, i.e. $\frac{1}{2}$″ past where thread was cut. Pinch the sides of the casing between thumb and forefinger to keep the tube out of the way:

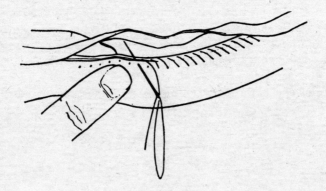

Pull stitches firm, but not so tight as to cut casing. Finish with a $\frac{1}{2}''$ overlap into original stitching. Layer cement on casing and inside of peeled-away tape and keep apart until dry. Position carefully and press together firmly.

Mounting a tubular

New rims and tires: inflate tire, deflate, place on rim (see below), inflate, deflate, remove.

Repaired tires and/or old rims: clean off old cement from rim with shellac thinner or solvent (bike stores).

There are two methods of mounting a tubular.

(1) Slow but sure. Deflate tire. Insert valve. Stand rim on soft surface with valve stem up, and working from above, work tire down over rim:

Be careful to distribute tire evenly around rim. Finish by grabbing with both hands and getting the last bit over by main force:

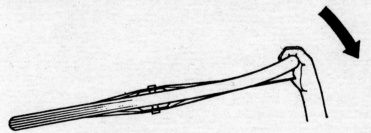

Check again that tire is evenly distributed and centered on rim. Roll back a portion of the tire and brush glue on rim and lining. Repeat all the way around and from both sides. Check again for evenness. Inflate hard. Allow half a day to dry before using or tire may creep (bunch up in spots) or simply come off the rim in a corner.

(2) Fast method. Apply glue to rim and tire and allow to dry tacky. Wear old clothes and assemble as above.

Road repairs: use the old cement on the rim and don't lean hard into corners going home. Double-sided rim tape (bike stores) is very handy.

Rims and Spokes

How They Work

The rim which supports the tire is laced (held) in position by the spokes, which are held fast at the hub and screw into the rim, so that they are adjustable:

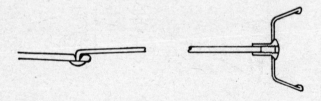

Adjustments

The tension on the spokes relative to each other determines both the strength and position of the rim. Positioning the rim correctly, both up and down, and side to side, is a long job requiring lots of patience and skill. Most times it is much more efficient to leave this to a bike shop. If you have no alternative however, or are determined to go it alone, here's how:

Hang up the bike or place the wheel in a jig. Spin the wheel while holding a pencil or some-such at a fixed point like the fork arm or a seat stay with the point near the rim to see how bad the wobble is. If it is over $\frac{1}{2}''$ pack up the entire project and take the wheel to a bike store. If they think they can save the wheel, fine, otherwise get a new wheel.

With less than $\frac{1}{2}''$ wobble: deflate tire. If job looks to be major, it will be easier if you just remove the tire altogether. Pluck the spokes with your fingers – they should all "ping" – and tighten any that are slack so that they all have an even tension. Spokes are tightened by turning *counter-clockwise*. If in the course of doing this you find spokes with frozen nipples (the part which holds the spoke to the rim) they must be replaced (see below). If it is more than 3 or 4 spokes I once again suggest resorting to your friendly bike shop.

Hold a chalk or pencil at the *outer edge* of the rim while you spin the wheel so that the high spots are marked. Working one half to 1 turn at a time, tighten the spokes at the chalk mark (*counter-clockwise*) and loosen them opposite the chalk mark. Continue until wheel is round.

Hold pencil or chalk at *side* of rim so that side to side wobbles are marked. Working $\frac{1}{2}$ to 1 turn at a time, and in groups of 4 to 6 spokes, tighten up the spokes opposite the chalk mark and loosen the ones next to it:

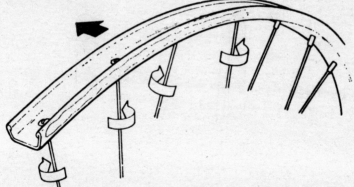

Tighten or loosen the spokes which are in the center of the chalk marks a little more than the ones at the edges of the marks. When you have finally succeeded, or compromised, run your finger around the rim and check for protruding spoke ends. File protruders down.

Replacing Spokes

Remove tire (p. 263). If you are dealing with spokes on a freewheel-equipped rear wheel that go to the freewheel side of the hub the freewheel will have to be removed (p. 304). Take broken spokes out of hub and rim. Get replacements which are exactly the same; many different kinds are available.

New spokes should go into hub so that head is on opposite side of hub from adjoining spokes and spoke is pointed in opposite direction:

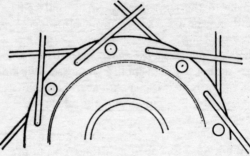

Be sure that it is correctly positioned in the hub with respect to the bevels:

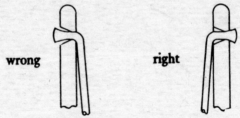

wrong   right

On almost all bikes the spokes touch where they cross. Weave new spokes through old as per other spokes on wheel. Place nipples on spokes and tighten. True wheel (see above), file down any protruding spokes which might puncture the tube, and remount tire.

Trouble-shooting

   * For side-to-side wobbles and elliptical wheels see p. 278.
   * For bulges in the rim caused by piling into curbs, stones, etc.: you will need vise-grips, channel-lock pliers, or a C-clamp. If

bulge is equal on both sides of rim place implement over bulge and squeeze *gently* until the rim is even again:

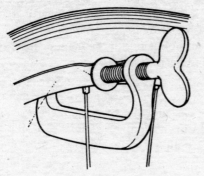

If the bulge is on the side of the rim, distribute the pinching force of your implement on the non-bulge side with a block of wood or some such:

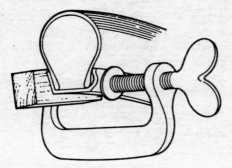

Fixing bulges almost invariably leave a slight dimple because the metal itself was stretched, but the wheel will probably be usable.

Wheel building

You may want to go the whole route and build your own wheels. This is at once straightforward, and an art. A good book on the subject is *Building Bicycle Wheels*, by Robert Wright (World Publications, P.O. Box 366, Mountain View, CA 94040, $1.95).

Hubs

Excluded from this section are sealed bearing hubs. These are by definition maintenance free. When they do require servicing or repair often special tools and techniques are needed for each particular make of hub. Consult the manufacturer for instructions if you have sealed bearing hubs.

How They Work

A hub consists of an axle, two sets of bearings, and a casing. The axle is held fixed, and the casing, to which the spokes are attached, spins around it riding on the ball bearings.

Adjustments

Wheel bearings are out of adjustment if, with the axle held firmly in place, the wheel can be wiggled from side to side (usually with a clicking noise), or if the wheel will not turn easily. Wheels held with nuts or lever nuts can be adjusted while on the bike Generally speaking however, the best procedure is to remove the wheel (p. 263). Wheels with quick-release hubs must be removed. You will need special thin hub wrenches (bike stores).

Undo locknut A from cone B:

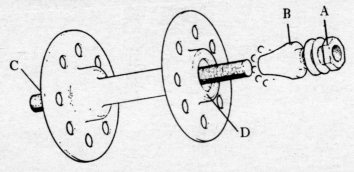

Holding axle or axle housing (quick-releases) still with wrench at locknut C (ten-speed rear wheels: if you can't get at it with a wrench use vise-grips or pliers), screw cone B fully home and then back off one quarter turn. Lock in place with locknut A. Test for side to side play. Wheel should spin freely, and on good hubs the weight of the tire valve will pull the wheel around so that the valve rests in the six o'clock position.

On a three-speed hub this adjustment is made on the side opposite the hub gear chain and sprocket:

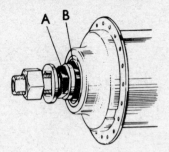

Loosen locknut A, turn cone B fully home, back off one quarter turn, reset lucknut A.

On a Sturmey-Archer SC coaster hub:

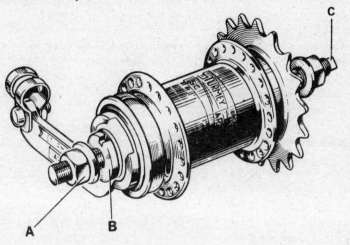

loosen locknut B, then turn C clockwise to tighten, anti-clockwise to loosen. Re-set locknut B.

Front wheel 'dynohubs' are adjusted at the left side, away from the dynamo, while rear "dynohubs" are adjusted at the left side next to the dynamo:

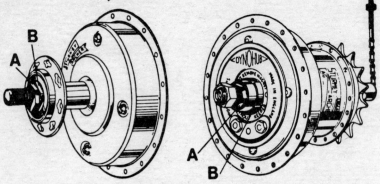

In both cases loosen locknut A, turn slotted washer B fully home, back off one quarter turn, and re-set locknut A.

Lubrication

Any front hub or 10-speed rear hub with oil clips or caps: ½ teaspoonful oil a month. If a grease fitting, one or two shots of grease per month.

Multi-speed rear hubs: 1 to 2 teaspoonfuls.

Coaster brake rear hubs: if oil fitting, 2 tablespoonfuls per month; if grease fitting, two or three shots of grease.

Hubs need to be cleaned and re-greased every six months for bikes in constant year-round use, and once a year for bikes retired for the winter or used only moderately. This requires disassembly.

Disassembly and Replacement

Remove wheel from bike (p. 263). Ten-speed rear wheels, remove freewheel (p 306). Lay wheel down on rags or newspaper to catch ball bearings. Undo locknut A from cone B and remove both while holding on to axle at C.

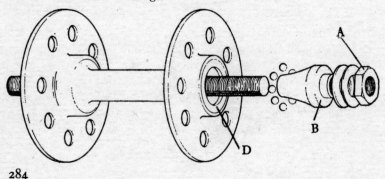

Remove dust cover D. To do this it may be necessary to let the axle drop in just a little way so you can pry the dust cover off with a screwdriver:

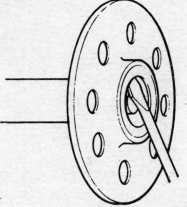

Prise out the loose or clipped ball bearings (or turn the wheel over and dump them out), count, and place in jar. Now slide axle all the way out and dump out remaining bearings. Garner and count. Undo remaining locknut and cone and remove from axle. Clean all parts in solvent. Examine bearings to see that they are not cracked or pitted. Clipped bearings should be secure in clip. Cups and cones should be even in color all around where bearings run and free of pitting. Test axle for straightness by rolling on glass surface. Replace any defective parts.

Reassembly: pack cups with grease. Not too much, excess will attract grit. Replace and lock one cone and locknut on axle. Slip dust cover on axle. Pack bearings into cup on one side of wheel. Gracefully insert axle and turn wheel over. Pack bearings into cup, replace dust cover, screw on cone and locknut, and adjust as per above.

Trouble-shooting

If something goes wrong it is usually because
  (1) the hub hasn't been serviced, or
  (2) a cone and locknut have come adrift.
In either case, if routine adjustment will not solve the problem, completely disassemble hub and replace broken or defective parts as per above.

5. Power Train

Contents

Pedals	288
How They Work	288
Adjustment	288
Lubrication — Disassembly	288
Trouble-shooting	289
Cranks	289
Adjustment and Removal	290
Trouble-shooting	291
Bottom Bracket	293
How It Works	293
Ashtabula One-Piece	293
Adjustment	293
Lubrication and Disassembly	294
Cranksets	296
Adjustment	296
Lubrication and Disassembly	297
Trouble-shooting	298
Front Sprocket	298
Adjustment	298
Replace	299
Trouble-shooting	299
Chain	300
Removal and Replacement	300
Fitting	302
Lubrication	204, 303
Trouble-shooting	303
Rear Sprocket	304
How It Works	304
Adjustment	305
Lubrication	306

Removal and Disassembly   306
Trouble-shooting   307

Gear Changers   307
  Multi-speed Hubs   308
   How They Work   309
   Adjustment   311
   Lubrication   311
   Disassembly and Replacement   311
    Hub   311
    Cables   314
    Shift Selector   315
   Trouble-shooting   315
  Derailleur Systems   316
   Shift lever   316
    How It Works   316
    Adjustment   316
    Removal and Replacement   317
   Cables   317
    Adjustment   319
    Removal and Replacement   320
    Trouble-shooting   320
   Derailleurs—Front   320
    How They Work   321
    Adjustment   323
    Lubrication   324
    Replacement   324
    Trouble-shooting   326
   Derailleurs—Rear   326
    How They Work   327
    Adjustment   334
    Lubrication   334
    Removal   334
    Disassembly   342
    The Positron
    Trouble-shooting   345

Power Train—
Trouble-shooting Index   346

Pedals

How They Work

A pedal consists of a platform of metal or metal and rubber for the foot, an axle (called a spindle) which screws into the crank, and two sets of ball bearings on which the platform rides as it spins around the spindle.

Adjustment

If pedal can be wiggled back and forth on the spindle it needs tightening. Remove dustcap A (pry with a screwdriver if it is the wedge type):

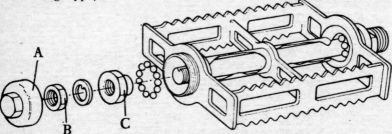

Undo locknut B from cone C. Screw cone C fully home and back off $\frac{1}{4}$ turn. Secure with locknut B. Check for play and that pedal spins easily. Replace dustcap A.

Lubrication and Disassembly

Pedals lead a hard, dissolute life and need cleaning and re-greasing every six months, more often if you ride a lot or favor wet weather. This requires disassembly. Remove pedals from crank. *Note:* right-hand pedal has a conventional right-hand thread and unscrews by turning counter-clockwise, but left-hand pedal has a left-hand thread and unscrews by turning *clockwise*. Work with pedal over newspaper or rag to catch ball bearings. Remove dust-cover A (see illustration above). Undo and remove locknut B and cone C while holding platform and spindle together with hand. Get all bearings out of dust cover end and place in jar. Remove spindle and place all bearings from crank end in jar. Clean all parts in solvent. Check ball bearings for pitting, cracks, disorderly conduct; cups and cones for uneven wear, pitting; spindle for straightness.

Reassembly: pack grease into cups on platform. Pack ball bearings into cup on crank side of platform (grease will hold them in place), and slide on spindle. Pack bearings into dust cover side cup. Screw down cone C fully home and back off one-quarter-turn. Secure with locknut B. Check for play and that pedal spins easily. Replace dustcover.

Note: When replacing pedals on bike be sure that left-side pedal, stamped "L" on end of spindle shaft, goes to the left side. It screws on *counter-clockwise*. The right-hand pedal is stamped "R" (surprise!) and screws on *clockwise*.

Trouble-shooting

* Pedal is tight to crank but askew. Bent spindle. Replace immediately.

* Grinding noises, hard to turn pedal. Try routine adjustment as above. No? Something is probably broken. Disassemble as above and replace defective parts.

* Loose pedal. Check that it is tight to crank. Left pedal tightens *counter-clockwise*, right pedal tightens *clockwise*. No? Loose bearings. Adjust as per above.

Cranks

Cranks support the pedals and transmit pedaling power to the front sprocket(s). They are attached to a bottom bracket axle which rides on two sets of ball bearings inside the bottom bracket shell. There are three types of cranks: one-piece; cottered three-piece; and cotterless three-piece:

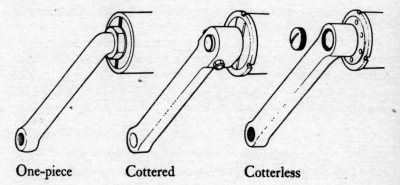

One-piece   Cottered   Cotterless

Since one-piece cranks include the bottom bracket axle, they are covered under Bottom Brackets. To test a cottered or cotterless crank for tightness, position the pedals equidistant from the ground. Press firmly on both pedals with hands and release. Rotate crankset one-half-turn and press pedals again. If something gives one of the cranks is loose.

Adjustment – Removal

Cottered Cranks
   Support the crank with a block of wood which has a hole or V-notch into which the cotter pin A fits:

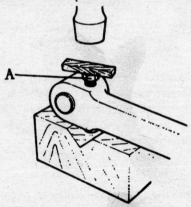

Be sure that the support block touches only the crank and is firmly in place. Otherwise what you do next will damage your bearings by driving the balls into the sides of the cup and scoring it (called Brinelling). Next: if you are tightening, give the head of the cotter pin A 2 or 3 moderate blows with a wooden mallet or hammer and wooden block combination. Then snug down nut firmly, but not with all your might or you will strip it. If you are removing, undo cotter pin 2 or 3 turns and then tap threaded end of cotter pin. Repeat if necessary. Be careful not to damage the threads as you will want to use the pin again. If you use a new pin and it does not fit, file down the flat side until it does.

Cotterless Cranks
   You will need a crank installer and extractor which fits your particular brand of crank. Cotterless cranks are made of an alum-

inum alloy called dural and must not be tightened with the same force as steel parts. To tighten or loosen first remove the dust cover A:

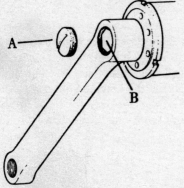

To tighten, apply socket wrench of installer to nut B and turn down, wiggling crank arm to make sure it is seated all the way. For new cranks retighten every 25 miles for the first 200 miles of use. To remove, first get chain out of way. Remove nut B. Back inner bolt A of extractor all the way out:

Screw extractor into crank, and then tighten down inner bolt. A *Do not do this with all of your might or you may strip the threads.* If the crank does not come loose with a firm tightening on the extractor bolt, give it 2 or 3 taps with a hammer, and tighten it one-eighth of a turn. Repeat until crank comes free. When replacing crank, be sure to wiggle it around a lot so that it is fully home before you give it the final tightening.

Trouble-shooting

 * There is a "click" as you bring the pedal around on the

upstroke and then a momentary dead spot and another "click" as you push it down. It may be a loose pedal (p. 289), bottom bracket (p. 291), or crank. If it looks to be the crank, test and tighten if necessary as per above.

* Stripped holding bolt on a cotterless crank. Get a new bottom bracket axle. If this is impossible, a machine shop may be able to re-thread the axle to accept a larger bolt. Be sure that the head of the larger bolt is small enough so that you can still use an extractor.

* Stripped thread for the extractor on a cotterless crank. First ask your bike shop if they can solve the problem. No? You may be able to find a substitute tool which will do the job. I have one which looks like:

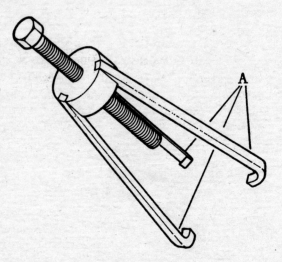

I have no idea what it is used for although I think it has something to do with plumbing. Anyway, the arms A will hook onto the crank or sprocket while the bolt passes against the bottom bracket axle.

If you can't find a substitute tool you and a machine shop may be able to manufacture a new extractor. It will be some trouble, but at upwards of $75 for fancy new cranks it is probably worth taking a stab at saving the old ones. Take your bike to a machine shop and explain that you want a steel plate or bar threaded in the center for an extractor bolt, and with holes drilled so that other bolts can be slid through and in turn be attached to metal plates which will hook behind the front sprocket:

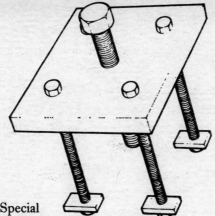

Backyard Special

If this Backyard Machine Shop Special Gizmo doesn't appeal to you, try jury-rigging your own conglomerate design of C-clamps, bolts, levers, bits and pieces and other materials. Just don't destroy your bike in the process.

   * Bent crank. Should be fixed by a bike shop with a special tool for the job.

Bottom Bracket

How It Works

The bottom bracket axle (called a spindle) spins on two sets of ball bearings contained within the bottom bracket shell, and holds the cranks. On the Ashtabula type one-piece crankset, the two cranks and spindle are one unit. Three-piece cranksets (cottered and cotterless) consist of two cranks and a separate spindle. Although service techniques are fundamentally similar, we will discuss one-piece cranksets and spindles for three-piece cranksets separately.

Ashtabula one-piece crankset

Adjustment

If axle is hard to turn, or slips from side to side in bottom bracket shell, first remove chain (p. 300). Then loosen locknut A by turning it *clockwise:*

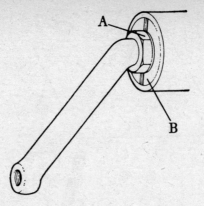

Use screwdriver in slot of cone B to turn it fully home (*counter-clockwise*), and then back it off one-eighth turn. Resecure locknut A (*counter-clockwise*), and check that cranks spin freely without side to side play.

Lubrication and Disassembly

Bottom bracket axles should be cleaned and re-greased once a year. This requires disassembly. Bearings for one-piece cranksets are held in clips so don't worry about losing them. Remove left pedal (*clockwise*) and chain from front sprocket (p. 300). Undo locknut A (*clockwise*), and unscrew cone B (*clockwise*):

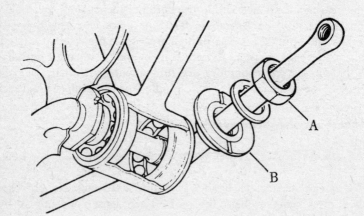

Remove ball bearing clip. Slide all parts off crank and place in a jar. Now move axle to right and tilt to slide whole unit through bottom bracket and out of frame. Take right side bearing lip off axle. Clean everything thoroughly with solvent. See that ball bearings are secure in clips and free from pitting or cracks; cups and cones are even in color where ball bearings run and free from pitting or scoring. If cups are deeply grooved replace. Remove with hammer and steel rod or screwdriver:

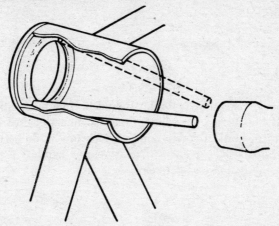

and make sure the new cups are well seated by tapping them in with a hammer and wooden block:

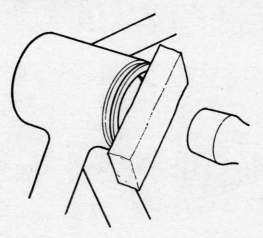

To resemble: pack grease into bearing clips and cups. Slide one clip on axle with solid side against right cone. Gracefully insert crankset through bottom shell from right side. Slide on ball bearing clips with balls in, solid side out. Screw on cone (*counter-clockwise*), and turn it fully home, wiggling and spinning the crankset as you do this. Back off one-eighth turn and secure with locknut (tighten *counter-clockwise*). Check that crankset spins freely without side to side play. Replace pedal (*counter-clockwise*) and chain.

Three-piece Cranksets –

Adjustment

Bottom bracket axle (spindle) should be free from side to side play and spin freely. To adjust, first disconnect chain from front sprocket (p. 300). Loosen notched lockring C on left side of bracket with a "C" wrench (bike stores) or hammer and screwdriver combination (*counter-clockwise*):

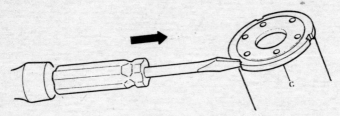

Then tighten (*clockwise*) adjustable cup D fully home with a screwdriver or center-punch inserted in hole or slot and *very light* hammer taps:

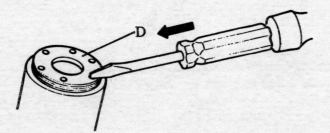

Back off one-eighth turn and secure with lockring C. Check that spindle spins freely and has no side to side play.

Lubrication and Disassembly

Bottom bracket assembly should be cleaned and re-greased once a year. This requires disassembly. Remove chain from front sprocket (p. 300) and cranks (p. 290). Lay bike right side down on newspaper or rags to catch loose ball bearings. Undo lockring C with "C" wrench or hammer and screwdriver combination and remove. Carefully holding axle in place against right side bearings, remove adjustable cup D:

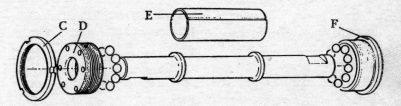

Lookout for the ball bearings! Some will fall out, others will stick to various parts. Get, count, and place in jar. Make sure you have them all. If your bearings are clipped, lucky you. Now pull spindle straight out. Garner all the right side ball bearings and jar 'em.

There may be a plastic tube (E, above) inside the bottom bracket shell. This is to prevent grit in the frame tubes from falling into the bearings. Take it out and clean it off. Clean out inside of bottom bracket shell with solvent. Examine the fixed cup F with a flashlight. If it is unpitted and wear is reasonably even, leave it alone. Otherwise unscrew and replace. Clean all other parts in solvent. See that ball bearings have no pits or cracks, and if clipped are secure in retainers; inside of adjustable cup and cones on spindle also have no pits and wear is even; spindle is straight. Replace defective parts.

Reassembly: pack cups with grease. If ball bearings are clipped, pack retainers. Replace plastic sleeve. Pack ball bearings into cups. Grease will hold in place. Clipped bearings go with solid side on cone (balls face out). Carefully insert spindle, long end to sprocket side of bottom bracket shell. Without jarring loose ball bearings fit on adjustable cup and screw home. Rotate spindle as you do this to make sure it goes in all the way. Back off one-eighth turn and secure with lockring. Be careful threading this on as it is easy to strip. Check that spindle spins easily with no side to side play. Replace cranks (p. 290) and chain (p. 302).

Trouble-shooting

    * Tight or loose crankset, grinding noises. Try adjustment as above. No? Disassemble and replace defective parts as above.

    * "Click" on pedal upstroke followed by dead spot and second "click" on downstroke. Could be a loose spindle, but more probably a loose crank or pedal (p. 289).

Front Sprocket(s) (Chainwheel)

    The front sprocket is the business with all the teeth attached to the right crank which pulls the chain around to deliver power to the rear wheel.

Adjustment

    The only maintenance needed is to check periodically for bent or chipped teeth. Remove chain (p. 300). With a strong light behind the front sprocket, rotate it, looking from the side for chipped teeth, and from above or in front for bent teeth:

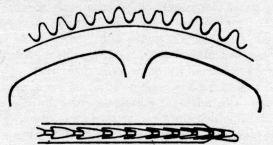

If teeth are chipped, replace sprocket (see below). If bent, take an adjustable wrench, snug it down over the bent tooth, and bend it back:

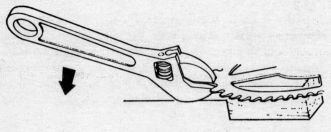

It helps a lot if you can brace the sprocket as you do this to avoid bending it.

Replacement

If it is necessary to replace your sprocket take a look at the chapter on gearing (pp. 93-105). You might be interested in changing the number of gear teeth.

Ashtabula one-piece cranksets require replacing the whole unit (p. 294).

One-speed and most 3-speed bikes have a one-piece right crank and sprocket. To remove see p. 297.

Ten-speed bikes generally have a sprocket which is bolted to the right crank:

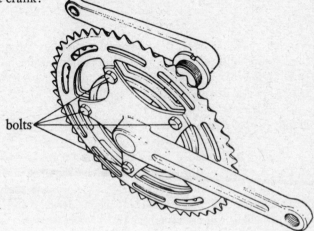

bolts

Simply undo the bolts (or allen screws) to remove sprocket.

Trouble-shooting

* There is a "clunk" every time you bring the front sprocket around. One possible cause is a bent tooth. Check by hanging bike up and slowly running sprocket. If chain suddenly jumps up where it meets the sprocket – bent tooth. Fix as above.

* Sprocket wobbles from side to side, hitting front derailleur cage or rubbing chainstays. If this is not due to incredibly loose bottom bracket bearings (p. 296), the sprocket is warped. Fixing is a job requiring both great delicacy and considerable force.

Techniques vary so much as according to the exact problem that I strongly suggest you leave it to a bike shop.

Chain

The chain is that innocent and simple looking business which transmits power to the rear gear(s). There are two kinds: one is used on non-derailleur bikes, is $\frac{1}{8}''$ wide, and held together with a master link:

which can be taken apart without special tools; the other for derailleur equipped bikes, is $3/32''$ wide, and has no master link (it would catch in the rear gear cluster), so that a special chain riveting tool is needed to take it apart or put it together.

Removal and Replacement

Chains should be replaced every two years on bikes that see constant use, and every three years on bikes that see average service. Although the chain may look perfectly sound, the tiny bit of wear on each rivet and plate adds up to a considerable alteration in size. A worn chain will chip teeth on (expensive) gear sprockets. To test for wear, remove chain (see below) and lay on table with rollers parallel to surface. Hold chain with both hands about 4–5″ apart. Push hands together, and then pull apart. If you can feel slack, replace chain.

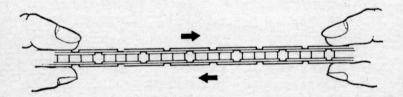

Test also for side to side deflection. It should not be more than 1″:

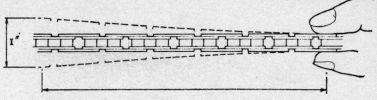

To remove and replace a master link chain find the master link

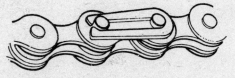

and pry it off with a screwdriver.

To remove a derailleur chain drive out a rivet with a chain tool:

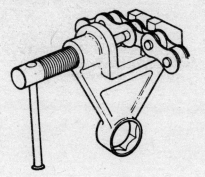

Be sure that the point of the chain tool centers exactly on the rivet. *Do not drive the rivet all the way out.* Go only as far as the outside plate. Stop frequently to check progress. Once rivet is near chain plate I like to free link by inserting a thin screwdriver and twisting gently:

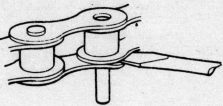

Another method is simply to twist the chain. Be careful that you do not bend the plates. To replace rivet, reverse tool:

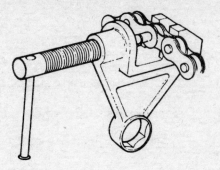

Again, be careful how far you go, or the link will jam (see Trouble-shooting to fix).

Fitting

Most new chains need to be shortened in order to fit properly. On a non-derailleur bike it should be set so that there is $\frac{1}{2}''$ up and down play in the chain with the rear wheel in proper position:

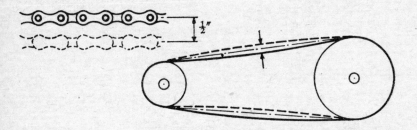

On a derailleur bike, the chain needs to be long enough to fit over the large front and back sprockets, and short enough to fit on the small front and rear sprockets. The less tension the better, but be careful the derailleur does not double up on itself. Remove links from end of chain that has two plates with no roller between them. Some adjustment can be made by changing wheel position with adjustable blocks on the rear dropouts:

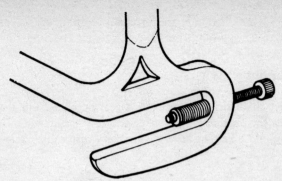

Lubrication

The scheme for lubrication depends on what kind of lubricant you use.

A dry film lubricant such as LPS-1 or (somewhat moist) LPS-3 is clean, does not attract dirt, and goes on in a flash. Apply every 1 or 2 weeks, and remove and soak chain clean in solvent every 2 or 3 months.

Oil is the common lubricant. The problem is that it attracts grit and the solution is to add more oil in the hope that it will float the grit away. Oil every link once a week, and remove and soak clean the chain in solvent once a month.

The most economical lubricant is paraffin, available in grocery stores. It is cleaner than oil. Remove and clean chain. Melt paraffin in coffee can, dip chain, and hang to dry so that drippings fall back into can. Once a month.

Trouble-shooting

* Jammed link. Use chain tool to free tight links by working the rivet back and forth a quarter-turn on the chain tool at a time. If your chain tool has a spreader slot (handy), use that:

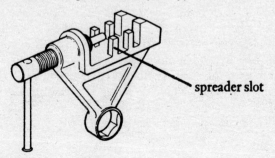

spreader slot

* "Klunk" sounds and/or chain jumping sprockets. Test chain for excessive wear as per above. May also be a bent sprocket tooth (see p. 298).

Rear Sprocket

All chain drive bikes have a rear sprocket. On 1- and 3-speed bikes this is a single sprocket and is extremely simple. Derailleur equipped bikes use several sprockets (also called cogs) mounted on a freewheel.

How It Works

The freewheel is in two parts, and there are two basic designs:

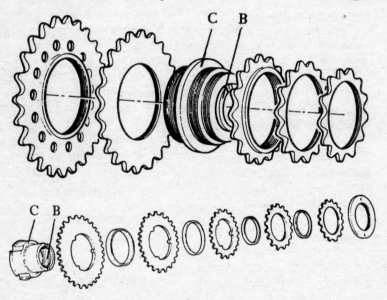

The inside part B threads on the hub. Sprockets slide or are threaded on the outside part C. The freewheel is ratcheted so that when the outside part C is driven clockwise by the chain, the inside part B (and hence the hub) is driven too. But when the bike is coasting, with the chain stationary, part C holds still while part B spins merrily along. This ratcheting is accomplished through the use of a clever maze of ball bearings, pins, springs, and other minute and complex parts inside the freewheel.

Periodically check for chipped or bent teeth by looking at them in profile:

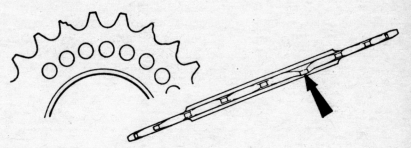

Replace cogs that have chipped or broken teeth, or an uneven U between teeth. Straighten bent teeth by removing cog (see below), gripping the bent tooth with an adjustable end wrench, and straightening:

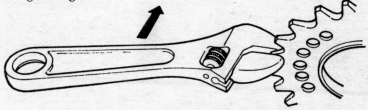

Alignment between front and back sprockets is important. Standing at the front of the bike and sighting between the two front sprockets, you should see the center cog of the back gear cluster:

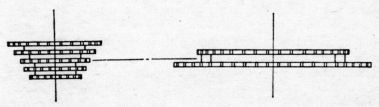

If back sprocket is too far out, so you can see the 2nd or 1st largest rear cog, the front sprocket must be moved out. This can only be done by installing a longer bottom bracket axle (p. 297). If you have Ashtabula one-piece cranks (p. 293) there is nothing you can do at all.

If back sprocket is too far in, so you can see the 4th to 5th largest rear cog, it must be moved out. This is done by removing the freewheel (below), installing a shim (bike stores), the freewheel again, and then possibly another shim so that the freewheel will clear the drop-outs. All this stuff usually makes it hard to get the wheel back in and may necessitate a little judicious bending. It is better to let a bike shop deal with problems of this sort.

Lubrication

A bi-weekly shot of LPS-3 is best. Remove freewheel (see below) and soak clean in solvent once a year.

Oil: a few drops once a month. Remove and soak clean in solvent every six months.

Removal and Disassembly

This requires a freewheel remover. There are two basic types, pronged and splined:

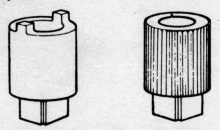

Look at your freewheel to see which kind you need. Remove wheel (p. 263). Remove nut and washers from freewheel side of axle. Quick release hubs: remove conical nut and spring from shaft of skewer and place spring in a jar. Fit freewheel remover. If it won't go on you may have a spacer nut. Remove with a wrench while holding axle stationary with another wrench on the left side cone or locknut. Fit freewheel remover into slots or splines. Replace nut on axle or skewer and screw down hand-tight. Use a wrench on the freewheel remover to break the freewheel loose (counter-clockwise). This may be difficult. As soon as it comes loose, remove freewheel and spin it off by hand.

Replacing freewheel. *Note:* a new freewheel or sprockets requires a matching new chain, especially if the existing chain is more than a year old. A stretched chain will probably kick up on new sprockets. Also, if you are getting a new freewheel, read the chapter on gears. You may be interested in changing gear ratios. If you do this, be sure to check chain tension after installing freewheel (p. 302). To replace a freewheel put a little grease on the threads and simply screw it on, being extremely careful not to strip the threads on the hub. Snug down with the freewheel remover secured by the axle bolt but do not bear down hard; it will tighten as you ride.

Changing cogs: For this you need a sprocket remover (bike shops) and, if you are removing all the sprockets, a freewheel vise (ditto). Incidentally, if you want a number of different gear ratios it is much simpler to have two fully set up freewheels with different gear ratios than to keep diddling with individual sprockets. However, if you are experimenting to work out the combination of cogs which is best for you and are impatient with bike shops (they can do this job very quickly), then by all means proceed. Removing a cog is simple – it unscrews or slides off the freewheel – but tools for the job vary considerably in design. Follow the instructions given with your particular tool. If you change the small or large cog, be sure to check chain tension (p. 302) after reassembly.

Dismantle freewheel. Uh-uh. This is another of those profitless jobs. If the freewheel goes, replace it.

Trouble-shooting

* A "klunk" two or three times per complete revolution of the front sprocket. May be a bent tooth on a freewheel sprocket. Check as per above.

* Freewheel won't freewheel. Try soaking in solvent to free up innards. No? Replace it.

* Freewheel turns but hub doesn't. Spin cranks while holding bike stationary and look carefully at freewheel. If both parts spin around the hub, threads on hub are stripped. New hub. If outside part of freewheel spins around inside part, freewheel is clogged up (frozen) or broken. Try soaking in solvent. No? Replace.

Gear Changer Systems

Except for the two-speed pedal-operated rear hubs, gear changer systems typically include a shift trigger, lever, or twistgrip, a cable, and the gear changing mechanism, of which there are two kinds, internal rear hub, and derailleur.

Multi-speed internally Geared Rear Hubs

These come in 2-, 3-, and 5-speed versions, with planetary or sun gears inside the hub. I consider these units too complicated to be worth disassembling, and so does any bike shop I have asked about doing such work. Here, for example, is an exploded view of a Sturmey Archer 3-speed hub and coaster brake combination:

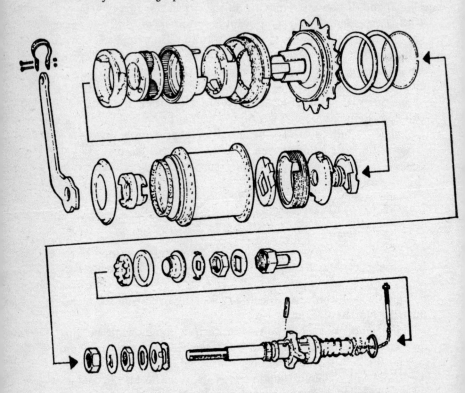

Believe me, if you run into trouble with your hub and can't solve it with routine adjustment or trouble-shooting (below), the best thing to do is remove the wheel (p. 263) and take it to a bike shop. The chance of problems arising is quite small. A regularly lubricated hub should last the life of your bike.

No adjustments are possible with 2-speed pedal-controlled hubs. There are two major brands of 3-speed hubs, Sturmey Archer, and Shimano. Service techniques for both are virtually identical, and so we will concentrate on one, the Sturmey-Archer.

How They Work

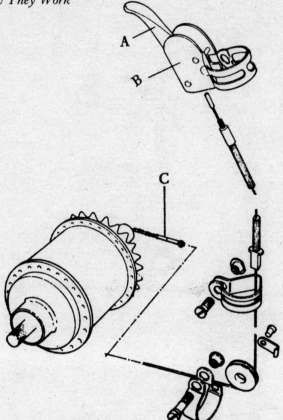

Shift trigger A connects to cable B, which in turn connects to toggle chain C on hub. Position of trigger determines gear.

Adjustment

Three-speed hubs –
To adjust a hub first run the shift lever to 3rd or H. Then take

up slack in cable by loosening locknut A and screwing down barrel sleeve adjustor B:

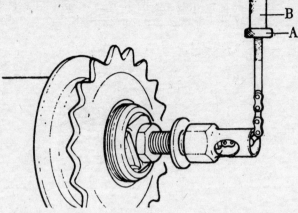

Leave cable very slightly slack. If barrel sleeve cannot do job, move the fulcrum clip which holds the cable housing on the bike frame forward:

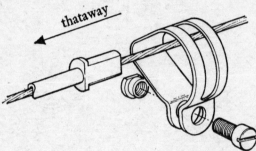

Test gears. No? Check position of indicator rod by looking through the hole in the side of the right hub nut. With the shift lever in 2nd or N position it should be exactly even with the end of the axle:

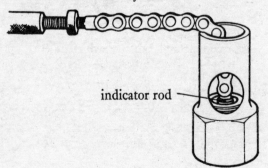

indicator rod

Adjust if necessary with barrel sleeve. Test gears. No? Remove barrel sleeve altogether. Check that indicator rod is screwed finger-tight fully into hub. Reassemble and adjust as above. No? Turn to Trouble-shooting, this section (p. 315).

Five-speed hubs –

For the righthand shift lever, follow the same procedure as for the 3-speed hub, above.

For lefthand shift lever, set it all the way forward and screw cable connector to bellcrank B two or three turns:

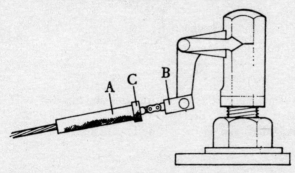

Then run shift lever all the way back, and take slack out of cable with cable connector. Secure with locknut C.

Lubrication

A tablespoon of oil inside hub once a month. I strongly recommend a quality oil such as is sold in bike and gun shops, or motorist's SAE 30 oil. Some household and other cheap oils leave behind a sticky residue when the oil evaporates. This is the last thing in the world you want. Once a month use a little LPS spray or a few drops of oil on the trigger control, cable, and inside the cable housing.

Disassembly and Replacement

Hub –

Remove wheel (p. 263) and take it to a bike shop.

Cable –

Needs replacement when it becomes frayed, the housing kinked or broken, or exhibits suspicious political tendencies.

Run shift selector to 3rd or H. Disconnect barrel sleeve from indicator and loosen fulcrum clip (for illustration, see Adjustment above). To free cable from a

Trigger: shift to 1st or L, pry up holding plate A with a small screwdriver, and push cable *in* until nipple clears ratchet plate:

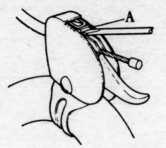

and then pull cable out. Remove entire cable and housing assembly from bike and set aside fulcrum sleeve.

Twist-grip: first take off the spring S with a screwdriver:

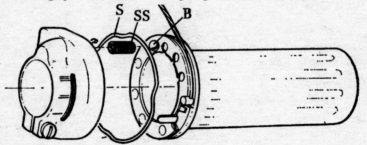

Slide the twist-grip off the handlebar and catch the ball bearing B and spring SS if they fall out. Release nipple from slot, and remove cable and cable housing assembly from bike.

Top tube lever: undo the cable anchor bolt near the hub:

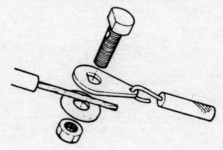

Unscrew the two shift lever halves A and B, and lift casing C away from bike:

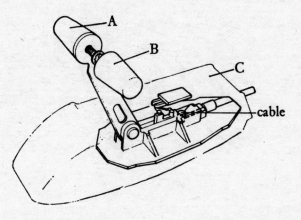

Push cable in to free nipple from slot and thread out cable.

Note: Take the old cable with you to the shop when getting replacement. This kind of cable comes in a variety of lengths. To replace a cable to a

Trigger: place the fulcrum sleeve on cable housing and thread through fulcrum clip. Pry up trigger control plate, insert cable through hole in trigger casing, and slip nipple into slot on ratchet. Run cable over pulley wheel if you have one, and attach to toggle chain. Shift to 3rd or H. Position fulcrum clip so cable is just slightly slack and tighten. Adjust if necessary as per above.

Twist-grip: insert nipple into slot. Grease and replace spring and ball bearing. Slide twist-grip on handlebar and secure with spring clip. Use a small screwdriver to work the spring clip in. Run cable over pulley wheel if you have one, and attach to toggle chain. Shift selector to 3rd or H and adjust as per above.

To top tube lever: thread cable through slot until nipple catches. Replace cable housing or run cable over pulley wheel, depending on the kind of system you have. Connect cable to anchor bolt, shift to 3rd or H, and adjust as per above. Replace casing, and screw together handle halves.

If you have a bashed or recalcitrant shift control the best thing is to replace it. They are not expensive. To replace.

Trigger: disconnect cable (see above) and undo bolt B:

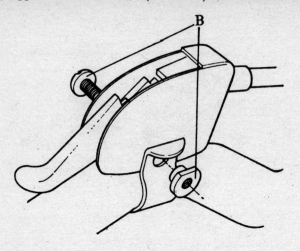

Twist-grip or top tube lever: I recommend replacing with a standard handlebar trigger, which is a much better mechanical design and more reliable. To remove old unit disconnect cable (see above) and undo bolt B:

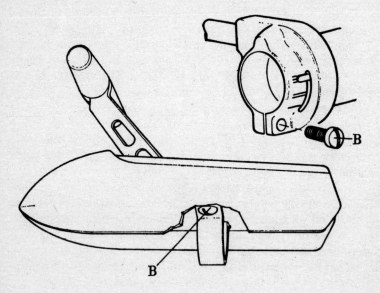

No gear at all (pedals spin freely) or slips in and out of gear.

* Is gear in proper adjustment (p. 309)?

* Is cable binding? Check by disconnecting barrel sleeve at hub (p. 311) and working cable back and forth through housing. Replace (p. 312) if it binds.

* Is shift mechanism together and functioning? Stick and twist-grip models are especially prone to slippage after the track for the ball bearing becomes worn:

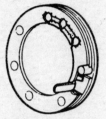

* Insides of hubs may have gotten gunked up through the use of too heavy or household oils so that pawls are stuck. Try putting in kerosene or penetrating oil and jiggling everything around. No?

* Uncle. Remove wheel (p. 263) and take to a bike shop.

Derailleur Systems

A derailleur system includes a shift lever on the down tube, but also on the top tube, or the stem, or at the handlebar ends, a thin cable and (sometimes) cable housing, and a front or rear gear changer (derailleur) through which the chain passes. When the shift lever is actuated, the derailleur moves sideways and forces the chain on to a different sprocket:

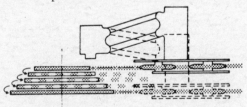

Although we are dealing here with a system, it will simplify everything to take it piece by piece first, and then deal with it as a whole.

Shift Lever

How It Works – Adjustment – Removal and Replacement

The shift lever should be set so that you can move it without undue strain, but be stiff enough to hold fast against spring pressure from the derailleur. This adjustment is made with the tension screw A:

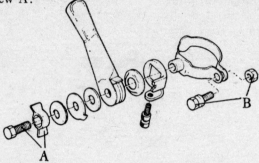

Some tension screws have a slot for a screwdriver (or coin), others have wings, and others have wire loops. All function the same way. To dismantle the lever, simply remove the tension screw. Be sure to keep all parts in order. To remove a down tube mounted lever unit undo bolt B above.

To get a top tube lever unit off remove the stem (p. 251). A stem mounted unit comes off by undoing bolts A & B:

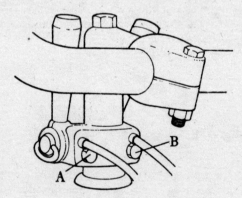

A handlebar end unit requires first removing trim nut A:

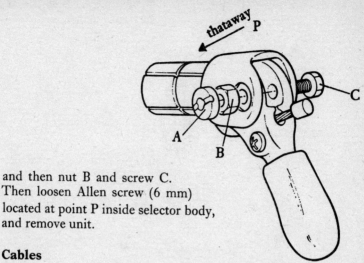

and then nut B and screw C.
Then loosen Allen screw (6 mm)
located at point P inside selector body,
and remove unit.

Cables
Adjustment

Cables of derailleur systems are frequently exposed, thin, and take a hell of a beating. Check them often for fraying:

Adjustment is needed when the shift lever has to be pulled all the way back to engage the large sprocket. Place the shift lever forward so that the chain is on the smallest sprocket. Some systems have a barrel adjustor, either at the derailleur or at the shift lever:

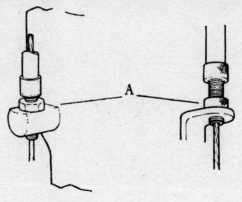

Undo the locknut A and move the barrel adjustor up until slack is removed from cable. If this will not do the job, turn barrel adjustor back down fully home, and reset cable anchor bolt.

All derailleurs, front and back, use a cable anchor bolt or screw to hold the cable. Here is the location (CB) on two representative types:

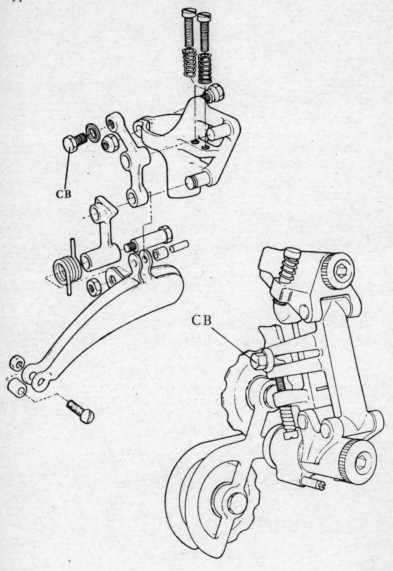

CB

CB

Loosen the bolt, take the slack out of the cable, pulling it through with pliers if necessary, and retighten bolt.

Removal and Replacement

Run chain to smallest sprocket. Screw home barrel adjustor, if you have one. Undo cable anchor bolt and thread cable out of derailleur. Check cable housings (not on all models) for kinks and breaks. Remove cable from lever by threading it out:

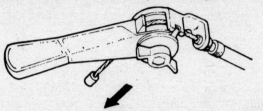

Reassembly: *Note:* do not cut new cable to size until it is installed or it will jam when going into cable housings. If you are cutting new cable housing, be sure to get the jaws of the cutter *between* the wire coils of the housing:

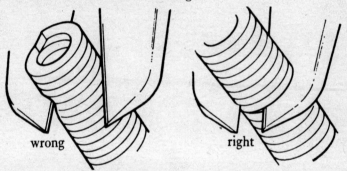

wrong   right

Start by threading through shift lever, and then through down tube tunnel, cable stops, cable housings, and whatever else is in your particular system. As you pass the cable through cable housings, be sure to twist it so that the strands do not unravel:

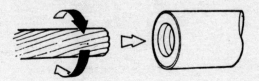

Finish at derailleur. Move shift lever to forward position, make sure that cable housing ferrules (if you have them) are seated properly, and attach cable to cable anchor bolt.

Trouble-shooting

Cable problems are evinced by delayed shifts, or no shifts at all. In any case, the procedure is the same: undo the cable anchor bolt and slide the cable around by hand, looking for sticky spots. Check carefully for fraying, and for kinks in the cable housing.

Derailleurs – Front

How They Work

There is a metal cage through which the chain passes as it feeds onto the front sprocket. The cage can be moved from side to side, and by pressing on the side of the chain, shifts it from sprocket to sprocket:

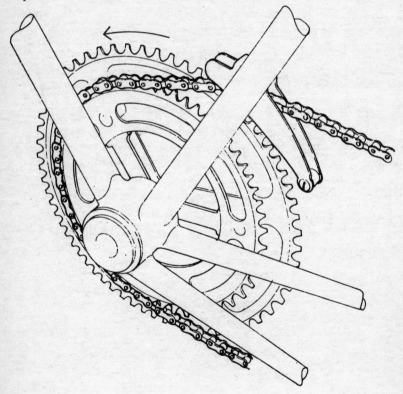

Virtually all derailleurs are built as a parallelogram. Heh. This design is used to keep the sides of the cage A straight up and down as the cage is moved from side to side on the pivot bolt P:

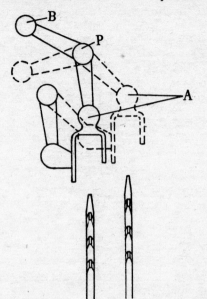

The cage is moved by pulling with a cable at point B, and when the cable is released, spring tension pushes it back. Details may vary, but this is the basic design.

Adjustment

The changer as a whole must be properly positioned, with the outer side of the cage about ¼″ to ½″ above the sprocket:

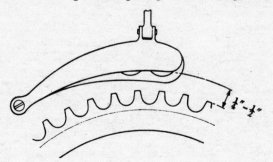

Raise or lower the unit by undoing the mounting bolt (S). The sides of the cage should follow the curvature of the sprocket. Some cages are adjustable in this respect, others (perfectly good ones) are not. Those that are usually swivel on a post between the cage and changer. Sometimes the post comes off the changer, and sometimes off the cage. Either way, there will be a locking bolt like C:

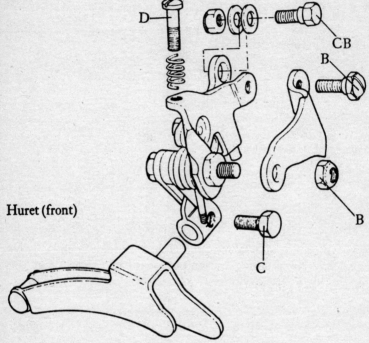

Huret (front)

Loosen, rotate cage to desired position, tighten.

Side to side travel of the cage must be set. First check that cable is properly adjusted (p. 317). Front derailleurs fall into two design categories, those with 2 adjusting screws, and those with 1. Look at yours to determine the type.

One-screw derailleurs

Run chain to largest back and smallest front sprockets. The first adjustment is made with the cage positioning bolt C (above). Loosen it, and move the cage so that the left side just clears the

chain. Tighten. Now back off the adjusting screw D 3 or 4 turns.
Run the chain to the smallest back and largest front sprockets.
Using the shift lever, position the cage so that the right side just
clears the chain. Turn down adjusting screw D until resistance is
felt, and stop.

Two-screw derailleurs

If you can't find your adjusting screws easily, get down close to
the unit and watch it carefully as you wiggle the shift lever back
and forth. Each time the body of the changer reaches the end of its
travel it will be resting on a spring-loaded screw or knurled ring:

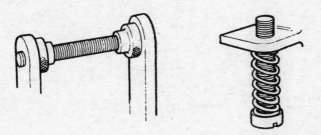

Run chain to largest and smallest front sprockets. It should just
clear the left side of the cage. Adjust left side (low gear) adjusting
screw (D, above) as necessary until it does. Now run chain to
smallest back and largest front sprockets. It should just clear the
right side of the cage Adjust right side (high gear) adjusting screw
(E, below) as necessary until it does. Test operation of gears.
Sometimes it is necessary to set the high gear adjustment a little
wide to get the chain to climb up on the big sprocket – but be
cautious, or the chain will throw off the sprocket.

Lubrication

A little LPS or a few drops of oil on the pivot bolts once a
month. If the unit becomes particularly dirty, take it off (see
below) and soak it clean in kerosene or other solvent.

Replacement

Remove chain (p. 300). Undo cable anchor bolt and slip off cable (p. 319). Now undo mounting bolt(s) B and remove unit:

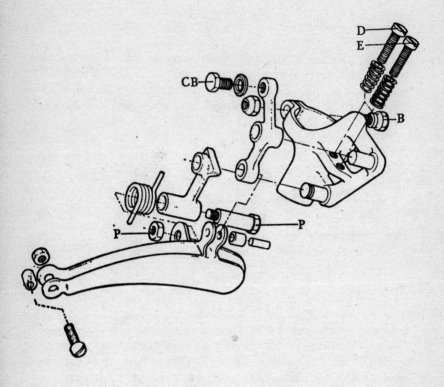

Reverse to replace. Other units may have different mounting bolts but their function will be clear.

Trouble-shooting

Most of the difficulties experienced with the front changer are actually caused by problems elsewhere in the power train. I am assuming that you have already set your changer as per Adjustment, above.

Chain rubs side of cage.

* Is shift lever tight (p. 316)?

* Can you stop rubbing by diddling with shift lever? For example, the amount of right travel necessary to shift the chain from the left (small) sprocket to the right sprocket may leave the cage too far to the right when the chain is on the large back sprocket, and cause the chain to rub the left side of the cage. In fact, it is frequently necessary with front changers to move the cage back just a trifle after a shift has been completed (p. 316).

* Is the sprocket warped (p. 299)? Or loose (p. 296)?

Chain throws off sprocket.

* Is shift lever tight (p. 316)?

* Cage travel may be set too far out. Adjust it slightly (p. 321).

* Is chain old? Test (p. 300).

* Are sprocket teeth bent (p. 298)?

* Are front and rear sprockets in alignment (p. 306)?

* If chain continually over-rides big front sprocket, take an adjustable wrench and bend the leading tip of the outside cage in very slightly – about $\frac{1}{16}''$:

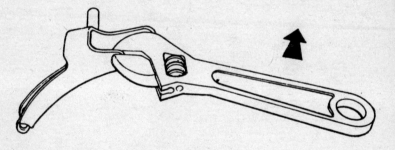

Delayed shifts or no shifts at all.

* Are pivot bolts clean? Try a little spray or oil.

* Is spring intact and in place?

* Is cable sticking or broken (p. 317)?

* If pivot bolts are adjustable, as P is on this Campagnolo unit (**opposite**) undo locknut, back P off one-eighth turn, reset locknut.

How They Work

As the chain comes back off the bottom of the front sprocket it passes through the rear derailleur on two chain rollers. The cage holding the rollers is fastened to the main body of the changer by a pivot bolt P, and is under constant spring tension so as to keep the chain taut:

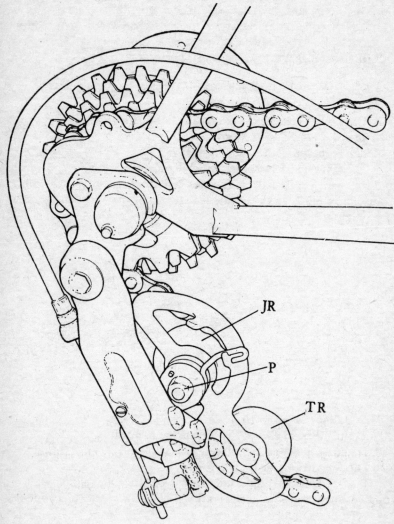

The lower roller is the tension roller (TR), the upper the jockey roller (JR). The position of the cage, and hence of the chain on the rear gear cluster, is determined by the changer body:

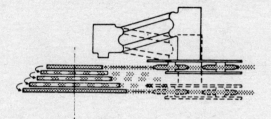

The changer body is under constant spring tension to carry it to the smallest sprocket. It is restrained from doing so by a cable and shift lever.

Derailleurs come in two basic designs, box, like the Huret Allvit or Simplex, and bare parallelogram, like the Campagnolo:

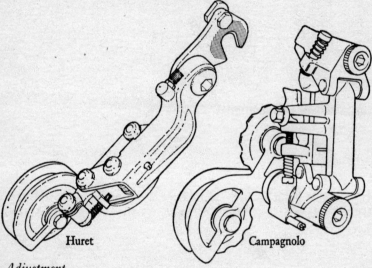

Huret   Campagnolo

Adjustment

– Position of changer with respect to bike.

The body of the changer should form an angle with the vertical of about 20° to 30°. Many derailleurs are not adjustable in this respect and are held by spring tension against a stop (Campagnolo, Simplex). Others like the Huret Allvit can be adjusted by loosening locknut A and then pivot bolt P.

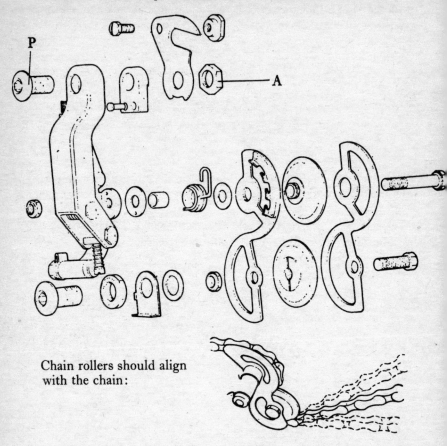

Chain rollers should align
with the chain:

If your derailleur is fastened to a mounting plate, remove it (see
below), clamp in a vise, and bend it with an adjustable end
wrench:

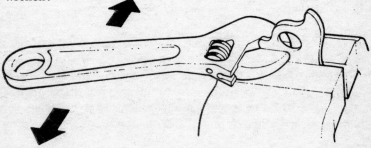

If your derailleur is bolted straight into the frame drop-out, snug wrench around the chain rollers and bend into alignment:

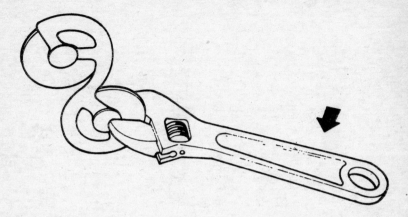

Bear in mind that this is a fairly drastic measure. I am assuming that the derailleur was bent in an accident, and that you have no choice. The alternative is replacement (see below), which you should consider if the old derailleur is on the way out. Box changers such as the Huret or Simplex are inexpensive and quite reliable, and a working derailleur, no matter how plastic and cheap, is miles ahead of a fancy job which is one shift away from disintegration.

Note: if it is a brand new derailleur which is out of alignment then the fault is with the frame drop-out. You can bend this into line yourself with an adjustable end wrench the same as you would bend the derailleur mount (above), but this is a very serious matter which should be left to a bike shop. Bending does cause metal fatigue, and if the rear drop-out were to shear unexpectedly you might have an accident.

– Side to side travel of derailleur.

First check with chain on smallest rear and biggest front sprockets, and with rear derailleur shift lever all the way forward, that there is only a little slack in the cable. Take up or give slack through barrel adjustor and/or cable anchor bolt (p. 317).

The derailleur needs to be set so that side to side travel is stopped short of throwing the chain into the wheel or off the small sprocket. This is done with two adjusting screws or knurled rings, and here is their location on 4 typical units (high gear – E, low gear – D):

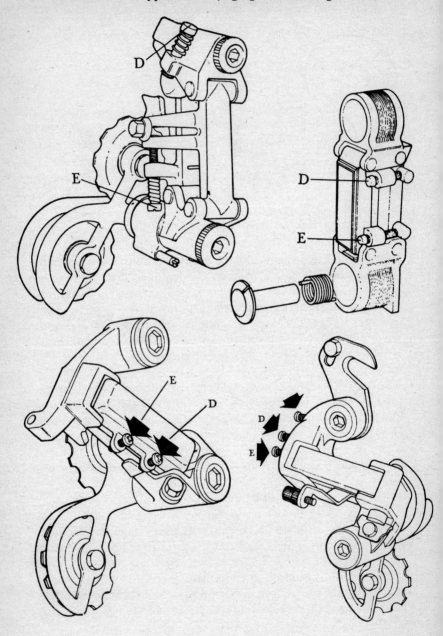

If your derailleur isn't included here, get down close to it and run it back and forth, seeing which adjusting screw does what. OK, now: if derailleur goes too far, throwing chain off, set in position with shift lever so that jockey wheel lines up with sprocket on the side you are working on, and turn in appropriate adjusting screw or knurled ring until resistance is felt. Stop. If derailleur does not go far enough, back the appropriate adjusting screw off until it does. If this does not work, check to make absolutely sure adjusting screw is backed off. Yes? Turn to Trouble-shooting, p. 344, for what to do next.

– Spring tension for roller cage.

Spring tension on the roller cage should be sufficient to keep the chain taut when in high gear. No tighter. Excess tension will cause unnecessary drag and rapid wear. On the other hand, too loose a chain will skip. If you have this problem and the chain tension seems OK, check the chain itself for wear (p. 300). Worn chains skip.

Adjustment procedure varies according to type of derailleur. Many have the spring set on a hook on the roller cage:

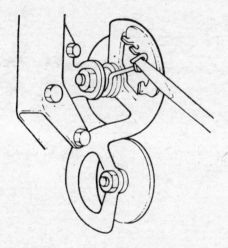

Move it carefully with pliers or screwdriver.

On the Simplex, remove screw and dust cap (not on all models) from bottom pivot bolt A (see next page).

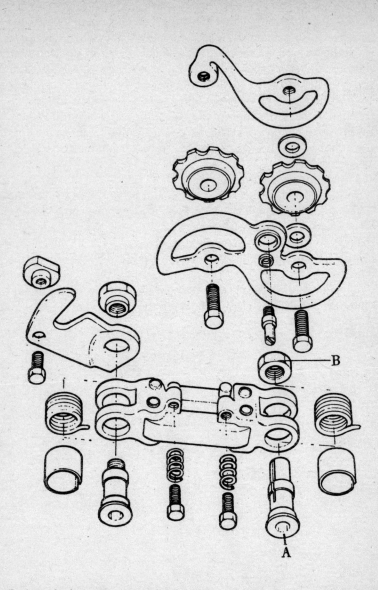

Loosen locknut B, use a metric Allen wrench to turn A clockwise
for more tension, counter-clockwise for less, reset locknut.

On a Campagnolo unit, first remove wheel. Then remove
tension roller by undoing bolt G:

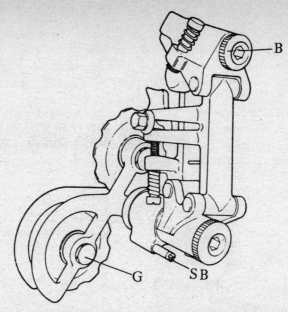

Use one hand to hang onto the chain roller cage and prevent it from spinning, and unscrew the cage stop bolt SB. Now let the cage unwind (about one-half to three-quarters of a turn). Remove cage pivot bolt with Allen wrench and lift off cage. Note that protruding spring end engages one of a series of small holes in the cage. Rotate cage forward until spring fits into next hole:

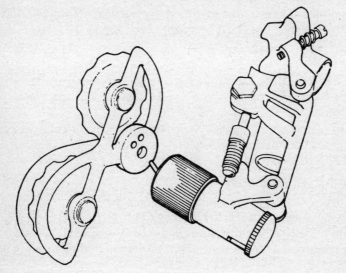

Replace pivot bolt. Wind cage back $\frac{1}{2}$–$\frac{3}{4}$ turn and replace cage stop bolt. Replace tension roller and go back to the races.

Shimano units: Remove wheel, tension roller, and cage stop bolt. Rotate entire cage one turn against spring. Replace cage stop bolt, tension roller, wheel.

The Maeda Sun Tour V–Luxe can be adjusted as per procedure for Shimano units, but this is likely to produce too much or too little tension. For a finer adjustment, disassemble (p. 286), noting the relative position of cage with respect to spring catch setting in castlated nut. If the normal position is as A:

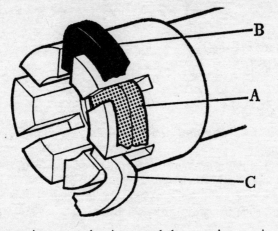

spring tension may be increased by moving spring catch to position B, and decreased by moving to position C.

Lubrication

LPS spray: once a month on the jockey and tension roller, pivot bolts, and cables. Once a year remove and soak clean in solvent.

Oil: a few drops monthly on chain rollers, pivot bolts, cables. Soak clean in solvent every six months. Regrease wheel bearings, if you have them (p. 336).

Removal and Disassembly

Disconnect cable from anchor bolt (pp. 318).

Remove tension roller by undoing bolt G (pp. 333 and 335). Undo mounting bolt B (Campagnolo) or slacken axle nut and remove adapter screw AS (Huret Allvit) according to how your unit is mounted (p. 333 and below).

Disassembly: the parts that need this regularly are the chain rollers. Otherwise do it only to replace parts. Chain rollers: get jockey roller off (tension roller is already off).

On the Campagnolo this is done by undoing the jockey roller bolt just like the bolt for the tension roller. On the Huret it is necessary to first unsnap the cage spring:

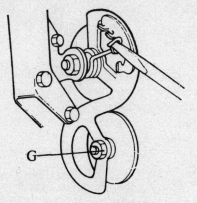

and then unscrew the cage mounting bolt CB:

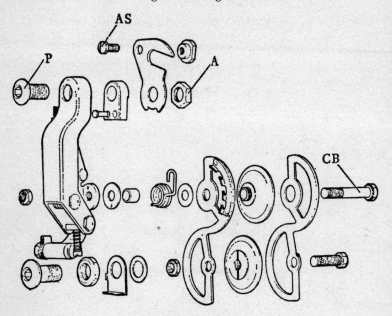

Be careful! of those shims and whatnots. Keep track of their order.

There are two kinds of chain rollers, those with washers and a metal sleeve, and those with a hub and ball bearings:

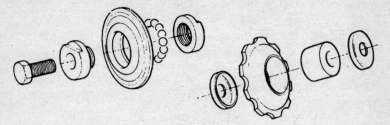

If you have the ball bearing type, disassemble the hub and remove the bearings. Both types: clean in solvent. Ball bearing type reassembly: lay one cone flat on table, place chain roller over it. Apply petroleum spray or grease. Put in ball bearings. More lubricant. Screw on second cone.

For the rest of it, the degree of disassembly possible, as well as the technique, varies somewhat from model to model. We'll do six: the Huret, Campagnolo, Simplex, Maeda Sun Tour, Shimano Crane, and Shimano Eagle.

The Huret Allvit

Undo locknut A and remove pivot bolt P with Allen wrench. Keep parts in order. Next: undo the upper lever arm bolt D:

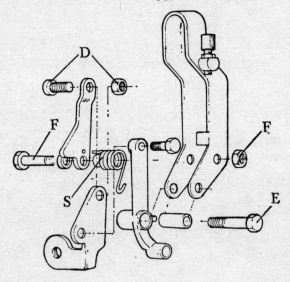

and then lower lever arm bolt E. Remove lever arm, and use pliers to pry spring S off changer body. Then remove bolt F to remove spring S. Replace any parts to be replaced. Clean everything in solvent.

Reassembly: *Note:* Be sure to set all locknuts with sufficient play for smooth derailleur operation. Assemble movement arm spring S, bushing, spacer, at housing and insert bolt F, secure with locknut. Replace spring hook on changer body. Put lever arm in place and secure with bolts D and E.

Reassemble cage (see above for illustrations): mounting bolt CB, outside cage, jockey roller, inside cage (has hooks for cage spring – these face changer body), washer, cage spring and bushing, washer; screw this assembly into the cage mounting plate. Set cage spring with screwdriver. Replace pivot bolt, stop plate, mounting plate. Mount derailleur on frame. Replace tension toller. Re-engage cable. Adjust side to side play as necessary (p. 330).

The Campagnolo

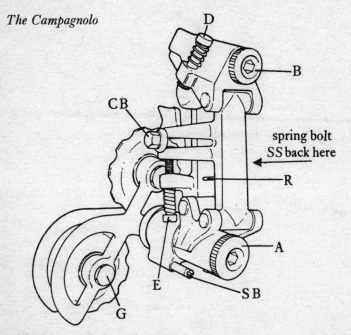

Hang onto chain roller cage to prevent it from spinning and remove cage stop bolt SB. Let cage unwind (about one-half to three-quarters of a turn). Remove cage pivot bolt with Allen wrench and lift off cage Slide out pivot bolt A and spring. Back off high gear adjusting screw E to minimize changer body spring tension, and undo spring bolt SS. Replace parts, clean everything in solvent. Reassembly: screw in spring bolt SS while holding changer body spring R in position. Replace cage spring and slide in pivot bolt. Put cage on changer with two half moon sides next to changer. Put nut on pivot bolt. Rotate cage back one-half to three-quarters of a turn and screw in cage stop bolt SB. Replace jockey roller. Mount derailleur on frame. Replace tension roller, cable. Adjust side to side travel as above (p. 330).

The Simplex

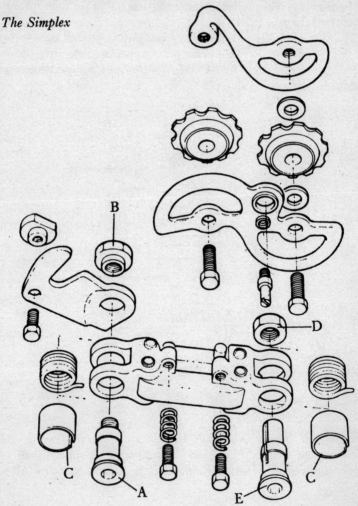

Remove dust caps from pivot bolts A and E. Spring off clips C (not all models). Undo locknut B for main arm pivot bolt A and remove bolt and spring. Ditto for locknut D and cage pivot bolt E. Some Simplex models have a circlip which can be removed so the anchor bolt F will slide out:

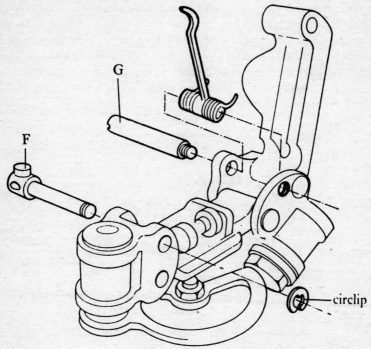

With the outer arm hinged up to relieve tension, unscrew the spring pivot pin G.

Other models lack this feature, in which case prise the spring up with a screwdriver:

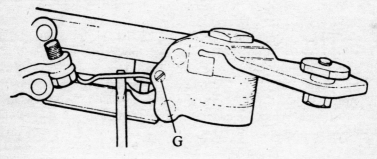

and then unscrew spring pivot pin G. Clean everything in solvent and replace defective parts.

To reassemble: Put main body spring in place and screw in spring pivot pin. Push down outer arm and secure with anchor bolt and circlip, or set spring in place with screwdriver. Put in cage pivot bolt and spring. Put on locknut and cage, and give cage pivot bolt one-half turn to right for proper spring tension before setting locknut. Repeat process for main arm pivot bolt, spring, and locknut. Fasten jockey roller to cage. Mount derailleur on frame. Mount tension roller, and then connect shift cable. Adjust side to side travel of derailleur as necessary (p. 329).

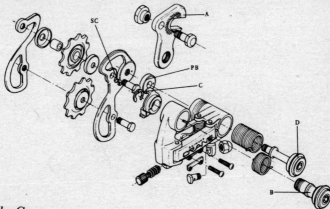

The Crane

The mounting bolt B has a spring. To get at it, prize off circlip C with a screwdriver or similar implement. It will come apart quickly. Clean parts in solvent, replacing spring if necessary, and grease. Reassemble by fitting spring, placing the head of bolt B on a hard surface, and twisting bracket A counter-clockwise while simultaneously pressing downwards. When it clicks into place, hold it firm with one finger, and with the other hand fit circlip C.

To get off the cage pivot bolt D back it off slowly with an allen wrench, and when the cage stop catch SC clears the little bump on the frame, let the chain roller cage unwind. Finish backing off bolt D. Remove spring, plate bushing PB, and bolt D. Clean and grease, replacing parts if necessary. To reassemble, fit bolt D, spring, and plate bushing PB. Fit roller cage to bolt D and turn down $1\frac{1}{2}$–2 turns. Wind cage clockwise until stop catch SC passes bump on frame, secure bolt PB.

To undo mounting bracket pivot bolt PB, slack off locknut N and then back out bolt PB.

To get off cage bolt CB, first undo cage stop screw SS and

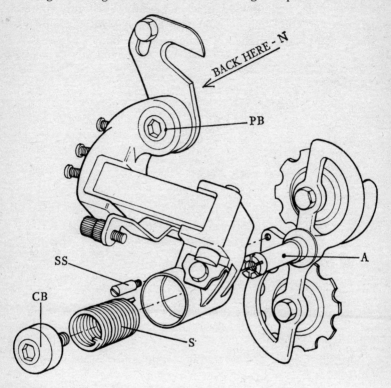

allow cage to unwind. Next, while holding cage and main body together, undo cage bolt CB and withdraw. Note position of spring S in slots of cage axle A, and of cage relative to main body. Separate cage and main body. Withdraw spring S, noting which of two holes the end catch fits into. Clean and grease, replacing parts as necessary. To reassemble: place in spring S, fitting to appropriate hole. Refit cage. If the spring tension of the cage has been weak, start from a position counter-clockwise of the original, and if it has been too strong, from a position clockwise of the original. A little diddling will get you what you want. Fit cage bolt CB .Wind cage clockwise until cage stop screw SS can be fitted.

To undo mounting bracket pivot bolt PB, remove dustcap D by twisting off or prizing up with thin screwdriver, prize off circlip C, and unwind bracket gently. When reassembling, be sure that CC catch on mounting bracket plate is wound past the corresponding catch CD on the derailleur body.

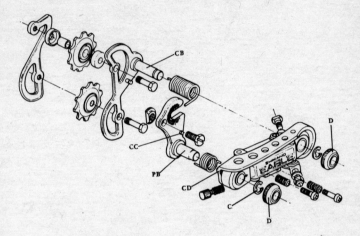

To get off the cage bolt CB do exactly the same thing as above.

The Positron

The Positron is a semi-automatic derailleur utilising a twin cable control.

Mount derailleur on dropout and axle. Move unit by hand until index pin lines up with numeral 3 on derailleur body:

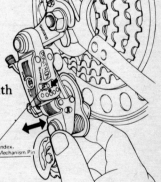

Check that guide pulley is aligned with the center sprocket of the freewheel:

If it is not, turn the adjusting screw
in or out until the two parts align.

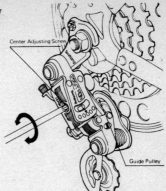

Thread through the chain:

And affix the shifting lever. Loosen
the cable fixing screw on the lever:

Fit the cable end with the head
into the slot provided on the cam
plate, and the cable end with no
head through the cable adjuster:

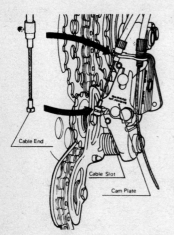

Thread cable through anchor bolt,
pull tight with pliers, and snug
down anchor bolt. Move shift
lever to 3 on lever plate and
tighten cable fixing screw. Check
operation of unit. If necessary,
adjust in or out with adjusting
screw. After about 50–100 miles
of riding, check the cables for
slack.

Cable replacement

Undo cable fixing screw and cable anchor bolt (preceding illustrations). Slide out old cable. Use the end of the new cable to poke through the hole in the side of the shift lever and move the cable fixing plate back:

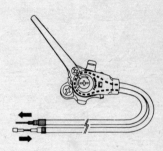

Thread cable through housings:

Fix and adjust as per instructions above.

Disassembly

Remove chain or remove tension roller by undoing bolt 14. Slack off rear wheel axle bolts, undo adapter screw and nut 11 and 12, and remove unit from bike. Undo jockey roller bolt 14.

Prise off dustcaps 1. Remove circlips 2. Pull out cage plate 15 until cage stop catch clears main body of unit and allow to unwind. Seperate. Ditto procedure for adapter 10.

Clean all parts in solvent. Be sure main body is thoroughly dry before lubricating. Assembly is reverse of above.

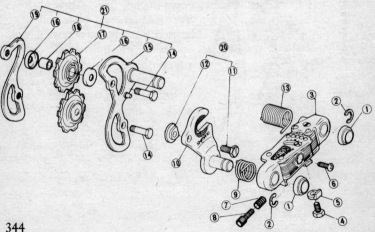

Trouble-shooting

Derailleur is sticky, won't always shift, sometimes shifts unexpectedly.

* Is shift lever working smoothly but with enough friction to hold derailleur in place (p. 316)?

* Are cables sticking (p. 317)?

* Are pivot bolts lubricated and clean? On some models (Campagnolo, Huret, among others) these bolts can be adjusted.

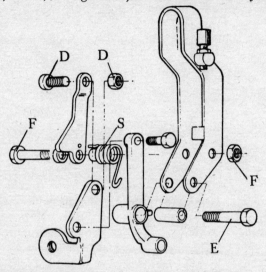

Undo locknuts for bolts D. E, and F, undo bolts one-eighth turn, reset locknuts.

Derailleur will not go far enough.

* Is cable slightly slack with shift lever all the way forward (p. 318)?

* Are adjusting screws properly set (p. 329)?

* Does cable slide easily (p. 317)?

* Is pivot or main changer spring broken?

* Are chain rollers lined up with chain (p. 328)?

* Try to wiggle the derailleur unit by hand. Can you push it to the desired position?

Yes:

works are gummed up. Clean in solvent and lubricate with spray or oil. Adjust (not possible with all models) by undoing pivot bolts one-eighth turn and resetting. (Illustration above).

No:
if it won't reach the big rear cog, remove mounting plate and bend it in a vise.
if it won't reach the little rear cog, bend mounting plate, or put in shims at the mounting bolt.

Chain throws off cogs.
* Are adjusting screws set properly (p. 322)?
* Are any teeth worn or bent (p. 298, 305)?
* Is chain good (p. 300)?
* If chain is skipping, is spring tension for roller cage sufficient (p. 331)?
* Is roller cage aligned with chain (p. 328)?

Power Train – Trouble-shooting Index
Noises

First make sure that noise is coming from power train by coasting bike. If noise continues it is probably a brake (p. 208) or hub (p. 282) problem. If noise persists, try to determine if it comes from the front (crankset), the chain, or the rear sprocket(s). Do this by disconnecting the chain (p. 300) and spinning the various parts.

Grinding noises:

Front –
* Bottom bracket bearings OK (pp. 293, 296)?
* Pedal bearings OK (p. 288)?
* Chain rubbing derailleur?
* Front sprocket rubbing cage or chainstays (p. 299)?
Back –
* Wheel bearings OK (p. 282)?
* Freewheel OK (p. 304)?

Clicks or Clunks:

One for every revolution of crankset –
* Pedal tight (p. 282)?

* Crank(s) tight (p. 290)?
* Bottom bracket bearings OK (pp. 293, ~
* Are teeth on sprocket(s) bent (pp. 298, 305):

Two or three for every revolution of the crankset –
* Are teeth on rear sprocket(s) bent (p. 305)?
* Is chain worn or frozen (p. 300)?
No go. Pedals and chain spin uselessly –
Three-speeds, see p. 315.
Ten-speeds, see p. 345.
Delayed shifts, no shifts, or not all gears
Three-speeds, see p. 315.
Ten-speeds, see p. 345.
For all other problems consult the trouble-shooting section for
the part which is malfunctioning.

Tricycle carriers like this late 1800 s model
are what we need now.

6. Dream-Ramode-Sunfighter-Dream-Birthright

Everybody has dreams and here is one of mine: cars are banned from central areas of all major metropolitan regions. Each city provides free bicycles (with adjustable seats and handlebars) scattered about to be used as needed. Because cities can buy enough bikes at a time to make special orders feasible, each city has a bike with unique and readily identifiable frame design. All bolts and screws have left-hand threads, like the light bulbs in subway stations, to discourage the stealing of parts for private use. There are repair centers throughout town, as well as special racks in which bikes in need of servicing can be left.

A dream? Perhaps. This is The Age of the Automobile, but faint upon the breeze is its swan song. The ecological and economic extravagance concomittant with the use of motor vehicles for private transport is so tremendous that they will of necessity go the way of the Dodo bird. In China, a country trying to embrace the fruits of technology as quickly and as efficiently as possible, there are no private motor vehicles. People ride bicycles or use public transportation. The savings in money and energy expenditure at every level is gargantuan. A bicycle factory, in comparison to an automobile factory, is a very low technology operation far easier to initiate and maintain. Bicycle production does not require vast support industries in petroleum, metals, rubbers, plastics, and textiles. Petrochemical and cement road building industries are minimal. There is no need for traffic regulation. There are no hundreds of thousands of maimed people requiring expensive hospitalization, emergency, and other medical services.

A dream? After all, this is the U.S. of A., home, rampart, bastion, and citadel of rampant consumerism. The freeways and highways regularly jam to surfit with massive automobiles conveying just one human each. CB'ers play spot Smoky the Bear to the ripping howl of 400 cubic inch engines. The sheer waste of it all is absolutely fantastic. But there are the beginnings of change. Not everybody wants to play the game.

Bikeways are paths or carriageways for cyclists in various grades or classes:

Class I   – A separate lane for bikes only.
Class II   – A restricted lane in a street with no autos allowed.

Class III – Streets with slotted speed bumps to slow down but not eliminate autos.

Class IV – Painted lane on a pedestrian path.

Class V – Signs on regular thoroughfares which say "Bikeway".

Class I and II bikeways are the only meaningful types, and where implemented have been a great success. The city of Davis, California, for example, has had Class I bikeways on the University of California campus, and Class II bikeways throughout town, since 1966. Davis has a population of 24,000 and approximately 18,000 bicycles. One survey found that during rush hour 40% of the traffic was bicycles, and 90% of the riders were adults.

Bikeways in the U.S. of A. come in all shapes and sizes. Many national parks such as the Cape Cod National Seashore in Massachusetts feature Class I bikeways. Wisconsin has a 300-mile mixed class bikeway through cities, towns, back roads, abandoned railroad beds, and the like. A number of towns make instant bikeways by closing parts to autos on weekends and selected weekday nights. A really enterprising town is Littleton, Colorado, which created 23 miles of bikeways. One side of the street is reserved and specially marked for two-way bicycle traffic. Cars are not even allowed to park on that side of the street, and violators get tickets. So do bike riders who disobey traffic regulations. The Littleton venture has been a great success (they should have about 50 miles of bikeways now), and inspired by this example other cities in Colorado – Boulder, Lakewood, Aurora, Denver, Englewood, Northglenn, Aspen, and Fort Collins – have either created or are creating bikeways.

Many traffic engineers and cyclists object strongly to bikeways. They contend that cyclists will be legislated off public roads and streets, where they have every right to be. Further, the design of bikeways which ajoin public roads is such that at intersections there is *increased* accident danger for the cyclist. Both criticisms are entirely valid, but blanket opposition to bikeways is not the answer.

The solution is to design total transportation systems in which the needs of all road users are met separately and without conflict. This is done by creating independent roads for motor vehicles, cyclists, and pedestrians. Use of one particular type of road is not obligatory; the charm of the system is that it works so well that most road users prefer to use the carriageway designed for them.

A dream? It has been done. Stevenage, Hertfordshire, England, a town of some 72,000 souls sequestered 32 miles north of London, is a transportation dreamworld, a kind of magical Walt Disney fantasy in which everything flows with perfect smoothness and problems evaporate. Stevenage was the first designated New Town under the provisions of the New Towns Act of 1946. which allows for development financed by the state with 60-year loans. Most or all of the credit for the design and engineering of Stevenage, and in particular its transportation systems, goes to Eric Claxton, now retired as Chief Engineer for the Stevenage Development Corporation, and a man who must be reckoned a one-of-a-kind genius.

With a population of 72,000 on 6,000 acres, Stevenage has a population density greater than that of Central London. Yet there is not one single traffic, cycle, or pedestrian stoplight or sign in the entire town. The flow of these different kinds of traffic, even at rush-hour periods, is so smooth and even that there does not appear to be anybody around. What rush hour? one asks, looking around for lines or packs of traffic. There are none. There is no congestion because nothing ever holds still.

The Stevenage system succeeds because it is a *total* transportation system. Roads for pedestrians, cycles, mopeds, and motor vehicles are separate and never conflict. It is possible to drive a motor car throughout the town without once encountering a cycle or pedestrian. As a result the average speed of rush-hour traffic is 20 mph, double the average of other cities, and better still than the average in major metropolitan regions such as London. You are guaranteed a parking space right near your destination except on the two Saturdays before Christmas. Bus services operate to and from the absolute center of town, literally only steps away from shopping and municipal centers. There are no dwellings more than a 5-minute walk from a bus stop. Most are much closer.

If you are cycling it is also possible to go anywhere you wish in town via the cycleways or footpaths (on which pedestrians, cycles, and mopeds have mingled freely and without incident for over 20 years), and never encounter a motor vehicle. For pedestrians, in addition to a comprehensive network of footpaths, the town center and many subcenters are completely pedestrianized, with no vehicle traffic and complete protection from the weather.*

The official cycleway system is 25 miles long, and is shared by all types of cycles, mopeds up to 50cc capacity, and pedestrians. The cycleways frequently run alongside main roads but are separated by grass verges and trees from both the roads and footpaths. There are in addition a number of crosstown cycleway links which run independently of roads. Some were originally country lanes from which vehicular traffic has been withdrawn. Additionally, cycles make free use of over 100 miles of footpaths so that most cycle journeys are door-to-door. There are no rules or regulations (and hence no need for the police to concern themselves with traffic regulation) governing the use of the cycleways and footpaths, no "cycles must or must not." Cyclists are free to use the vehicle carriageways if they prefer. The existing cycleway system is so attractive, however, that only the odd racer in training buzzing along at 25-mph-plus chooses to mix it up with the cars.

The different types of roads are kept separate through the generous use of underpasses. These are a study in sensitive design and architecture. An overpass for cycles must rise at least 16 feet over the road, necessitating either a long or steep gradient. An underpass for cycles only requires 7' 6" headroom, and by excavating to a depth of only 6 feet, and using the excavation material to gently raise the road 3 feet, the differences in gradient are still further minimized. The cycleways are normally 12 feet wide and carry two-way traffic. Construction is similar to a footpath, with minimal lighting and drainage. The main costs derive from the earthworks and concrete underpasses needed at intersections to keep cycleways and motor roads apart.

Equal in importance with underpasses to the success of the Stevenage system is the frequent use of ingeniously improved traffic circles described here as part of the "Good Ideas To Keep In Mind" campaign.

In the classic traffic circle vehicles must fairly well stop before entering, and the tendency is for paths through the circle to conflict, creating four crossroads where formerly there was only one:

---

* Traffic bans increase business in shopping areas. The Organization for Economic Cooperation and Development reports that vehicle bans increased business by 25–50% in Vienna, 15–35% in Norwich, and 10–15% in Ruen (1972).

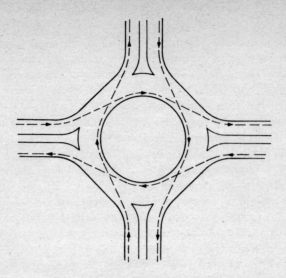

When the right of way of vehicles already in the circle is observed, traffic flow is improved, but heavy traffic from one road will impede lighter traffic from another for long periods of time. Enter the Stevenage traffic circle:

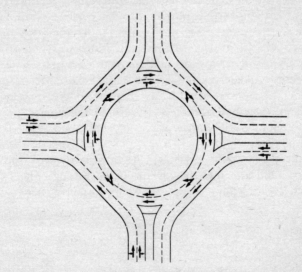

Under this system the crossroad conflict points are replaced by weaving areas. Before arriving at the circle the motorist positions him/herself in the correct lane for the intended route. It has been found that at busy periods most of the motorists know where they are going. Those few who need to read signs before selecting a lane can manage a shuffle without difficulty.

Vehicles then enter the traffic circle at between 15 and 25 mph, the same speed (by design) as traffic already in the circle. Merging is simple, and under the Stevenage system vehicles may go before or after vehicles already in the circle as long as there is no abrupt dislocation. Vehicles turning left have no problem at all and can just motor through.* For skeptics, I can only say that I have tried this system myself and it works like a charm.

The benefits of a system such as Stevenage's are often intangible and not easily reckoned on a balance sheet. What is the worth of never, ever, having an obstruction or aggravation in traveling? That whole series of abrasions, conflicts, and problems for which most of us armor up each day just doesn't exist in Stevenage. What price a mother's peace of mind, knowing that her children can walk or cycle anywhere – and never encounter a motor vehicle? Sixty per cent of the workers in town go home for lunch. How do you measure the value and effect of this increased home life? These are alterations in the quality of life, perhaps describable as similar to the relaxed pastoral peacefulness of a "primitive" society – but with full technological benefits! The worth of this sort of thing can only be determined by each individual.

Other benefits are more tangible:

The cycleways serve the interests of a large segment of the population aged 6 to 16 who cannot drive cars. Of 16,760 children, 1,420 (8.4%) cycle daily to school. This figure is low, because Stevenage's primary schools are located within easy walking distance of home. Of secondary school children, 17.4% cycle to school.

Such few accidents as do occur on the cycleways are minor. Pedestrians, cyclists, and moped riders are all equally vulnerable and take equal pains to avoid each other. Stevenage's safety record is 4 casualties per 1,000 population per year as against a national average which is more than 50% greater. The direct savings in medical service costs is considerable, to say nothing of life and limb.

* For an American system this would be right-turning vehicles.

By encouraging cycling and walking, the Stevenage system promotes mild exercise. There are 4,000 regular cyclists, about 11 percent of the people working in Stevenage, and 10,000 recreational and shopping cyclists. This health benefit may seem minor, but for many people it is the only exercise they get, and as such may extend their longevity up to five years.

An immense amount of time is saved. There is a car ownership rate per household of .80, which is high. People walk and cycle because it works better than using cars.

As a New Town, Stevenage has had considerable freedom in designing and implementing a transportation system. But the difficulties encountered with already existing towns are surmountable. For example, Peterborough, England, is currently creating a 72 mile long system of four types of cycleways: cycle path, completely separate from motor traffic; cycle lane, by the side of a road and separated by a painted line or curb; cycle route, low-traffic streets marked with signs giving priority to cyclists; and cycle trail, through park, countryside, and forest, utilizing bridle paths, disused railway tracks, and footpaths. The proper cycle path is the ideal, of course: at one-sixth the per square yard cost of a road, with a 12-foot wide cycle path yielding five times the carrying capacity of a 24-foot road, it is a bargain. In existing built-up areas, however, cycle lanes, routes, and trails are often a better compromise. Construction of a proper cycle path can await general redevelopment although sometimes, if there is no suitable alternative, it cannot. This costs, but in the end a lot less than sticking with what we have; also, expenditures can be spread out over a period of time. For the most part, a great deal of special provision for cyclists can be made right away, with minimal construction and expense.

The first step is to arm yourself with information. A really first-rate book is *A Handbook for Bicycle Activists*, by Ernest Del, *et al* (Stanford Environmental Law Society, Stanford Law School, Stanford, CA 94305, $2.95). Another good one is *Cyclateral Thinking* (Urban Bikeway Design Collective, W20-002 MIT, Cambridge, MA 02139, $3). The *Cycling Traffic Engineering Handbook*, by John Forseter (Custom Cycle Fitments, 782 Allen Court, Palo Alto, CA 94303, $12) is full of nitty-gritty particulars. Helpful is *Bicycle Transit: Its Planning and Design*, by B. L. Balshore, *et al* (Praeger Publishers, 111 4th Ave., New York,

NY 10003, $14). If you'd like to, you can even go to school. John Forester gives a course in traffic engineering – ITC Extension Programs, 12 North Gate Hall, University of California, Berkeley, CA 94720.

Action. Write your local authority and ask them what they are doing to encourage cycling. What about bikeways? What about parking for cycles? Twenty cycles will fit into the same space as one car.

Design a bikeways system for your area. Mark on a map all the schools, factories, offices, shops, and places of interest that need to be served by a bikeway. Work out routes from residential areas to these areas which are as direct as possible (going along back streets, footpaths, bridle paths, etc.) and necessitate the minimum of construction. Some conflicts are unavoidable, and once the plan is accepted, will be resolved with traffic lights, bridges, or underpasses. Provide for recreational cycling and access to leisure facilities and the surrounding countryside. Cycle the routes yourself. Note where parking should be provided and what major problems, if any, exist. You can get help and advice with this project from:

Nicholas Cole
British Cycling Bureau
Greater London House
Hampstead Road
London NW1 7QP
England

The Bicycle Institute
of America
122 East 42nd Street
New York, N.Y. 10017

Once you have completed your plan/proposal, send it to your local authority asking for their comments, and send copies to the Bicycle Institute of America and your local newspapers. If you have done your homework – and both the BCB and BIA will innundate you with a blizzard of information on the advantages of bikeways – you'll get action. Despite the fact that some bikeways are sheer tokenism distinguishable in no way whatsoever from a regular highway or street, there are some good ones, and the idea is sound, especially if you push for Class I and II bikeways. I hope that you will engage in such activity, but there are some other things to keep in mind.

An integrated traffic system such as Stevenage's is a masterful

study in efficiency where each modality of transportation comple-
ments the other. The question arises: Should efficiency be the
prime value? What about the need to preserve health, or to expend
energy wisely? Stevenage shows clearly that the car is not the
enemy of the bicycle unless they share the same road. Create an
integrated system, and this problem evaporates. But the car
remains an enemy of man, a tool with a backlash of millions of
dead and grievously injured. More Americans and Britons have
died in accidents since the inception of the auto than in World
War II. The simple fact is that humans cannot master the safe
operation of motor vehicles. And even if they could, the motor
vehicle is indictable on account of air and noise pollution and
energy waste.

We may mourn the loss of an early morning run into a rising
sun, the thrill and satisfaction of fast motoring, the love and fury
we feel for our machines – but the price is too stiff. The actions of a
Jack-the-Ripper-style sniper or mass murderer, while a predictable
outcome of society, are seen as aberrant and "unacceptable,"
whereas the hundreds of thousands killed and mangled by motor
vehicles are seen as an unfortunate but necessary by-product of
modern transportation needs.

Bilge. It is not necessary on two counts. First, we do not need
the high mobility which cars provide. Second, even if we insist on
having it, there are other, safer ways to get it.

Let us start with the idea of banning the motor vehicle as an
unwarranted assault on human rights and life. Many must feel
that such an action would severely depreciate our quality of life,
and would therefore be completely unrealistic. Not so. The precise
point is that an excess of transportation efficiency is not good for
us, but bad. We do not own our transportation; it owns us.

Mobility and the nuclear family are products of an industrial
society. The extended kinship family is not necessarily the model
for relationships, and relationships are not needed by everyone,
but relationships must exist for most people most of the time. An
industrial society, particularly a hyper-industrial society such as
ours, inhibits relationships. Men and women are sorted into
worker and nonworker groups. Employability is privileged, and
nonworkers, who include females, the old, the foolish, the poor,
the incompetent, and the uncooperative of whatever form and for
whatever reason, are discriminated against. They simply have

fewer human rights.

It is the nature of industrial processes that it is difficult to employ groups or families or even couples. For the sake of worker mobility males are given the dominant, central economic role in a nuclear family, and females, less desirable in the labor pool, are made accessories.

So we have a situation where a large segment of society has been relegated inferior status and rights, and where even the structure of relationships is subordinate to industrial needs. The rewards are not job satisfaction or the furtherance of the good of society, but consumerism – the use of the products and services created. Quite simply, we have no choice. We do not reap benefits, rather we are compelled to adopt certain behaviors if we wish to live. We do not own the machines and the technology and the products therefrom; they own us.

It is my feeling that some loss of mobility would be a good thing. Negatively, in that employability for the sake of consumerism is worthless and destructive, and positively, in that loss of mobility may encourage relationships, foster wholesome goals, and increase self-awareness. The consumer society is built on promises and the hoax of future progress. Expectancy blinds us to the realities of the moment. The "primitive" societies that functioned without technological innovation or expectancy that the future would be different enjoyed a far richer here and now.

But it goes deeper than not perpetuating the evils of consumerism. If the members of society are to engage in management and share privileges and responsibilities, there must be a relative equality of experience. The creation of privilege – in this example, mobility – for the purpose of administering, coordinating, or whatever worthwhile activity is terrible a mistake which confers discriminatory power. And power corrupts and perpetuates. It is more important to maintain power equality.

Ivan D. Illich, in his wonderful book *Tools for Conviviality* (Harper & Row), New York City), says that the upper limit of transportation technology should be the bicycle. A genuinely socialist society cannot support anything more advanced. Properly limited technologies "serve politically interrelated individuals rather than managers."

The point of this discussion is to show that "alternate transportation" does not necessarily mean just another way of doing the same thing. This is more than a matter of perspective, because the form of our transportation is related to the content of our culture. The car, for example, is a tool of alienation. Giant shopping complexes are created to promote the use of cars. Gone is the local butcher, fishmonger, greengrocer, and frequent contact with known people, replaced by uniform packaging and uniform employees who work with customers the same as a nut-and-bolt assembler on a production line. If we are conscious of the desirability of other goals besides employment mobility and consumerism – goals such as human contact – then transportation design may be influenced in evolution.

But I. D. Illich directs his ideas toward influencing the lifestyle possibilities of countries which have not yet industrialized. No one standing by the endless streams of cars blaring through our cities and countryside can realistically hope that it will end quickly. In one important sense the energy crisis is a boondoggle, a hoax, not the harbinger of a new and different time, but a manipulation by the petro-chemical companies and governments to maintain consumerism – and power. "Shortages" are basic operations of a 1984 Fascist society. We may need to want the things now in short supply about as much as rectal cancer, but it is just too much to expect that the hyper-industrialized society, in dying, will do anything but promote to the utmost the values which have preserved it in the past.

No major concessions will be made to cyclists and human beings as long as the automotive and petro-chemical industries hold the economic clout. A glimpse into the future was provided a while ago in France.

Paris is famous for traffic. Cars are everywhere, moving in a constant rushing stream, and creating an incredible din. Cars have the right of way and pedestrians have to fend for themselves. In Paris the auto is King. Mr. Pompidou has even announced, "We must adapt Paris to the automobile and renounce a certain aesthetic idealism."

Not all Parisians agree. They want alternate means of transportation and an end to noisy traffic jams. On April 23, 1972, the Organizations Les Amis de la Terre, Comité Anticuleaire de Paris, Comité de Liberation, Ecologique, Etre, Objectif Socialiste, and the Federation of Users of Public Transport staged a massive bike-in to dramatize their demands. It was beautiful.

Some 10,000 bicycles of every conceivable type and condition rendezvoused at Porte Dauphine. A few forward-looking Frenchmen showed up on roller skates! Harried police tried to route the demonstrators to exterior streets, but the procession went straight down the Champs Elysées to the Place de la Concorde, up the Blvd. St. Germain, and on to Bois de Vincennes (a park). Bus loads of riot police tried to stem the tide on the Champs Elysées but failed, possibly because they did not want to be violent in full public view. As the procession wound along replete with signs and streamers, some sympathetic motorists blocked side streets with their cars to add to the confusion, and pedestrians shouted "Bon Courage!" One spoilsport who refused to be stymied ran into several bicycles with his car. Surrounded by several thousand angry bicyclists he paid damages on the spot.

When the cyclists reached Bois de Vincennes, they were greeted with victory hymns by the Grand Magic Circus troupe. An hour of dancing, singing, and good times followed. Then the CRS riot police arrived. Helmeted troops on motorcycles charged the crowd and tear gas flew. Efforts at reason failed. About 50 people were arrested. The CRS used the shelter of the woods to smash up bicycles with their night-sticks.

Now Les Amis de la Terre and other groups are pressing on with their demands: the creation of pedestrian streets; one million free bicycles at the disposition of Parisians; non-polluting public transportation à la Rome; the closing of Paris to more automobile traffic, and a halt to the creation of inner-city expressways. *Yeah!*

The French experience points the way to real victories. Theirs was an *ecological* demonstration stressing the needs of both pedestrians and bicycles. Bikeways are not enough. What is needed is the elimination of polluting transportation. In urban areas the car accounts for up to 85% of the air pollution, and for 85% of the noise pollution. In Vienna the intra-city ban has reduced air pollution levels by 70%; a 1971 closing of New York City's Madison Avenue resulted in a threefold drop in carbon monoxide levels. The absolute elimination of internal combustion engines from urban areas is the practical solution which benefits everybody.

And the curious thing is, if we do define mobility as a prime value, then in urban areas a car is the last thing we need. It just does not work. George Washington, riding a horse, made better time between his home in Alexandria, Va. and the capitol, a distance some six miles, than today's Washingtonian does driving a car. Trains, buses, bicycles, roller skates, and steam- and electric-powered delivery vehicles are more than adequate – they are better. At present motor vehicles are very heavily subsidized by the general public, and if the users of this form of transportation were to pay the full cost they could not afford it. Support must now go to alternative (and cheaper) methods. Trains and buses must have racks for the free carrying of bicycles. Stations, terminals, businesses, and residences must have parking facilities. There must be a comprehensive system of bikeways serving not only industry and consumer outlets, but areas of recreation and sport. It has to be possible to go anywhere in the country on a bicycle without getting involved with motor vehicles. No road or street should exist without a corresponding bicycle path. Instead of squandering funds on expressways and heavy streets and traffic regulation, cities must provide free, simple, easily adjustable bicycles for intracity use. And as for the car and truck, in urban areas – Ban it!

Which is of course easier said than done. The industries with vested interest in maintaining a motor age are large and powerful to the extreme. Petro-chemical companies are a law unto themselves. They routinely buy and sell governments. Steel, mining, rubber, textiles, cement, and plastics are automotive-related industries, each with a profit and make-work situation to protect. Each, curiously enough, is a major pollutor in its own right. Ultimately, the only solution to this vicious conglomerate of vested interest and power will be to take the profit out of their activities by nationalizing all transportation – bicycles, cars, trucks, buses, trains, airplanes – and all related service industries. In the technology-oriented U.S. of A. this is economic and psychological revolution.

What we are more likely to see is a long series of minor reforms, tokenism, and other concessions to public unrest. If we are lucky, there will be a major smog disaster in which thousands of people will suddenly die all at once, instead of piecemeal as they do now. This might spur improvements which would ultimately save more lives than were lost. But the power of vested interests in maintaining a motor age is such that there will probably be a long, drawn-out struggle, and concessions will not be won without a fight.

So don't be too surprised if you are beaned at a bike-in by a club-swinging cop who calls you a dirty communist, and don't back off because of it. *You have a right to live.* Arguments which present the roller skate or bicycle as more economical, efficient, etc. are all well and good, but the situation is extremely simple: present transportation systems are filling the air with deadly fumes and noise and recklessly wasting a dwindling supply of natural resources. *They are killing and injuring people.* You have a right to live – it is your birthright – but you will have to fight for it.

The U.S. of A. is an engine of destruction unlikely of spontaneous redemption. The opportunity for radical change and transformation, of revolution, of destruction, reorganization, and creation – if it comes at all – is a matter of individual assessment and decision. I can't tell you to pick up the gun at such and such a time or, alternatively, that if you do pick up the gun all is lost. We all move according to our best understanding of right and wrong, and act according to our ability to do so. If the chance comes your way,

Take it.

A MIDDAY HALT

Index

Accessories, 177-87
Accidents, 129-30
  and bikeways, 348-53 *passim*
Adult bicycles, 13-59
Africa, touring in, 170
Airplanes, bikes and, 151
Air pollution, 7-9, 116-17, 359
Air pump, 177
Animals, 136-39
Ankling, 109-10
Antique bikes, 189-91
  reproduction, 72
Arnold, F., 116n
Asia, touring in, 171
Assaults, on cyclists, 90-92, 117
Automobiles, 3n, 9, 348-61 *passim*
  air pollution and, 7-9, 116-17, 359
  bicycles carried by, 19, 150-51
  riding and, 117-18
Australia, touring in, 171

Baby seats, 185
Baggage, on bikes, 144-46, 185
Bearings, 200-3
Bells, 187
Bicycles, inspection of, 82-84
Bicycle stores, 81-87
  maintenance and, 195
Bike-ins, 358-59
Bikeways, 348-61
BMX bikes, 75-76
Bottom bracket, 37-38
  maintenance index, 286
Brakes, 27-31
  emergency, 111-12, 120, 129-30, 136
  fitting, 97-98
  maintenance index, 208
  riding and, 111-12
  see also Center-pull brake; Coaster brake; Disc brake; Side-pull brake
Bryce-Smith, Derek, 116
Buses, bikes and, 151

Cables, 206, 210
  brake, 219-21, 224-28
  gear, 287, 311, 317
Cadence, 110-11
  touring and, 139-40
  traffic jamming and, 121-22
Caliper brakes, *see* Center-pull brakes; Disc brakes; Side-pull brakes
Camping equipment, 147-49, 162
Canada, touring in, 172
Cantilever brakes, 30-31
Car bicycle carriers, 150-51
Carriers, on bikes, 144-46, 185
Center-pull brakes, 27-30, 209
  maintenance index, 208

Chain, 286
Chainwheel, 37-39, 286
  see also Front sprocket
Children, 126
  bikes for, 73-76
  carriers for, 185
Claxton, Eric, 350
Cleats, 144, 177
Clothing, 146
Coaster brake, 27-28, 209
Commoner, Barry, 7n
Commuter bikes, 42, 77-80
Cranks, 37-38
  maintenance index, 286
Cyclists Touring Club, 153-56
Cyclo-cross, 141, 175

Derailleurs, 34-37
  gear capacity, 104-5
  maintenance index, 287
  shifting, 107-9
Disc brakes, 28, 209
  maintenance index, 239-41
Dogs, 136-39
Duker, Peter, 171

Ecology, bikes and, 7-9, 348
Economics, of bikes, 3, 348
Europe, touring in, 152-70
Exercise, from cycling, 5-7, 354

Fenders, 144, 186
Flats, 169-78
Folding bikes, 63-64, 79
Food, 149
Forester, John, 124
Forks, 242
  see also Headset
Frozen bolts, 205
Frame, 20-27
  custom, 58-60, 159-60
  fitting, 93
Front sprocket, 37-39
  maintenance index, 286

Gear changers, 34-37
  maintenance index, 287
  shifting technique, 107-9
Gearing, 99-105, 159

Handlebar bags, 144-46
Handlebars, 41-42
  fitting, 96-97
  maintenance index, 242
  taping, 183, 248
Headset, 242
Health
  air pollution and, 7-9, 116-17
  cycling and, 5-7, 354
Heilman, Gail, 9n

Helmets, 182-83
Hi-riser bikes, 75
Horns, 187
Hubs, 33-34
   maintenance index, 263
Hyperventilation, 16-17

Illich, I. D., 357, 358

Ladies' bikes, 48-49
Lights, 126, 143-44, 177-82
Locking bikes, 89
Lubrication, 200-4
   see also specific maintenance indexes
Lugging, of frames, 21

Maintenance, 194-206
   see also maintenance indexes for
   specific components
Maps, 146, 161-62
Mexico, touring in, 172
Mini-bikes, 61-62
Mirrors, rear view, 186
Multi-speed hubs, 287

Nail catchers, 186

Panniers, 144-46
Pedalling, 109-10
Pedals, 39-40
   maintenance index, 286
Pedestrians, 126
Public transport, bikes by, 19, 151-52, 163
Pump, air, 177

Quadricycles, 70

Racing, 173-76
Railroads, bikes and, 151-52, 163
Rear sprocket, 286
Reflectors, 182
Reinow, L. & L., 7n
Rice, Professor, 9
Riding
   country, 134-38, 158-59
   learning to, 74
   technique, 107-13, 139-40
   tires and, 268
   traffic, 117-26
Rims, 31-34
   maintenance index, 263
Road races, 174-76

Roller lever brakes, 222-23

Saddle, 40-41
   fitting, 93-95
   maintenance index, 242
Saddlebags, 144-45, 184
Sailing tricycle, 70-71
Sanders, William, 90-91, 129
Security, bike, 78, 79, 88-92
Shifting gears, 107-9
Shift levers, 36-37, 314, 316
Shoes, bicycle, 144, 177
Side-pull brakes, 27-30, 209
   maintenance index, 208
Sleeping bags, 147-48
Sloane, Eugene, 5
Small wheel bikes, 61-62
South America, touring in, 172
Spokes, 263
Sprockets, see Front sprocket; Rear sprocket
Stem, 242
Stevenage, England, 350-54
Stolle, Walter, 170

Tandem bikes, 64-66, 68
Tape, handlebar, 183, 248
Taxicabs, 122
Tents, 148
Tires, 31-32, 141-43
   inflating, 267
   maintenance index, 263
Toe clips, 87, 110, 177
Tools
   bags for, 184
   for maintenance, 197-99
   for touring, 143
Touring, 131-72
Track races, 175-76
Traffic, 4, 115-26
Trailers, 185
Training wheels, 74
Transportation, of bikes, 19, 151-52, 163
Tricycles, 66-70
Turning, 112-13, 121, 124

Unicycles, 71
Used bikes, 87-88

Wheel
   removal, 263-66
   truing, 278-88
Woods bikes, 141